RABBI PAUL

RABBI

· an intellectual biography ·

PAUL

BRUCE CHILTON

IMAGE BOOKS

DOUBLEDAY

New York   London   Toronto

Sydney   Auckland

AN IMAGE BOOK
PUBLISHED BY DOUBLEDAY
a division of Random House, Inc.

IMAGE, DOUBLEDAY, and the portrayal of a deer drinking from a stream are
registered trademarks of Random House, Inc.

A Peekamoose Book

Book design by RLF Design

The Library of Congress has cataloged the hardcover edition as follows:
Chilton, Bruce.
Rabbi Paul : an intellectual biography / Bruce Chilton.
p.   cm.
Includes bibliographical references and index.
1. Paul, the Apostle, Saint.   2. Christian saints—Turkey—Tarsus—
Biography.   3. Tarsus (Turkey)—Biography.   I. Title.
BS2506.3.C47 2004
225.9'2—dc22
[B]   2003070121

ISBN 0-385-50863-8

December 2005

First Image Books Edition

1   3   5   7   9   10   8   6   4   2

for the members of the
Institute of Advanced Theology

CONTENTS

PART THREE
THE APOSTLE OF CHRISTIANITY

MAPS AND ILLUSTRATIONS

PREFACE

Paul has been reviled and revered throughout Western history. A visionary thinker who combined Stoicism, Judaism, and nascent Christian theology, he transformed all of them in the mix. Any single designation we choose for him proves incomplete. He is one of the most frustrating and tantalizing figures in our intellectual tradition because he tried to change every group he joined, every idea he embraced. He wove his thoughts from his complex background and his volatile temperament and produced a new way of thinking and feeling about what it means to be human. He emerged as an innovator and a radical ideologue by synthesizing the popular philosophy of the Greco-Roman world and his passionate Judaism into a new hybrid.

The first Christian dogmatists—the fathers of the Church—considered Paul their premier theologian and referred to him simply as "the Apostle." To this day he is widely considered responsible for separating Christianity from Judaism by teaching that God does not require people to obey him, but only to love him and believe in him. Paul made Jesus the center of a new religion, the Christ who offered a special relationship with God despite any human fault or failing. That established him as the principal architect of the Church, the thinker who gave Christianity its doctrine and form.

Paul's influence over the Church has actually grown with time. The Protestant Reformation pinned its hopes for a comprehensive program of reform on Paul and made him the only theologically correct thinker. For all the vehemence of its stand against Protestantism, Roman Catholic Christianity since the Second Vatican Council has increasingly emphasized Paul's teaching that God's favor cannot be earned by obedience to convention, and Orthodox Christianity has always venerated "the Apostle."

Meanwhile, revisionist theologians and critics—ancient and modern—have pilloried Paul, making him responsible for whatever is wrong with Christianity. They have portrayed Paul as antifeminist, homophobic, and doctrinaire—while Fundamentalist Christians often embrace such attitudes as part of their Pauline inheritance. Paul's own letters do give support to this picture. He wrote that women in Corinth should shut up in church, he despised homosexuality and prostitution, and he fussed endlessly in an effort to get the churches he addressed in his letters to behave decently and think coherently.

All these images of Paul have their merits, but they inevitably distort "the Apostle" because they don't fully trace the sources of his ideas, explain why he combined them the way he did, or account for how he changed, often chameleon-like, to impress his vision on the different communities that he proselytized. They do not convey the passion of a man who lived his ideas. It is my hope in presenting an intellectual biography of Paul, and placing his thought within the environment of the Mediterranean world, that we will begin to see who Paul was and understand the thinker who has given us so much of what is most beautiful and most troublesome in Christian faith.

· · ·

PART I of *Rabbi Paul* explores the wellspring of his theology within the ferment of first-century Judaism and the Stoicism of his native Tarsus (as this city in modern Turkey is still called). We follow him from Tarsus to Jerusalem, where Paul went at the age of twenty-one and studied to become a Pharisee, an expert in the practices and customs of the Judaic Law. Proudly advancing in that role, he could claim the mantle of rabbi,[1] a teacher knowledgeable in the Torah. Part 1 ends with Paul's famous conversion on the road to Damascus, but, as we shall see, this was a *Jewish* experience. We disentangle Paul's conversion from the fallacy that Paul deliberately separated himself from Judaism: Paul saw himself as one in a long line of Israel's visionary prophets.

In Part 2, we see Paul debating the significance of Jesus' Resurrection with other Jewish leaders in the fledgling Christian movement and crafting his teaching about Jesus for the different communities of Christians in the Mediterranean world. Christianity in the Mediterranean basin varied enormously from city to city, congregation to congregation. But in setting after setting, a single, radical theme reverberates in what Paul, as a rabbi, taught: The chosen people, "Israel," are defined, not by kinship and not by obedience to the Torah, but by their belief that the risen Jesus, the Christ, is the Son of God. That view, passionately embraced and fiercely argued, put Paul at odds not only with most other rabbis of his time, but also with those who were apostles before him: Peter, James (the brother of Jesus), and Barnabas.

We will see how Paul played a crucial role in the division that later occurred between Christianity and Judaism, religions often described as having parted ways, each going off in its own direction. But the relationship between them is much more fraught than a parting. It is more like a divorce, in which the partners keep returning to common experiences and affections that are no less potent for having soured. Following Rabbi Paul's journey permits us to trace the roots of the rancor and regret that emerged when Judaism and Christianity became separate, antagonistic religions—and I hope this biography will help readers ford the gulf that separates the two faiths.

Part 3 of the book deals with Paul's extraordinary ambition: to speak as an apostle for the whole of Christianity. Paul devoted his massive talent and energy to achieve a prophetic breakthrough in Jerusalem, the heart of Jesus' movement. He wanted to bring a sacrifice on behalf of Gentile Christians directly to the Temple and, by doing so, unite pagan and Jewish believers in a single Israel. His vision of all humanity worshiping one God challenged every Christian constituency he addressed, whether they were converted pagans or practicing Pharisees. He had to admit that some people refused to call him an apostle (1 Corinthians 9:2). Even in his own eyes, he was (1 Corinthians 15:9) "the least of the apostles, who is not worthy to be called an apostle, for the reason that I persecuted the church of God."

Still, we will see that Paul's perspective, controversial as it was, shaped the formation of the New Testament after his death, and we inherit that influence today. Perhaps more than any other single person, Paul defined Christian spirituality. We will examine how he has left his imprint on the way all Christians—Catholic, Orthodox, and Protestant—understand the basics of their faith: Spirit, revelation, faith in Jesus as God's "son," conscience, sexuality, what defines religion as an institution, and the nature of the religious personality. The Church has grappled with Paul's thought for two millennia and will probably continue to struggle with it in centuries to come.

· · ·

HOW CAN WE GET at the truth about Paul as a human being and appreciate his thought? It takes more to encounter Paul than reading an ancient text or two. The New Testament gives us Paul's life and thought in fragments, sometimes through secondhand sources.[2] His letters are the earliest documents in the New Testament, when they are genuine. But some are spurious, and one of the most important of the authentic letters (2 Corinthians) is pasted together from separate pieces of correspondence. Even when we have whole and genuine letters, we are in the position of an eavesdropper who can hear only one side of a conversation, since we don't have letters written back to Paul. We need to parse his words to access the person speaking, and we have to appreciate the settings and milieus that he addressed. We can do that by examining the historical and archaeological evidence of the cities and towns in which Paul taught.

Paul helped make Christianity, and we can see that happen in his letters, written just as this new faith emerged. That is why these documents are priceless to anyone interested in religion, for any reason. But his letters are also as limited as Paul was. He did not write one line about his physical environment during the thousands of miles he traveled by foot, caravan, and ship. He mentioned many people by name, sometimes with tenderness and sometimes with anger, but only for what they did or didn't do in the service of his message and its announcement. Paul, in his own mind, was merely a herald of the only truth that mattered. His emotional restraint was always at war with his unreserved passion for Christ.

What Paul does not say makes the Book of the Acts of the Apostles an extremely valuable resource in any attempt at biography. A broad consensus of scholars puts the date of Acts around 90 C.E., some thirty years after Paul had stopped writing. But the writer of Acts clearly incorporated earlier material in his narrative: the travel notes of one of Paul's companions, for example.[3] The likely author of those notes was Timothy.

Many details in Acts correspond to historical and archaeological evidence. That doesn't make Acts more reliable than Paul's letters, but it does mean that what Acts says should be assessed, not simply rejected.[4] Sometimes there is good reason to infer that Paul keeps a self-interested silence that Acts breaks, while sometimes Acts' myth of peace and unanimity in the early Church is simply implausible.

Perpetually restless, reckless with his own life and the lives of others, Paul careened around the Mediterranean—Asia Minor, Judea, Syria, Greece, and Italy[5]—wrecking the tranquility of synagogues, forums, and churches, making friends and breaking friendships with the compulsive abandon of a man possessed. Paul is inexplicable apart from the environment of apocalyptic zeal, intense mysticism, and incipient violence that characterized first-century Judaism and Christianity. As I have read his own words over the years, he has never seemed to me an armchair theologian or a self-possessed saint. He is not nearly as pious or serene as his reputation among dogmatists and hagiographers suggests.

A professor at my seminary thirty years ago liked to tutor me privately in Paul's letters. Officially, the tutorial was in advanced Greek. His real agenda, though, was to get me to see that some of the other courses I was taking were watering Paul down. Usually he had me read a passage in Greek aloud, and then translate, analyzing the grammar as I went. One spring morning I came to Paul's catalog of how he paid personally and physically for his honesty (2 Corinthians 11:24–27): "From Jews five times I got the forty lashes less one; three times I was beaten, I was stoned one time, three times I was shipwrecked—a night and day I spent at sea. With frequent journeys, in dangers of rivers, in dangers of thugs, in dangers from my race, in dangers from Gentiles, in dangers in city, in dangers in wilderness, in dangers at sea, in dangers from false brothers, in toil and hardship during frequent sleepless nights, in famine and thirst, in frequent fastings, in cold and nakedness. . . ." Reading aloud, I didn't need to think about the vocabulary or the grammar; the sense of Paul's Greek came home directly. When I had finished, I couldn't quite get my breath. But Professor Barr said I didn't have to translate the passage, since I had obviously gotten the point. So I did, and it has never left me.

Paul is the most complex, brilliant, troubled figure in the New Testament. He speaks for himself—inviting us to trace his turbulent, dramatic life. In *Rabbi Paul*, I have focused on the places he went and the people he knew as well as the evolution of his vastly influential theology. The more we delve into the man and his thinking, the closer we approach the inner flame that once ignited a new religion.

part one

PATH OF VISION

· I ·

TENT-MAKER'S SON

FROM TARSUS

TWO MILLENNIA BEFORE PAUL, there was Tarsus. His native
city lay near the southeast coast of Asia Minor on a fertile plain
called Cilicia. Tarsans were famous for a loudmouthed ambition that flaunted exotic festivals for their gods and flamboyant commerce in foreign products. Their city gobbled up immigrant groups
such as its Jews and boasted a bustling academy. Pagan, commercial,
part Jewish, and philosophical all at the same time, Tarsus was complex
and conflicted. Knowing Tarsus is basic to knowing Paul. He mirrored
the city that raised him.

To the end of his life, Paul cherished his association with the people
he called "kinsfolk": fellow Jews and fellow citizens from the city that
had nurtured him from the time of his birth in 7 C.E. In his letter to
the Romans he refers to Andronicus and Junia[1] (Romans 16:7),
Herodion (Romans 16:11), and Lucius, Jason, and Sosipater (Romans
16:21). Their names fit Greco-Roman custom generally, except for
Herodion, which recalls the famous Jewish client-king of Rome. By
Paul's own testimony, we can say that he identified with the Judaism of
the Diaspora and with the fierce pride of his native city.

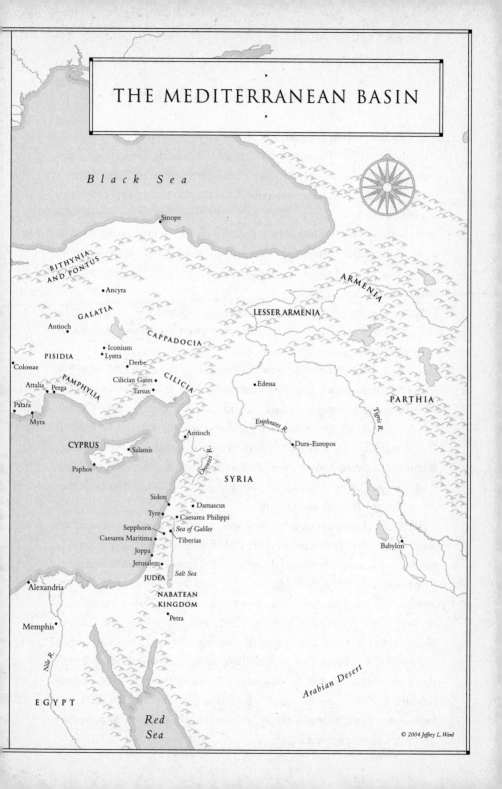

THE MEDITERRANEAN BASIN

Black Sea

Sinope

BITHYNIA AND PONTUS

• Ancyra

ARMENIA

LESSER ARMENIA

GALATIA

Antioch •

CAPPADOCIA

• Iconium
• Lystra

• Edessa

PISIDIA

• Derbe

PARTHIA

Colossae •

CILICIA

Cilician Gates •

Attalia •

PAMPHYLIA

Tarsus •

Euphrates R.

Tigris R.

Perga •

Patara •

Myra •

Antioch •

Dura-Europos •

CYPRUS

• Salamis

Orontes R.

SYRIA

Paphos •

Sidon •

• Damascus

Tyre •

• Caesarea Philippi

Babylon •

Sepphoris •

• *Sea of Galilee*

Caesarea Maritima •

• Tiberias

Joppa •

Jerusalem •

Salt Sea

JUDEA

• Alexandria

NABATEAN KINGDOM

• Petra

Memphis •

Nile R.

Arabian Desert

EGYPT

Red Sea

© 2004 Jeffrey L. Ward

COMMERCIAL TARSUS

The city thrived on markets but produced only a fraction of the merchandise on offer. Trade was the key to the wealth Tarsus had established and would long retain. Still a considerable city in Turkey with a population today of some 150,000, it has six thousand years of history buried beneath its streets. With only half that population during the first century, Tarsus dominated Cilicia. Even Dio Chrysostom, an itinerant philosopher who had little regard for the city, grudgingly admitted it was "the metropolis" (*Discourses* 33.17, 34.7), the pivot of the regional economy.

Since the Bronze Age, deforestation has exposed the Turkish highlands to wind and water, forces that have silted up flatlands and coasts beneath. Shifting coastlands and riverbeds as well as decimated forests and bare highlands attest to how human beings alter the land they live in. Here, as in Israel, the environment can be modified dramatically without a big change in climate. Centuries of mountain runoff made Cilicia's soil fertile, fit to produce grain and wine and flax. The Cydnus River provided for a city's thirst for water: to drink, to dispose of effluent, to navigate down to the Mediterranean Sea. After all that, abundant supplies were left over for the decorative, cooling fountains that cities all over Asia Minor prized.

Between Tarsus and the coast some ten miles south,[2] a natural lagoon made for a protected harbor; that distance helped keep pirates at bay from the city, if not from shipping. The Tarsans enhanced what nature provided, fitting their lake out with docks and an arsenal. That access to the sea was crucial to the city's success: Tarsus occupied a crossroads for international trade. Thirty miles north lay the Cilician Gates, a pass through the Taurus Mountains. These "gates" had begun as a natural formation that provided a rough, narrow trail for trekkers; the Tarsans then carved the pass into a highway through rock, cutting beneath a cliff face—sometimes between five and six hundred feet high—to permit animal-drawn caravans to ply their trade across an otherwise inhospitable range.

This city was a commercial bridge between caravans to the north (where east and west also met by land routes) and shipping to the south. Even without the Cilician Gates, fertile soil and diligence would have provided for Tarsus's survival; with the Gates, Tarsan markets made for wealth, and its people had every reason to take pride in their achievement.

The people of the highlands benefited from Tarsus by trading rugs and tapestries, somewhat as they do today. Their bartering over high-quality carpets was comparable to their Persian and Indian counter-parts, but the designs they wove were different. Although some of the high court styles of Greece and Egypt and Persia were imitated, carpets from the Taurus range were renowned for the vivid, primitive designs of a people who resisted assimilation. Abstract symbols in red wool—a diamond with eight limbs and a mandala within, an insect sketched around an inverted triangle—stand for a scorpion, admired because ac-cording to myth a scorpion would rather sting itself to death than ac-cept capture or defeat. Whatever its scientific merits, that claim applied more directly to the people of the mountains, who profited from their Greek and Roman masters without actually submitting to them.

The bazaars that sprang up due to trade were polyglot. Merchants came in from the mountains and the sea, some from far afield, setting up their wares under tents. Tent-making firms such as Paul's family ran made a huge profit—providing portable stalls and accommodations, and repairing damage to the canvas and felt that protected a caravan's wagons and to the leather that harnessed its animals. The mountain people spoke their own Cilician language but made themselves under-stood in Greek and sometimes Latin to the bulk of their clients, the servants of wealthy nobles and Roman colonists. Aramaic was also spo-ken by the Syrians who traded there as well as by many of the local population from the time of the Persians. Merchants from the Black Sea and Europe also passed through and did their business in Aramaic, Greek, or Latin: whichever worked best. When trade involved not only finished products and handiwork, but silver and lead from the Taurus Mountains as well as iron from Pontic Cappadocia, dealers and customers had every reason to find a way to make themselves understood accurately. Multicultural commerce and haggling surrounded Paul from the time he could speak.

Tarsus had long provided an axis of regional commerce not only for the people of Cilicia, but also for the great empires that had conquered the city. Antiochus the Great had settled two thousand Jewish families from Mesopotamia in the region, providing them with land, tax incentives, and a measure of self-government[3] in exchange for their loyalty in this troubled sector of his Seleucid empire.

The Jews formed a civic "tribe" (*phule* in Greek, not to be confused with the clans of Jacob), comparable to the tribes to which all citizens belonged during the Seleucid and Roman periods. Families such as Paul's enjoyed the rights of citizenship. Seleucid monarchs found that Jews generally made good subjects, loyal to the rulers who assured them civic status and protected them from local hostility. The Romans reinforced the Persian policy when they took power during the first century B.C.E. Jews in the Diaspora prospered because imperial powers sheltered them from the worst of classical anti-Semitism, and they knew where their loyalty was owed.[4] Local pretenders to power attracted them no more than local gods did. Their security depended on the rule of imperial law.

Mark Antony bolstered the prospects of Paul's family, and every family of citizens, during a visit to Tarsus when he came east to represent the Triumvirate in 42 B.C.E. He showed his gratitude to a city that had been loyal to Julius Caesar, confirming its autonomy and granting it exemption from Roman taxes. Antony's generosity was stoked by his passion; Tarsus was the site of Cleopatra's famous ride in a barge, in which she sailed up the Cydnus River to meet her paramour, dressed as Aphrodite.[5] For the ambitious and often libidinous population of the city, this was Tarsus's finest hour.

PAGAN TARSUS

Every year, Tarsus mounted a spectacle for Tarku, the people's favorite god among the many they worshiped.

The city was built on Cilicia's swampy coastal plain, drained for agriculture over the centuries. Dio Chrysostom made fun of how far short Tarsus fell from classical norms of civic beauty (*Discourses* 33.24–30). With its flat landscape and dirty river, Dio Chrysostom accorded Tarsus the kind of respect that Manhattan's young professionals give The Bronx. Tarku more than compensated for that.

Tarsus had passed from Hittite control to Assyrian control (during the ninth century B.C.E.); after that came the Persians (during the sixth century B.C.E.), with their powerful bureaucracy and an insistent policy of speaking Aramaic for official purposes throughout their vast empire. The coming of Alexander the Great in 334 B.C.E. and the dynasty of his general Seleucus that succeeded Alexander preserved many Persian ways, increasingly leavened with Hellenistic art, philosophy, and language. The culture that shaped Paul from the beginning of his life was pagan as well as Jewish; even the Aramaic he learned at home had been imported by the Persians. Greek was the intellectual oxygen of his thought. And when it came to his proud Jewish heritage, cultural memory taught him that Rome was its indispensable guardian.

The Romans had to wrest control of Cilicia from the pirates and local kingdoms that plagued Tarsus during the last years of Persian rule. Rome's firm measures revived the underlying economy of the region; the new rulers had little to do but police the place to enjoy the contribution of loyal, prosperous subjects and citizens. Yet Tarsus never lost its affinity with the Near East; its natives retained their customs and language when foreigners took over the reins of power. Cilician pride was almost as famous as the fine linen that bore the name of their region, and it came out in religious festivals.

Four teenage men held a canopy for the image of their divine hero as they stood on the corners of a garlanded wagon that oxen drew through the streets along the Cydnus River. They sweated under linen tunics in damp, alluvial heat. An effigy of Tarku, handsome as his bearers, stood tall atop a winged lion on this platform inside four poles erected to form a pyramid. Impassive within his palanquin, Tarku paraded through clouds of incense.

Thousands of people made way for their painted god. Forever as young as his bearers, Tarku's feet did not touch the base of the platform: he stood on top of a winged lion with horns.[6] He stands there now, on the many coins of Tarsus that have survived to this day, minted with the emblem of a proud city.

The palanquin approached a temple while crowds chanted the god's name. Some people hailed the god as Perseus or Hercules, familiar names in the Hellenistic world that Greek-speakers often applied to the heroic and virile founder-gods of cities in central and eastern Asia Minor. But other enthusiasts—as we know from the same coins that bear Tarku's likeness—spoke Aramaic, calling him Ba'al-Tarz (Lord of Tarsus), a designation from the Persian period, used long after Greek became a lingua franca in the region; still others acclaimed him as Tarku in the primeval language of Cilicia.

Tarku had been the people's god since before time could be reckoned. He wore an Anatolian headdress as he rode standing on his celestial beast, holding a blossoming flower in his right hand and a battle ax in his left, sword and bow case strapped to the same side of his body. He conveyed fertility, protection, the commanding strength of youth. Offspring of a father-god and a goddess, every spring he was carried to his temple, and there he was burned in effigy. As the flames leaped up to heaven in the midst of sacrifice and incense, he became a god, and Tarku's apotheosis—symbolized by an eagle at the apex of his pyramid—brought the promise that the spring planting would be successful, that another year would see Tarsus healthy and prosperous.

The crowd clamored its praise and petitions and hopes and fears to its god. Pleas for rain, for healing, for personal success were mixed with sacrificial chants and cries of local patriotism. Women keened Tarku's approaching immolation, at the same time celebrating his ascension into heaven. Sorrow and festivity, tears and joyful song had joined in this moment long before written or oral memory. Festival unleashed the passion and vitality of a proud people, roused by feasting to make their fortunes the coming year from the soil, from the river, from the mountains, from the marketplace. With the process of his dying, the god lived eternally. He fused death and life in a way comparable to Osiris in Egypt, Dionysos in Greece, Tammuz in Syria.

Some of the women who sang this moment were veiled from head to toe in the old Cilician manner, so thoroughly they could not see well enough to walk in the street without assistance (Dio Chrysostom *Discourses* 33.48), a bizarre sight next to Roman ladies in their flimsy linen. Priests presided over the rituals in long-robed, ceremonial dress, proud to underwrite feasting as well as mediate the divine. Tarku perhaps gave his name to this city, and in any case he was an appropriate icon for a diverse population up and coming with civic ambition. Every year Tarsus brought itself to birth in the cycle of planting and harvesting, trekking and shipping, wheeling and dealing that made it rich.

Paul's ancestral Judaism probably prevented him from taking part in the festivals of Tarku. But he had to have seen them, and their significance was embedded in his culture; his own words show how deeply they shaped his religious consciousness. In one of his rhetorical flourishes, he describes himself as being led in procession amidst clouds of incense, on the way to a personal apotheosis (2 Corinthians 2:14–16a):

> Thanks to God, who always leads us in procession in the Messiah, and manifests the fragrance of his knowledge through us in every place, because we are Messiah's aroma for God among those who are being saved and among those who are perishing, either a fragrance of death for death or a fragrance of life for life.

Burning in his experience much as Tarku did on his pyre,[7] the mature Paul spoke in the idiom of his youth. He had never carried Tarku on his palanquin, but the faith he embraced in his maturity enabled him to carry the message of a new divinity, and to embrace the ambition that he himself might taste the fragrance of immortality and become divine. This son of Tarsus—passing through the flames of persecution and resistance on behalf of Christ at the time he wrote these words— had in his own mind become a new Tarku.

JEWISH TARSUS

Judaism's most basic teachings prohibited actually cheering Tarku or fawning over Cleopatra's pretensions to the charms of Aphrodite. The Jews of Tarsus steered clear of that behavior (no doubt with exceptions), yet maintained their standing in the city. They owed their position of privilege to their loyalty, not to local custom, but to great conquerors: Cyrus the Persian, Alexander and the Seleucid monarchs who followed him, Julius Caesar and his successors. All those military geniuses had enforced the view that citizenship was compatible with Judaism, and Jews had thrived.

They still encountered local prejudice, and for centuries would feel little confidence in those who appealed to "democratic" sentiments. But at least the provincial mobs that remained a fact of life did not enjoy official sanction in Tarsus, and the Jews of Cilicia were notable for their absence from first-century delegations of complaint to Rome and from armed revolts, while Judea, Galilee, Egypt, Libya, and Cyprus all saw major unrest.

The Jews of Tarsus could freely pursue trades, tent-making among them. This skilled craft required expertise and tools—and therefore investment in people and material—to work the leather and felt from which tents were made. But the investment offered excellent prospects: any army or caravan of traders had need of professionals to get their camps set up and keep them in good repair. Travel meant wear and tear, even on the heavy materials the best tents were made from, so contractors in the business, keeping a row of shops with tenements for a couple dozen workers and slaves upstairs, were richly rewarded.

References in Paul's letters speak of manual work as onerous (1 Thessalonians 2:9; 1 Corinthians 4:12; 2 Corinthians 11:7), and some commentators have concluded that his skill was acquired late in life and grudgingly. But these references don't settle the question. People then as now often complain about their work, even when it is rewarding. In any case, tent-makers in antiquity formed up into guilds of masters and apprentices, and to imagine Paul just picking up tools as an adult and quickly mastering the skills and social networks required to make tents commercially seems implausible. Even Hillel—a far more important Pharisee than Paul ever became—had to make his living from unskilled journeywork. Hillel also came from the Diaspora (in Babylonia rather than Cilicia) a generation before Paul and shows us how tough it was to earn a living without established professional contacts.

Paul's family in Tarsus in all likelihood brought him up in this trade. As prominent citizens of Tarsus—and Roman citizens—they shared the huge tax advantage that Rome gave the city, and profitable contacts came their way. As citizens they were expected to extend their patronage to the city, but they had means enough to do that without difficulty. Citizenship was well worth the expense in terms of the commercial advantages it gave: access to business with the Roman army and magistracy as well as the tax break.

Jewish families congregated on the Sabbath to hear their Bible—the Scriptures of Israel—read in its Greek version, and lived in easy proximity to one another. This enabled them to gather for worship within the walking distance allowed on the seventh day, and made sure that they frequented only those shopkeepers who observed the laws of kashrut. Theirs was an enclave community, perhaps seven thousand strong, a town within a city rather than a ghetto. The civic authorities did not segregate them, but they insulated themselves from the worst excesses of promiscuous Tarsus.

Families of wealthy men such as Paul's father could afford real mansions with courtyards, space for the extended family, and servants' quarters. We can't estimate the size of Paul's family exactly, but the Book of Acts does mention a sister whose son was in Jerusalem when

Paul was arrested there toward the end of his life (Acts 23:16). Wealth meant that Paul's parents could beat the odds of infant mortality in Tarsus as a whole better than most; he probably had several brothers and sisters. Because Paul freely traveled to Jerusalem once he had grown, it seems unlikely that he was the only son, or even the eldest son. "Be fruitful and multiply"—the primordial command to the first man and the first woman (Genesis 1:28)—was also the advice the prophet Jeremiah had given to Jews in exile (Jeremiah 29:6), and Diaspora Jews saw to the extension of their pious families as a bulwark against dissolution in the Roman Empire. Paul's father must have assured the stability of the family and its business (including his commercial successor) before he allowed number two or three son to experiment with the beat of distant drummers.

But his father did let Paul go, evidently supporting him in his vocation to train as a Pharisee in Jerusalem. His son returned the favor by saying absolutely nothing about his family—father, mother, brothers, sisters, or any other relation—in his many letters. Ruthless independence shaped his personality from first to last.

· · ·

MANY BOOKS have been written on the topic of Paul and the religion of the territorial Israel of his time (usually referred to as "Palestinian Judaism" in the secondary literature). But the Hellenistic Diaspora, not "Palestine," was the seedbed of Paul's life and thought. Asia Minor's Judaism had its own flavor and character, venerating the memory of Noah, for example, whose ark was said to have landed locally, on Mount Ararat. Jews in Tarsus even claimed that their town was identical with the primeval city mentioned in connection with Noah called Tarshish (Genesis 10:4, connected to Tarsus by Josephus, *Antiquities* 1.127). Legends of this kind express the religious sensibility of the Diaspora during the first century, where the vast majority of Jews lived.

Classicists are familiar with the oracle called the Sibyl—the premier prophetess of Greco-Roman culture. She was such a pivotal figure of prophecy, Judaism claimed her as its own. The *Sibylline Oracles* (3:809–29), a popular Diaspora book written in Greek and never included in the Bible (whether in Hebrew or Greek), presents the Sibyl as Noah's daughter-in-law! Sometimes obviously made-up history is the most accurate measure of an ancient people's faith, because it shows us what they wanted to believe was true.

For Israelites in the Diaspora, the most noble of non-Jewish people (such as the mantic Sibyl), even if they did not fully embrace Judaism by circumcising their males, could acknowledge the God of Israel by following the commandments of Noah: refraining from idolatry, from consuming blood, and from promiscuous sexuality. Such people were known as worshipers of God or God-fearers, who—like their Jewish contemporaries—held themselves aloof from some of the civic religions of Tarsus.

Avoiding idolatry and blood, of course, meant not taking part in sacrifices for Tarku and similar exercises. Yet in the bustling market, even ordinary meat might appear under the icon of a god or goddess to whom it was notionally sacrificed at the moment of slaughter. Idolatry of this sort was an ancient form of advertising (unless it is truer to say that advertising is idolatry in modern dress). Jews and God-fearers avoided that, just as they insisted that animals for consumption should be killed by cutting their throats rather than by strangling, so the meat was well bled. Even the program of avoiding promiscuity was not an easy matter; the Torah prohibited marriage with near relations (Leviticus 18:6–17), a customary practice among the elites of the Hellenistic world.

Jews and God-fearers stood apart from the ordinary life of the city; often they even sat apart. At several archaeological digs, inscriptions carved in the ancient stone benches of theaters and stadiums in Asia Minor indicate that seating was especially designated for "God-fearers" and "Jews," away from those devoted to blood sausage who chanted praises to diverse gods and cultivated prohibited liaisons. Jews themselves also kept the Sabbath, which opened them to charges of laziness, and their food laws were held to be more than odd. Why would any-

one prohibit eating a meat as good as pork? Gentiles in fact contributed
to making the pig into a primary symbol of impurity for Jews, rather
than having it remain one animal among many proscribed in the
Torah; in times of persecution they would attempt to force pork into
the mouths of their hapless victims.

Gentile mockery included the taunt: Do they worship pigs, or
something? Otherwise respected authors such as Cicero provide noto-
rious examples of this kind of anti-Semitism. In peaceful Tarsus this
silly rhetoric appeared trivial to God-fearers. It didn't lead to anything,
and Judaism offered them access to a rational deity: a single creator,
consistent with philosophy and moral in character. Even the most an-
thropomorphic images of Israel's God competed favorably with Zeus
and company. And Jews could rejoice in the commandments intended
for them especially—circumcision and kashrut and sacrifice in
Jerusalem—which marked them out as the bearers of the covenant.
They led the meetings in synagogues that God-fearers also attended
and arranged for pilgrimage to Jerusalem for wealthier families as well
as the collection of tax for the Temple there.

Wealthy Jews did more than gather in pickup meetings on the
Sabbath. Their synagogues were "gatherings," as the term *sunagoge*
means in Greek, but also buildings, whether converted private homes
or purpose-built. Each stood in stark contrast to the ornate temples of
Greco-Roman cities. The pagan acropolis dominated the urban landscape in city after city, lavishly decorated with statues and altars and the
paraphernalia of sacrifice, while modest synagogues nestled in the midst
of Jewish neighborhoods, advertised by their plain design and aniconic
simplicity. Each was a triumph of understatement amidst the baroque
competition of god vying with god in the streets of Tarsus.

The rectangular synagogue in Tarsus faced Jerusalem and was
arranged around a central portion of open space framed by pillars.
Around the pillars, stone benches arranged seating for Israelite men and
women and God-fearers in separate sections. Within that central area,
Paul watched the leaders of his community as he grew up; these teachers guided worship, spoke about the Torah, taught children such as

himself, collected revenue for the Temple in Jerusalem, and settled disputes. To become one of these men was the height of his ambition.

Paul no doubt had heard of the most famous teacher of international Judaism, Philo of Alexandria. Philo came from a family of aristocrats; his brother served the Romans as a treasury official in Egypt and enjoyed excellent relations with Herod Agrippa (Herod the Great's grandson, who died in 44 C.E.). Philo's own vast, erudite corpus of work flowed from a cosseted life whose ornament was well-spent leisure. In all the ornate twists and turns and genuine complexity of his thought, Philo was committed to the fundamental Diaspora principle that the best that Greek philosophy had to offer and the Torah of Moses together attested to the power and moral character of one God, the God of Israel.

Paul once wrote directly about his own Jewish heritage (Philippians 3:4–5): he had been circumcised on the eighth day, a true Israelite by parentage, birth, and practice, not merely an admirer of Judaism. He was descended from the clan of Benjamin and spoke Aramaic[8] as well as Greek from his birth. By means of his family and their synagogue, he was acculturated as a Jew in a thoroughly Hellenistic city.

Paul also says he attached himself to the Pharisees (Philippians 3:5); they became the first intellectual influence on Paul at the earliest stage of his adult life. Pharisaism was originally a movement in Jerusalem; its aim was to influence the conduct of worship and sacrifice in the Temple. Outright control of the Temple's operation eluded the Pharisees, but they did manage to gain access to the Sanhedrin, the most important Jewish governing body in Jerusalem. Outside Jerusalem, initially in the cities and towns of Judea and Galilee, the Pharisees pursued their agenda: they convinced local populations to immerse themselves for purification in the kinds of bathing pools they mandated (the *miqvaoth*), to observe regulations of tithing, and to exert particular care in the storage and preparation of foods. In all of this the purity of the Pharisaic household was analogous to the order the Pharisees desired to see in the Temple; fellowship at table in their practice became commensurate with sacrifice.

Because Pharisaism was a town and city movement, it could be exported from Jerusalem to metropolitan centers of the Diaspora such as Damascus, Alexandria, and Antioch. As it went further and further afield from the Temple, the movement lost appeal, yet the Book of Acts (23:6) has Paul calling himself "a Pharisee, a son of Pharisees." Some scholars have vehemently denied that there could have been any genuine Pharisees in Tarsus.[9] They are technically right because, apart from the Temple, the movement could focus on the sanctuary and its holiness only in the abstract. But this statement in Acts needn't mean Paul had been a Pharisee in Tarsus. The reference to Paul's being a "son" of Pharisees is an Aramaism, indicating that Paul had *apprenticed* with Pharisees; the city of the apprenticeship is not specified.

In a similar way Jesus is called a journeyman's son (Matthew 13:55), indicating his trade as a worker with primitive skills rather than who his father was. To be the "son" of Pharisees or journeymen or whatever meant to belong to that group. In the cases of both Jesus and Paul, family involvement in the designation is implicit. Jesus did not become a journeyman without Joseph's training and contacts, and Paul did not get to Jerusalem without his family's support and encouragement. He became a zealot for values his family before him had embraced.

The New Testament says the Pharisees "cross land and sea to make a single proselyte" (Matthew 23:15), and—hyperbole aside—that description is informative. Judaism may not have been a missionary religion in the same sense that Christianity eventually became, but it won admirers, and some of its branches—Pharisaism included—clearly did actively seek support among Jews and Gentiles. If Paul's parents passed on their attitudes to their children, that would accord with what is said of many religious teachers in antiquity, and with common experience today.

After all, Paul's nephew was in Jerusalem at the same time he was near the end of his life (Acts 23:16): a family connection with the city, the center of Pharisaism, is pretty obvious. Back in Tarsus, Paul must have been exposed to the devotion to the Temple and its worship, and the maintenance of Israelite purity as demanded by the Torah that characterized Pharisaic sympathizers. One method of Pharisaic propaganda was written communication. Both the authorities of the Temple and their Pharisaic competitors wrote letters to urban communities in the Diaspora to encourage them to maintain the practices and attitudes they preferred. This epistolary literature, missives from Jerusalem to the Judaic community at large, was an important feature of life within Paul's synagogue, and he aligned himself with Pharisaic sympathizers there. Writing as an apostle years later, he showed himself a master of just this sort of communication.

His letter-writing also shows that Paul's parents schooled him to a level beyond the bare ability to read and write. Yet for all his attainments in rhetoric, he offers remarkably little by way of references and allusions to classical literature. He quotes a scrap of Menander while writing to his Corinthian readers (1 Corinthians 15:33), and the Book of Acts has him reel off a little Aratus during a speech in Athens (Acts 17:28). But that is pretty much it.

In this regard Paul contrasts sharply with Philo of Alexandria, his older contemporary. Philo was no mere controversialist, but a public intellectual who contributed a commentary on the whole of the Pentateuch in elegant, literary Greek, with philosophical cadenzas and a thorough mastery of classical allusions. The Diaspora never produced a more committed, better-read, brilliant representative than Philo of Alexandria. He wrote more than Paul, better than Paul, with philosophical accomplishment. In comparison with him, Paul would not merit a footnote within the intellectual history of the first century, except that he became a Christian. When you read Philo, you realize what Paul was not, could not have been, and never wanted to become—any more than any Pharisee of his generation.

In the style of his letters, Paul deliberately eschewed the kinds of classical references that Philo rejoiced in. He wrote to the Corinthians, "I decided not to know anything among you except Christ Jesus" (1 Corinthians 2:2); he avoided the classical allusions we might expect from a master of rhetoric so consistently that it looks like a lifelong habit, not just a consequence of his conversion to Jesus' movement.

Paul's family enjoyed the services of slaves and had contacts with many other Jewish families who owned slaves. They could easily afford to detail one or several of them to teach the children their letters and numbers and higher subjects, making sure they eased up on the classics of Greece and Rome in order to instill their own classic: the Greek Bible, which was their pride and glory.

The Diaspora's Bible differed from the Hebrew Bible. Rabbis in the land of Israel during the first century typically grouped the books of the Hebrew Bible into a canon of the Torah, the Prophets, and the Writings. But the Bible of the Diaspora was Greek in language, Hellenistic in conception, and followed a distinctive order that reveals a special significance.

An early surviving manuscript of the whole Greek Bible orders the books in a sequence so that the climax is marked out as prophecy. As in the Hebrew Bible, the Five Books of Moses commence the whole; narratives of Israel's past come next, making a category, not of law, but of historical writing. Then a series of poetic works follows, starting with Psalms. Finally the prophetic section starts with the minor prophets and reaches its climax with the imposing books of Isaiah, Jeremiah, Ezekiel, and Daniel.[10] The message of this presentation is clear: the ultimate meaning of the Bible is prophecy, and its apogee is the apocalyptic vision of Daniel.

This grouping was by no means fixed. Even the *content* of the Greek Bible varied. The Diaspora Scriptures contained books not included in the Hebrew Bible: That produced the Apocrypha, works whose Hebrew originals were "hidden" (as St. Jerome during the fifth century put the matter, although in most cases there just weren't any Hebrew originals). This Diaspora Bible varied from community to community: there was no central authority capable of fixing it, so synagogues differed in what they read as Scripture, and in what order.

The triumph of the Greek Bible is the crescendo leading to Daniel, now emphatically one of the *Prophets* (rather than one of the Writings, as in the Hebrew Bible). That change over the centuries exerted a powerful influence on Christianity, whose own "New Testament" closes with the Revelation of John, which develops the imagery of Daniel. Early Christian preachers seized upon Daniel's references to the Resurrection (12:2) and to the angel like a person or "a son of man" (7:13, 10:16) as predictions that Jesus fulfilled.

They forged those associations so effectively, it is difficult for Christians to think in any other terms. But in the young Paul's time, Diaspora Judaism saw that angel and the Resurrection he brought as predicting *Israel's* triumph, not Christianity's. This "one like a person" was the angel of Israel, whose elevation before God marked the eternal dominion (Daniel 7:13–18) of "the holy ones of the Most High."

The Bible in Greek commonly circulated with what amounted to a preface, called the *Letter of Aristeas*. Aristeas's story shows the kind of revelatory power Diaspora Judaism attributed to its Scriptures. Aristeas says he was a go-between in arranging for a translation of the "Bible" (which is called just that, *Aristeas* 316) from Hebrew to Greek in Alexandria. King Ptolemy acts on the advice of his librarian Demetrius and sends Aristeas and a companion to secure the services of seventy-two elders (six from each clan of Israel) from the high priest in Jerusalem. Amid much pious gift-giving and lavish banqueting, they are set up in a mansion on an island near Alexandria, miraculously accomplishing their task in just seventy-two days, the same as the number of translators. No wonder this version was called the Septuagint, meaning "the Seventy," in Greek.

Aristeas delivers its punch with its characterization of the principal characters. Ptolemy is a just ruler who frees hundreds of thousands of Jewish soldiers and slaves and donates a golden table to the Temple in Jerusalem, all because—although a Gentile—he is devoted to "the Most High God." His librarian insists on the translation, since the Bible is philosophically accomplished and can teach his master to govern wisely (*Aristeas* 28–40). Together, the legendary Ptolemy and Demetrius are just what Egypt lacked at the time of the exodus: wise rulers who acknowledge the God of Israel.

Eleazar, the equally idealized high priest they appeal to, is the key figure in the narrative: the supremely rational teacher at the heart of the lavish, gorgeous Temple in Jerusalem (*Aristeas* 41–51, 83–120). He explains that he represents the one true God of all creation and that all the laws of Judaism—even those that may seem trivial or irrational— are intended to fit Israel to serve this God (*Aristeas* 128–71). The translation Eleazar and Ptolemy authorize is embraced by the priests and the community of Jews in Alexandria amid warnings that any change of wording would bring about a divine curse (*Aristeas* 308–11).

A noble Gentile king, a wise Gentile librarian, an enlightened Israelite high priest, and a loyal Jewish subject—Aristeas himself— together show how the whole world could one day be if only obedience to the Torah could be secured by means of accurate translation and pious effort. The Greek Bible was not only a translation of the Hebrew Bible in a new language; because the Septuagint spoke the language of empire (as founded by Alexander and inherited by the Romans), it held out the prospect for converting the world to worship of the true God. Here the mantic utterances of the Sibyl, the imperatives of the Prophets, the Torah delivered to Moses, and the poetry of Israel's sages all met in a single climax of power, revelation, and philosophy. This was the only classic literature of which Paul the Pharisee (and later, Paul the Apostle) had any need.

PHILOSOPHICAL TARSUS

Roman Tarsus was also a city of philosophy. Between 52 and 50 B.C.E., none other than Cicero—lawyer, broken statesman, Stoic philosopher, master of intrigue—served as governor of Cilicia. From his elitist perspective, Tarsus was a step away from a pirate-plagued backwater, whatever its wealth. The new governor devoted his correspondence from Tarsus to politics and gossip back in Rome, not to concerns of the city he governed.

Cicero did nothing for philosophy in Tarsus, but Augustus Caesar did. His father, Julius Caesar, had found a warm welcome in Tarsus when he had passed through in 47 B.C.E.; people there even started to call their city "Juliopolis" (Cassius Dio, *Roman History* 47.26). Augustus's affections for distant Cilicia were cemented by his own tutor, Athenodorus of Tarsus.

Athenodorus, a prominent Stoic philosopher, was brought up in a village near Tarsus. Widely traveled, he had tutored Augustus at Apollonia in Macedonia. By then Athenodorus had already studied in Rhodes and journeyed to Rome, and was famous enough to warrant Cicero's recommendation for his teaching on nobility (*Letters to Friends* 3.7.5). That made him more notable in Cicero's mind than Tarsus itself. The later Stoic master Seneca (Paul's contemporary) also quoted Athenodorus. Seneca embraced Athenodorus's teaching that, during a period of political corruption, a man can serve the body politic by means of private virtue among friends (*On Tranquility of Mind* 3). Seneca also cherished and developed the theological side of Athenodorus's Stoicism (*Moral Epistles* 10.5), "Know that you are freed from all desires when you have attained this: that you ask God nothing except what you can ask openly."

Augustus had studied with Athenodorus in 45 B.C.E., and Athenodorus came back to Rome with him the next year. The old philosopher eventually asked the emperor for retirement around 15 B.C.E.; he took up a commanding position in Tarsus. Athenodorus ruled by imperial warrant, which gave him the ability to exile corrupt local leaders and insist upon a philosophical oligarchy centered on the local academy.

Academies in the ancient world were loose affiliations of seminars rather than formal institutions. Teachers would lecture to students and engage in dialogue, sometimes at public expense and sometimes in the hope of attracting private students. Provided they posed no threat to public order, these floating talk-shops were considered an ornament to an ambitious city. In exchange for offering both wisdom and entertainment, shelter in buildings or porticoes was a small price to pay.

Tarsus's academy, for all its accomplishment, did not compete with those of Alexandria or Athens or Rome; it even trailed Antioch, Corinth, and Carthage in influence. This was apparent to Strabo

(*Geography* 14.5.13) even during the city's intellectual salad days under Athenodorus: "Yet it differs in this: the men who are fond of learning there are all natives, but foreigners are not prone to sojourn there. Neither do these natives stay there, but they finish their education abroad. And when they are finished, they are pleased to live abroad, and few go back home." This was a provincial setup at the best of times. Gifted students were encouraged to acquire their expertise and standing abroad and then stay abroad, securing private and public benefaction in another city. Such is the insecurity of provincial universities then and now.

Budding philosophers from Tarsus were not helped in this quest during the first century by the growing reputation of Tarsus's intellectuals for superficiality. Apollonius of Tyana (also in Asia Minor) complained that Tarsan students were mere jesters, caring more about their fine linen than the Athenians did for wisdom (Philostratus, *Life of Apollonius* 1.7).[11] Both he and Dio Chrysostom (*Discourses* 33:36–43) compared the rude sounds Tarsan audiences made to swans honking on the Cydnus.

Wounded pride might lie behind these typically academic jabs at Tarsus. Strabo observes that "the city of Tarsus has all kinds of schools of rhetoric," so its students are adept at speaking "offhand and unceasingly on any given subject" (*Geography* 14.5.13, 14). Maybe Apollonius and Dio had lost an argument or two in Tarsus.

PAUL

In any case, history does know at least one debater from Tarsus who pursued arguments, if not offhand, then incontrovertibly—some would say incorrigibly—at length. Some of Paul's readers in Corinth remarked that his letters were weighty and strong, while his physical presence seemed weak and his delivery pathetic (2 Corinthians 10:10). Neither in body nor in voice could he ever approach the boundless ambition of his mind, which included a desire to replicate the soaring rhetoric of teachers he had first heard in Tarsus.

Like many other gifted young intellectuals from Tarsus before and after him, Paul knew that he needed to make his reputation abroad to have any impact in his native city or elsewhere. And "abroad" for a fledgling Pharisee could mean only one place: Jerusalem. His ship set sail one day during the summer season when travel was easiest, a steady wind blowing from the west across the Mediterranean. The ship was one of the many merchant barks that plied their trade along the coast, filled with grain, amphorae of wine and oil, ingots of metal, and commercial merchandise. They hugged the shore despite their large size and the danger of rocks, to facilitate sightings for navigation and to make frequent harbor stops well away from the threat of pirates and the open sea.

Before he set foot on this tubby bark, he had seen such vessels put in at Tarsus and observed the loading and unloading of their cargo. But only at sea could he witness the ceaseless activity of a gnarled, skilled crew whose feet gripped mast and deck with a confidence he (and his stomach) could only envy. Even during the summer, a storm at the west end of the Mediterranean can make sea conditions treacherous at the east end and digestion for new sailors parlous at best.

A citizen had the right to wear a toga,[12] but Paul did so only occasionally. He had in any case probably left his best clothing at home after a last, formal leave-taking from his family prior to his journey. After all, a toga would be no recommendation to any Pharisee he might study with in Jerusalem, his ultimate destination. But his linen tunic would have been new, with a woolen cloak and leather sandals stowed below with his few affairs.

Judging from a description written during the second century (*Acts of Paul* 3.3), the twenty-one-year-old who stood on deck—proud as a college freshman—was short, bowlegged, and a little thick around the middle. We can infer that his hair was thinning already because he became quite bald as a mature adult. Perhaps, given the chronic condition that developed later in his life, he felt a little stinging in one eye; but he might have been aware of the sensation only as a vagrant tear in the salt air.

This journey and the many that followed it brought him countless new sights and beguiling possibilities; the cities of Antioch, Sidon, Tyre, Ptolemais, and Caesarea Maritima were centers of empire, commerce, and the dominant paganism of the first century. Antioch, named after the same Persian emperor who had given Tarsus its status as an autonomous city, was the Romans' window on the East, inflated with trade into the third largest city in the Roman Empire. In exchange for Tarsan grain and wine in amphorae, trade gave the boat tapestries and spices to continue the journey south to Sidon and Tyre, ancient biblical cities of idolatry and wealth, guardians of the Phoenician secrets of cosmetics and dyes. Any room left in the vessel—a bobbing cork for new travelers like Paul, burdened to the danger point in the eyes of its captain—was filled at Ptolemais with fresh farm produce of the Galilee and western Syria. Then the groaning bark made its final leg south, unloading the bulk of its wealth at the Roman garrison port of Caesarea, one of the most sybaritic cities of the whole area. By the time they reached Joppa, the comparatively modest port that served landlocked Jerusalem, the crew loaded leather goods and agricultural produce so as to continue its profitable journey.

He saw people and customs and attire and buildings and armies and vessels and piers he had never dreamed of. A different man, or perhaps Paul at a more formative age, would have been turned into a curious sophisticate by such travel. But Tarsus had already formed him, and he kept Jerusalem, his goal, at the center of his attention. Paul the Cilician believed in maturity what he had been taught in Tarsus: that it was a shame for a woman to be unveiled in public. He also said she ought to have all her hair shorn off her head if she disagreed (1 Corinthians 11:5–6). Paul the Stoic felt, like Athenodorus of Tarsus, that humanity could be linked into a single body by a divine principle (1 Corinthians 12:12–27), and that prayer and behavior should be open to the light of day (1 Thessalonians 5:5–9). In a well-worn Stoic image, he compared himself to a runner competing for a prize (1 Corinthians 9:24–27), an experience that his youth in Tarsus offered him. Rhetoric of this kind earned many Tarsans the reputation of conceited posing: such flights belonged to Paul's mental warp and woof.

When Paul left Tarsus for Jerusalem on that sultry day in 28 C.E., he brought persistent traits of attitude and temperament derived from his home city. He was a Cilician, a Stoic, a tent-maker, and—by deliberate ambition—a Pharisee. The resolution of those distinct personae within a single mind required years of struggle and the development of Paul's own unique thought. He made his way from Tarsus as an intellectual in the making, and his intellect eventually made him more influential than even his adolescent ambition could conceive.

"AT THE FEET" OF GAMALIEL,
IN SERVICE OF CAIAPHAS

ARRIVING IN JERUSALEM from Tarsus, Paul couldn't have put off visiting the Temple, God's only true dwelling on earth. On the eastern side of the city, dazzling in the sun, giant stone blocks extended the modest hill called Zion into a huge white platform. On that expanse, massive courts and porticoes surrounded the altar of Israel's Adonai, the "LORD" whose personal, ineffable name was "Yahweh" (according to the current estimate of scholars).

Jerusalem's Temple, the biggest religious structure in the ancient world, competed with the great pilgrimage sites of antiquity. Gold and silver and polished bronze covered so much of the edifice, Josephus said, that, depending on weather conditions, travelers to Jerusalem saw the Temple (*Jewish War* 5.222–23) as a second sun on the horizon or the white peak of a mountain.

For the 7 million Jews of the Mediterranean world, this was not just an acropolis such as pagan cities boasted, but the single place in the world where the LORD, who was uniquely God, could be worshiped with the offerings he desired. God might be known anywhere, but he accepted sacrifice—the supreme expression of devotion throughout the ancient world—only on Mount Zion.

Diaspora Jews cherished a special feeling for this place. Even when separated by hundreds or thousands of miles from Jerusalem, they knew that sacrifice offered there made them Israelites, different from other peoples, and that sense of difference kept them from the idolatry that surrounded them. They read their Scriptures in Greek, but as far as they were concerned, the high priest in the Temple had authorized the Septuagint and assured its inspiration, and the Temple alone was where "the overseer and creator of all" (*Aristeas* 16) was worshiped by means of perpetual sacrifice. In Tarsus, Paul had learned to love the Temple as much as he adored the Greek[1] Scriptures.

Even during the second century B.C.E.—long before Herod began to enlarge the Temple into the magnificent structure Paul saw— Aristeas said of its beauty (*Letter of Aristeas* 99): "I emphatically assert that every man who comes near the spectacle of what I have described will experience astonishment and amazement beyond words, his very being transformed by the hallowed arrangement of every single detail." When Paul stood in the sanctuary he was at the crossroads of earth and heaven, embodying the link between Aramaic and Greek, Diaspora and Mount Zion, the mind of Greece and the heart of Israel.

· · ·

IN JERUSALEM, Paul of Tarsus spoke his ancestral Jewish language freely in public as well as in private. He even took a new Aramaic name to replace his Hellenistic name—calling himself Saul *(Saulos)* after the most famous hero from the clan of Benjamin, Israel's first king. The name "Saul" carried no cachet in purely Greek company because the adjective *saulos* in Greek refers to a mincing walk such as a prostitute might affect.[2] What proud young man would want to be known by a name that sounded like "swisher"? In Jerusalem he could boast his self-attributed, Benjamite name—"Saul, my name is Saul"—without the pathetic, jokey puns that would have come his way at home.

At the age of twenty-one, Paul claimed his birthright—the right of his circumcision, the right of his commitment to purity—by entering all the way into the Temple's sanctuary court, where the altar stood. He had bathed in a *miqveh* (a Pharisaic bathing pool) south of the Temple, leaving his traveler's cloak and sandals and purse with the owner, and climbed the vast, torch-lit stairs of the great court. In that porticoed expanse he was immersed in the chants and songs and dances and prostrations and cries of thousands of people caught up in pious fervor—or tourists' amazement—and expressing themselves in dozens of different languages.

Crossing through the crowds, Paul bumped and jostled against other worshipers and travelers. Most of them either knew their way around or had guides who did, and moved in large enough numbers—twenty or thirty to a pack—that they could make a path through the huge throng. They came from villages in Galilee, from Rome and Corinth and other major cities, from Syria, Egypt, and Mesopotamia as well as from local communities of Pharisees, priests, and Essenes. In the great outer court he even bumped up against Gentiles who had come to pay their respects or satisfy their curiosity. Paul had to slip in at the tail of one of these groups to make his way, and finally passed the balustrade that threatened death to any Gentile who entered the interior court of the Temple, its sanctuary.

Only Israelite males were permitted in the central court proper; the sacred choreography of priests sacrificing to Israel's God was the privileged family treasure of Israel's enormous household. Here the LORD took pleasure in his people; inside the hidden shrine behind the altar the high priest entered once a year (on Yom Kippur) and addressed Yahweh personally with his own name. Paul had no real role here as yet. From his words and gestures one might have guessed that the earnest youth was a pious tourist: provincial accent, provincial tunic, not knowing what he should do as he gawked in awe. But he had come to the most sacred spot on earth to master the Pharisaic disciplines that, to his mind, would make this Temple truly his own. For him the sanctuary would become not merely the aim of pilgrimage and devotion, but also the constant center of his daily actions. From that ambition, only the power of heaven itself could dissuade him.

He brought the devotion of his Cilician homeland to this place. The Septuagint contains many Greek additions to the Hebrew text of the Bible. One of them relates the psalm sung in a furnace of fire by three young men whom a Gentile king tried to incinerate (Daniel 3:53–54), and it is a psalm of praise for the Temple. This singing draws an angel who protects them from the flames as the young men sing to God:

You are blessed in the Temple of your holy glory:
    Hymned and glorified above all forever.
You are blessed on the Throne of your kingdom:
    Hymned and exalted above all forever.

The faith and practice of Israel all over the world saw this place, this Temple, as the physical focus of God on earth, the lens that concentrated his power from above. This was the hub on earth of the indescribable glory of Israel's LORD on his celestial throne. For an ambitious intellectual from the Diaspora, Jerusalem was a city of unimaginable promise and pride, the place from which—in God's own apocalypse of fire and judgment—the whole earth would be transformed. Paul cannot have felt better or more fulfilled at any other moment of his life.

· · ·

IN THE NEXT four years, Paul accomplished in Jerusalem what he could never have managed in Tarsus: fervent in worship, prayer, and study, he learned well and emerged as a fledgling master of the Pharisees, a rabbi. Jerusalem was the center of the Pharisaic movement as a whole, its influence reaching out to affect the character of Judaism in territorial Israel and beyond. Paul says that as a Pharisee he "advanced in Judaism beyond many contemporaries in my race, remaining exceedingly zealous for my patriarchal traditions" (Galatians 1:14). He could have done that only in Jerusalem, the city that always occupied a place in his heart and mind.

Paul's letters refer to this period in the compressed, almost veiled way he adopted when speaking of his life prior to his conversion. As a result, he did not say in so many words that he spent this time in Jerusalem, although the Book of Acts emphatically does. Jürgen Becker, a leading scholar, concludes from Paul's silence that he never was in Jerusalem at this time, but instead resided in Damascus.[3] That conclusion goes beyond using Paul's letters to correct Acts. Instead, it invents readings of Paul *in order to contradict Acts*, ignoring the cultural reality that Jerusalem, and Jerusalem alone, was the place to be for any Pharisee who considered himself advanced. To Paul's mind this was the mainstream of Israel, and the Pharisees in fact became prominent among the founders of Rabbinic Judaism,[4] surviving in many varieties to this day.

In this most sacred but confusing city, Paul bumbled his way to the Pharisees' neighborhood as best he could, asking directions of friendly faces he hoped might speak Aramaic or Greek. He heard all the languages that rang out in the agora of Tarsus and then some, spoken by Jews and tourists who were driven by piety, commerce, and sheer curiosity. New dialects of Aramaic as well as unusual inflections of Greek sounded both intimidating and comic to his ears. Like many visitors to unfamiliar cities who hear their own language in the mouths of strangers, he had to ask himself: Is that really the same tongue I learned at home?

And is this the same religion? Essene preachers, whose doctrines are spelled out in the Dead Sea Scrolls, must have seemed outlandish to Paul. They proudly dressed in plain linen raiment, refusing to use oil on their bodies out of concern about the impurity that fluids could carry. They did not even use the same bathing pools other Jews frequented, but withdrew to their own baths. These zealous puritans believed they were the masters of the Temple in waiting, who would take over Jerusalem and destroy all those who opposed them in the final eschatological war. They looked forward with deadly, apocalyptic precision to that day when they would take the Temple over and slay their enemies, "the sons of darkness," by which they meant Gentiles—*and* any Jews who failed to agree with them.[5] Secrecy was their watchword where it concerned their most esoteric teaching, but the Essenes eagerly recruited Jewish converts to their cause in Jerusalem and other cities.

In contrast to the rigorous simplicity of the Essenes, Paul also saw styles of dress and cookery in Jerusalem as exotic as could be found anywhere, but crammed into the narrow streets of what was already a thousand-year-old city. The Romans and their Herodian client-kings had occupied Jerusalem for nearly a century, adding their own characteristic structures—most prominently the Temple Mount, Herod's Palace, and the Antonia Fortress—but they had not superimposed their typical grid plan of wide streets and avenues at ninety-degree angles. Visitors negotiated a tangle of alleyways and streets. Above them all, the Temple stood out on its gleaming white pedestal, a sacrificial engine spouting flame and smoke in its colossal testimony that the God of Israel alone ruled here and one day would rule everywhere.

High priests, priests, and their Levitical retainers lived an easy walk west of the Temple, while the Pharisees were quartered a little south of that wealthy district. Paul found some Pharisees' houses standing between the priests' on the north and the Essenes' further to the south. Families lived cheek by jowl, pressing into the streets with their wares and often setting household items out for cleaning and airing. Here Paul found his dream fulfilled: the Pharisees drew adherents from all the family lineages of Israel in common dedication to the ideal of living with one another. In such constant purity, they had ready access to the Temple. So in terms of both physical and metaphysical proximity, they lived as close to the LORD as any Israelite in any age could live.

The Pharisees were proud of their distinctive sets of cups and pots used for daily acts of purification. Airing in the street outside their houses, these utensils marked the way to Paul's new neighborhood. The most famous patriarch of the Pharisees, named Gamaliel, taught his family that, if they had to share an alleyway with priests,[6] they should awaken early to put household wares outside *before* the priests did. You didn't want to let them set out their vessels first, because then they could claim that the alley could be used only for priestly receptacles that day (Erubin 6:2 in the Mishnah). Living at close quarters meant battling for territory, staking claim to the demands of Pharisaic purity against the claims of all comers, priests and Essenes included.

The Pharisees, like the Essenes and the priests, preferred to live in their own neighborhood and practice their religion in their own way, the way God wanted. The aspiring Pharisee from Tarsus who claimed Benjamite genealogy had little in common with visionaries from Galilee like Jesus' disciples, with privileged priests, or with apocalyptic fanatics. He was much more inclined to fall in with the enthusiasm of the *Letter of Aristeas* in portraying the Temple in its grandeur as a transforming edifice, the living hope that all people might one day recognize the single true God, the LORD of Israel. He speaks of himself during this period as "zealous" (Galatians 1:14). In this time when the religion of Israel included many different kinds of belief loosely united by sacrifice in the Temple, there were as many sorts of zealots as there were varieties of Judaism. Paul was a zealot for the Pharisees' way of life.

· · ·

THE PHARISEES committed much of the Hebrew Bible to memory; even illiterate Pharisees—the majority of them—knew the Scriptures. Yet devotion to the Torah went beyond that. On Sinai, Moses indeed received written tablets of the Torah, but during his forty days on that mountain God also gave him personal instruction. Those mysteries had been passed on from sage to sage in an unbroken chain of tradition that linked every master of the Torah to Moses, and therefore to God. A tractate of the Mishnah called Aboth, "Fathers," sets this principle out in its introduction. A rabbi became the "father" of his disciples,[7] and that relationship shaped the spirituality of Paul in Jerusalem.

Fresh into Jerusalem from the boat-and-overland journey by way of Joppa, the young Tarsan at first had no standing whatever as a Pharisee. But from resources his family gave him, he could more than compensate the cost a household might run up to maintain him. He needed to identify a Pharisaic sage in Jerusalem who was in financial straits—scarcely a difficult task. Once he started to write his famous letters, he had no interest in relating the details of his time as a Pharisee in

Jerusalem, and so he never named his personal teacher. But for these four years in Jerusalem, this anonymous master was the conduit of the Torah for Paul, his "father."

Pharisees were famous for the hospitality they extended to masters and aspiring disciples; eating together, living together, they investigated how everything they did could reflect the divine revelation to Moses and prepare them for worship in the Temple. For a disciple, staying in close quarters with his rabbi was vital in order to learn the living Torah. The Talmud (Berakoth 62a) tells of a disciple hiding under his master's bed one night to learn how the *halakhah* of making love might work out.

Acts goes so far as to say (in fact, to have Paul say in a speech, Acts 22:3) that he sat directly "at the feet of Gamaliel," the most famous rabbi of his generation. This reference doesn't put Paul under Gamaliel's bed, but it does speak of a relationship as close as Mary the sister of Martha enjoyed with Jesus (Luke 10:38–42). In the view of most critical scholarship, the claim that Paul studied personally with Gamaliel goes over the top. A Pharisaic aspirant from Tarsus, even a well-heeled one, can't have had much to recommend him to the greatest patriarch in the whole movement. Still, there is no escaping how much Gamaliel's teaching shaped Paul's mind, for the simple reason that he influenced every Pharisee's practice.

Gamaliel's influence on the Pharisaic movement was so great, the Mishnah conveys his teaching not only by what he said to disciples but also by arrangements in his household and by what he did. The patriarch's every act could be taken as an example. Before the destruction of the Temple, the Pharisees did not have formal academies, and as far as the Roman Empire was concerned, the priests—rather than Pharisees like Gamaliel—were the men on top. Gamaliel's influence came from who he was, not what he was: His power did not derive from office, qualification, or the occupier's favor, but from his living embodiment of the Torah. No Pharisee, whether aspiring or well established, could ignore him, even though the Pharisaic movement was in no way monolithic.

Men in the Pharisaic neighborhood of the city bound little leather boxes with Scripture texts to their foreheads and their left arms as Moses taught them to do (Deuteronomy 6:8), so that the words most sacred to Israel would be always on their minds and by their hearts (Deuteronomy 6:4–5):

> Hear, Israel *[Shema' Yisrael],* the LORD is our God, the LORD is One, and you shall love the LORD your God with all your heart and with all your soul and with all your resource.

Shema' Yisrael: Words that opened the moments of prayer, morning, noon, and night, marking the interstices of the day with sacred presence.

The Pharisees' every gesture, each act, reflected the will of heaven. They were careful, as Moses commanded (Leviticus 19:19), not to mix fibers in their clothing, an all-too-easy mistake if one relied on the jumbled markets of Jerusalem. Pharisees favored their own vendors and wore long robes with their trademark blue tassels (Numbers 15:38–39) at the corners, as Rabbi Jesus also did (Mark 6:56). Appearing in their neighborhood in any other attire would not have been smart. Newly embarked on his Pharisaic career in Jerusalem, Paul would have likely made a tasseled robe one of his first purchases. His ambition burned for genuine advance in Pharisaic practice, starting with prayer.

Prayer was not the still, passive affair it has become in the practice of most Christians and Jews. The Scriptures of Israel are filled with allusions to the physical exertion of prayer. Positions referred to in the Book of Psalms, Israel's perennial manual of prayer, include lying, standing, sitting, kneeling. By assuming these postures, you could rejoice in the sinews of your body, celebrating that you had been "wonderfully made" (Psalm 139:14), or feel the pain of human frailty—the sensation of "bones . . . out of joint" (Psalm 22:14) that really came when an ill, old, or anxious body was pressed into positions designed for a healthy, fit sage. Clapping hands, moving feet, singing aloud, moaning to oneself all featured in the aerobics of prayer, communal and individual, for which the Psalms are the songbook.

Extreme physical demands often accompanied high attainment in prayer. When Elijah prayed for rain, "he put his face between his knees" (1 Kings 18:42). Leaning forward over his legs (either straight or crossed), he turned his body inward, restricting his own breath. Elijah later approached the very presence of God when he fasted on Mount Horeb, passed through wind, earthquake, and fire, and heard a still, small voice. At that climactic moment he wrapped himself in his own prophet's mantle (1 Kings 19:13). Those who later practiced the vision of the divine presence imitated this gesture, covering their heads and faces in a practice that lives on in Jewish liturgies to this day.

Gamaliel allied himself with priests in order to practice his own distinctive disciplines. Within the Temple's inner court, where sacrifices took place, it was customary to engage in what were called "the thirteen acts of prostration in the sanctuary." These prostrations were not little bobs of the head or bows of the knee. To prostrate oneself was to lie facedown on the stone pavement—whether hot in the sunlight or cold in the morning, whether damp from washing or spattered with the soot and grease of offering—in obeisance to the sanctity manifested there. To this ritual of thirteen acts of reverence, Gamaliel and Rabbi Hananiah, prefect of the priests, added a fourteenth (Sheqalim 6:1 in the Mishnah), and their followers took up the practice.

Why add this innovation, which—like any change in ritual—could only arouse comment and controversy? Because Gamaliel and Hananiah, the patriarch and the priest, believed they knew from ancient tradition just where the ark of the covenant had once been located in the Temple, and they suited their practice to their special knowledge. Under Gamaliel's authority and Hananiah's permission, Paul and other Pharisees would sweep into the Temple at the time of sacrifice, fringed robes swirling. At sacred point after sacred point they raised their hands to heaven in the ancient position of prayer, and then lowered themselves fully to the stone pavement, taking their weight on the tip of one toe on the way down. It was a smooth, powerful adagio, all the more impressive for the number and strength of the young men, muscled limbs under rippling fabric.

Ritual bath in Jerusalem (photo courtesy of Daniel Frese/BiblePlaces.com). This ritual bath had once been a covered cistern; converted into a stepped pool for purification, or miqveh, it offered privacy for those who prepared themselves to ascend to the Temple. Its date, design, and proximity to the Temple are discussed in Eilat Mazar and Benjamin Mazar, *Excavations in the South of the Temple Mount. The Ophel of Biblical Jerusalem:* Qedem, Monographs of the Institute of Archaeology 29 (Jerusalem: The Institute of Archaeology, 1989) 53 (Locus 7037).

On any occasion, visitors and worshipers alike thrilled at the sight of priests, Levites, Pharisees, Essenes, and assorted adepts in their various choreographies of prostration, punctuated by their Psalmic incantations of Yahweh's praise. But the cognoscenti of the Temple—among whom Paul quickly numbered himself—appreciated the significance of Gamaliel's fourteenth prostration.

The ark of the covenant had once led Israel into battle. A portable box capped with a golden platform where two winged cherubim (griffinlike monsters) faced each other, it defined the sacred space where the God of Israel sat enthroned in their midst. It was a holy and dangerous source of divine power (1 Samuel 6:1–11): to treat it lightly meant instant death (2 Samuel 6:1–10). Solomon understood that the Temple was the only safe place for it (1 Kings 8:1–13). But this ark had been gone for almost a thousand years; pillaged by Shishak of Egypt (1 Kings 14:25–26), it disappeared from history. Nonetheless, Gamaliel and Hananiah believed they knew what its location in the Temple had been: they could identify the locus on this earth where God's presence dwelled.

Other teachers held that it was dangerous to know this location. The Mishnah tells the story of one priest in the Temple observing to another that a paving block was slightly different from the rest, and showed where the ark had been (Sheqalim 6:2). The result? He died before he could finish speaking.[8] You don't have to believe such stories to appreciate what they are saying: People believed that the ark and the vision of God on his many-wheeled angelic throne above the ark could kill.

Along with adding a fourteenth prostration to the usual thirteen, Gamaliel encouraged an extra effort for each prostration. His son, Simeon ben Gamaliel, used to put his finger on the ground, bend to kiss the pavement, and straighten up in a single, smooth movement (Tosefta Sukkah 4:4), the liturgical equivalent of a one-handed push-up. At festivals he would dance and juggle with eight flaming torches so that none touched the ground. Simeon was more adept at such feats than his contemporaries—Rabbi Paul included. He exemplified an intensity of prayer that modern rationalists, children of the Enlightenment and its materialism, can barely fathom: communing with the divine physically as well as intellectually and emotionally.

·   ·   ·

SPEAKING SPECIFICALLY of his Pharisaic formation, Paul said, "Things that were gain to me I regarded forfeit because of Christ" (Philippians 3:7). As Paul saw his life in retrospect, his conversion to Christ put everything else in its shadow. But that followed Paul's *first* conversion—to the Pharisees. He broke with his former way of life to embrace values and practices his family endorsed, but with Paul's ferocious dedication. That conversion, from Diaspora Judaism to Pharisaic practice, made him change his clothing, behavior, and associates, give up his native city for Jerusalem, and make the Temple the center of his zealous devotion. He could no more shake off the effects of his Pharisaic conversion than he could conceal his origins in Tarsus, although at the time no one could have predicted the kind of zealot he ultimately would become.

Paul's letters sometimes show that he shadowboxed with his past. Gamaliel wrote letters to the Diaspora; so eventually did Paul. It can't be sheer coincidence that the apostle who pioneered the art of writing personally to particular communities had studied in Jerusalem as a Pharisee during Gamaliel's time. Gamaliel deliberately tried to get the recipients of his letters to keep the calendar of Judaism, while Paul tried just as hard to *stop* Gentiles from observing that practice (Galatians 4:10–11). Even when he rebelled against his Pharisaic formation, Paul betrayed his knowledge of its strengths.

Gamaliel's influence was so great that he could enforce his teachings—even in the Temple—by means of his devoted disciples (his *talmidim*). If the high priest had his Levitical heavies and the Temple police, Gamaliel had his Pharisaic homeboys. When he gave in the annual shekel tax in the Temple, Gamaliel had a member of his household throw it right in front of the collector to make sure his money went for public sacrifices (Sheqalim 3:3 in the Mishnah) rather than for general maintenance. If the collector needed prompting to pick up the shekel and put it in the right container, a little gang of Pharisees loyal to the patriarch gathered, yelling out, "Take up, take up, take up!" It did not take long for the collector to get the point and set aside Gamaliel's shekels for sacrifices alone.

Gamaliel's gang also insisted on their own rules for determining when an animal should be excluded from sacrifice on the grounds of a blemish (Bekhorot 6:9). To do that, they had to deploy themselves on the ground in the great shambles on the north side of the Temple to make any Levite or owner who disagreed with them back off.

Being part of the gang meant more than yelling a lot. Enforcing a Pharisaic position might involve the art of a discrete shove, a cuff to an animal, a shot to the ribs of a man, and—under cover of a ring of partners blocking the view of any Temple police—a punch thrown with the frank power of all one's weight. Those skills coupled with more elegant means could exert Pharisaic power in the Temple, although its official rulers were the priests, whose protectors were armed police backed by Roman might. Direct mob action against the priests would lead only to disaster (as the case of Rabbi Jesus and other revolutionaries proved). Gamaliel mastered discreet force, moral persuasion, brilliant argument, and strategic alliance with some high priests in order to get his way, and Paul became a proud soldier in his service.

Gamaliel had keyed himself into the same sort of eschatological fervor that had motivated Jesus to enter Jerusalem in the last year of his life. A major difference between them was that Gamaliel had exactly the kind of local knowledge, influence, and finesse in Jerusalem that Jesus had lacked. The prophet Zechariah had predicted that all the nations of the earth would stream into Jerusalem to offer worship there. The rabbi from Galilee tried to realize that prophecy directly, even organizing his followers in a raid to throw merchants out of the Temple, because Zechariah said in the very last words of his book, "There shall no longer be a trader in the house of the LORD of hosts on that day" (Zechariah 14:21).[9] There is no room to doubt the passion of Jesus' commitment, but that doesn't mean he was unique in that passion.

The followers of Gamaliel cherished Zechariah's injunction to insist on just and peaceful judgments in Jerusalem (Aboth 1:18, citing Zechariah 8:16). God's apocalyptic plan centered on justice, so that all the nations of the earth would converge on Jerusalem (Zechariah 8:23); "ten men from all the languages of the Gentiles will take hold of the hem of one Jew, saying, We will go with you, because we have heard that God is with you." Gamaliel did not share the rustic program of direct action that Jesus committed his life to, but that did not make him any less committed in his own way to the prophetic vision of how all humanity would one day flow toward Mount Zion.

In fact, Rabbi Gamaliel's affinity with Rabbi Jesus caused Paul to shift his own allegiance within the Pharisaic movement. Gamaliel had no problem with contradicting the high priest Caiaphas when it suited him. After all, Caiaphas had moved merchants into the Temple. That was his innovation, and the Pharisees did not take well to the high priest's habit of changing arrangements on his own authority. In addition, Caiaphas had pushed the Sanhedrin, the local council in which the Pharisees' influence was important, out of the Temple and onto the Mount of Olives. That is why Jesus found so many ready participants for his raid on the Temple.

Caiaphas had hoped, following Jesus' execution, to put down the remnants of a troublesome challenge to his authority. Gamaliel gave him no support, even though that meant expressing tacit sympathy with Jesus' movement.

When some of Jesus' followers claimed that God had raised him from the dead, Caiaphas wanted to ban them and their teaching from the Temple. He even arrested some of them and kept them in the custody of his police (Acts 5:12–26). But Gamaliel resisted Caiaphas (Acts 5:34–41), arguing that no one could yet discern whether Jesus' followers were deluded or not. The Sanhedrin prevailed on Caiaphas to release Peter, James, and John, the triumvirate among Jesus' apostles. Gamaliel's opposition undermined the high priest's already waning power.

Politically, keeping Jesus' followers around the Temple hastened the day when the Sanhedrin could be brought back where it belonged, the vendors returned to the Mount of Olives, and Caiaphas sent off to retirement. All of that was accomplished by 37 C.E., along with the removal of Pontius Pilate. But you needed to be cagey, experienced, and patient to follow Gamaliel's strategy. After all, he was putting pressure on Caiaphas, the legitimate (if ruthless) high priest, by means of tolerating a movement whose leader the Romans had punished with their ultimate penalty.

For Paul, immature and not in direct contact with Gamaliel in any case, all this was too subtle. In contrast to the confident patriarch and his willingness to tolerate a strange visionary form of Judaism within the Temple, Paul was a more staid loyalist of the Temple's status quo.

In the contest between Caiaphas and Gamaliel, he went with the high priest.

. . .

IN THE SUMMER OF 32 C.E., Paul broke with Gamaliel, publicly taking part in the execution of Stephen, a follower of Jesus, by stoning. Like his name, Stephen's natural language was Greek. He belonged to one of the Greek-speaking synagogues of Diaspora Jews that dotted Jerusalem. The influx of these Hellenists (as the Book of Acts calls them, see 6:1–8) strained the patience and resources of the apostolic group that looked to Peter for leadership. Not only was the Hellenists' preferred language Greek rather than the Galileans' Aramaic; the Galileans were living communally, and the arrival of these new believers put a strain on their common purse. Stephen emerged as a natural leader (a "servant," *diakonos*) of this subgroup, reputed for his practical wisdom and miracles as well as his skill in debate.

Taunted for his belief in the risen Jesus by a crowd of skeptics,[10] including members of other synagogues (6:8–15), Stephen harangued his opponents and finished by saying that, at that very moment, he was having a vision of Jesus, raised from the dead and standing at the right hand of God (7:1–56). Fatally, he also declared—at least according to his opponents—that this triumphant Jesus would destroy the Temple (6:14). While Peter and those around him worshiped tranquilly in the Temple and broke bread in their communal home (Acts 2:46), Stephen insisted on confronting people in the Temple with a vision of Jesus that he claimed would change everything. The crowd reacted by stoning him.

Stoning was laid down in the Torah as the punishment for blasphemy and, prior to execution, the judges who inflicted the punishment removed their outer garments in conformity with the practice mandated in the Mishnah (Sanhedrin 7:5). Acts reports that in this case, they left their clothing with a young man named Saul (Acts 7:57–60), who agreed with what they were doing.

This is how Acts introduces Paul, so it offers no analysis of why Paul was so opposed to Stephen while Gamaliel was tolerant of Jesus' followers. The difference in their ages and experience had something to do with it as well as the tendency of a Diaspora Jew to prove his loyalty to the Temple in a way the established patriarch of the Pharisees would not. That tendency was exacerbated because Stephen himself came from the Diaspora and impugned the inviolability of the Temple. In fact, some of those who disputed with Stephen came from Cilicia (Acts 6:9); they may have been the first source of Paul's information about Jesus' movement.

Jerome Murphy-O'Connor has characterized Paul at this stage in his life as "an immature religious bigot working out his personal problems."[11] That expresses forcefully and well a conviction that many scholars and popular writers have shared. Paul's vehemence both before and after his conversion seems pathological by the standards of our time.

But perhaps that judgment reflects on us as much as on Paul. Whether or not he was a bigot, his motivation will inevitably escape routine psychology, because we have nothing like the data that a case history requires. Besides, religious persecution has had a relentless history: why assume that every persecutor suffered from some identifiable maladjustment? Such assumptions have the look of facile dismissal.

At a more explicit and profound level than psychology, a person's commitments explain behavior. These are the markers within an individual's development of directions chosen, of relationships valued, of people and paths rejected. In the midst of a swirling, violent crowd converging on the hapless Stephen, Paul was moved by the very force that had brought him to Jerusalem and planted him in Acts' description at the feet of Gamaliel: his love for the Temple.

The members of the Sanhedrin who had agreed earlier in 32 C.E. that Jesus should be denounced to Pilate did so because Jesus had stormed into the Temple with his followers, disrupting its operation. Caiaphas had personal grounds for animosity, but any Israelite might well have been offended by Jesus' raid. When Jesus was unable to return to the Temple, he started to call the wine he shared with his disciples during meals his "blood" and the bread his "flesh," as if those meals supplanted offerings in the Temple within God's affections. In Jesus' mind, wine and bread did not stand for his personal blood and body, but they did take the place of sacrifice. That was enough to get some people on the council to agree with Caiaphas, despite the reluctance of teachers such as Joseph of Arimathea and Gamaliel, so that Jesus could be identified to Pilate as a threat to the public order and Rome's hegemony.

To a young Pharisee such as Paul, assaults on arrangements authorized by the high priest threatened covenantal worship in the sanctuary, and talk of meals replacing Temple sacrifice was blasphemous. Visions such as Stephen's and his prophecy of doom insulted the sanctuary. The focus of God's presence was the Temple, specifically the mercy seat over the ark—spiritually still to be acknowledged in the Temple according to Gamaliel's teaching—where men of Paul's discipline regularly devoted their prayers, their thoughts, and their bodies. Now Stephen, a Greek-speaking Jew, announced that he had seen what the Book of Daniel called "one like a person," an angel of God with a human face and form, and that he was none other than the renegade from Nazareth who had challenged the high priest.[12] Blasphemy was too light a word for this nonsense. Paul, never one to take things lightly, was revolted. He joined in the stoning of Stephen.

Paul's career as a persecutor of Jesus' followers was no flash in the pan, and he refers to his anti-Christian activity in his letters (Galatians 1:13; 1 Corinthians 15:9; Philippians 3:6). But at the time what he did was more for the Temple than against Jesus; from the altar, recognition of the one true God radiated to the whole Diaspora. The figure of the high priest appealed to any young aspiring Pharisee in the Diaspora. Caiaphas held the same office as Eleazar in *Aristeas*. From Jerusalem— the very center of Israel—Eleazar had authorized the Greek Scriptures that Paul could read and appreciate on the basis of the literary and rhetorical training he benefited from in Tarsus. Without the Temple, and the sacrificial good order the high priest maintained there, what would become of Israelites all over the world?

Acts even portrays Paul as taking letters to Damascus on behalf of the high priest, to order the arrest of Christians there (Acts 9:1–2). That attributes more direct power to Caiaphas than he actually had, but it is perfectly plausible that the high priest communicated with synagogues in Damascus, asking members to denounce followers of Jesus there to the Romans. For this purpose he needed educated zealots who could deliver, read, explain, and defend the letters he sent out, both in Aramaic and in Greek. Paul was an ideal candidate, with the added cachet of his nascent standing with the Pharisaic movement and the cultural advantage of being bilingual. Co-opting a young rabbi out of Gamaliel's own stable must have given Caiaphas pleasure, and Paul had enough standing to bring some junior colleagues along with him.

Besides, Caiaphas simply needed help. Stephen's public claim of a vision came on top of a series of reported sightings of Jesus risen from the dead, attributed to Cephas (as Peter was called in Aramaic), the Twelve, a Galilean throng of more than five hundred people at once, and James (the brother of Jesus) as well as other apostles. That is the list given by Paul (1 Corinthians 15:5–9), the earliest writer to refer to Jesus' Resurrection. Starting it all, some women who had been going to tend Jesus' corpse had an angelic vision (Mark 16:1–8) that told them to go back to his followers and say that he had risen from the dead.

Because these were visions, teachers devoted to disciplines of mysticism such as Gamaliel were reluctant to dismiss them out of hand. For the same reason, the claims about Jesus could not be refuted just by finding his corpse and displaying it:[13] At this stage the Resurrection was a visionary experience, not a claim of resuscitation. Caiaphas feared the threat to his own authority and resented the insult to the Temple implicit in the claim that his antagonist—as Stephen explicitly stated—was the angelic protector of Israel prophesied in the Book of Daniel. Caiaphas desperately needed to denounce Jesus' followers to Rome as insurgents, much as he had arranged for Jesus to be denounced. He delegated men like Paul for this task, and Paul—in awe of the high priest much as he was of the Temple and the secret place of the ark—was all eagerness.

Paul made his way to Damascus in the service of the high priest to convince synagogues there to join in the denunciation of Jesus' movement. In a police state such as the Roman Empire, denunciation—whether formal or anonymous—was often the best way to deal with an opposition group rather than direct conflict. This commission gave Paul some standing, and the young Pharisee's younger companions called him "Rabbi Saul" on the way from Jerusalem to Damascus. No one could have convinced him that people would come to see the risen Jesus rather than the Temple as the gateway to heaven. No one could have predicted, Paul least of all, that devotion to Jesus would convert *Gentiles* to the God of Israel. And how could he have known that his own vision would have a part in those impossible events?

· 3 ·

ON THE ROAD

URING THE CHANGES and challenges of travel, prayer remained a constant. The Mishnah expected Jews, even on a journey, to recite the words *Shema' Yisrael* that should commence each act of prayer:

"Hear, Israel, the LORD is our God, the LORD is One. . . ." Chanting this ancient creed (Deuteronomy 6:4), the sage plunged into his personal discipline, shaped by his master and crafted by experience.

Young Rabbi Paul was no exception. Praise and supplication of Israel's God, memorized Scriptures and remembrance of oral Torah, images and mantras of meditation came easily to him. He had mastered the physical postures of prayer as well. Fasting and wakefulness set the scene for revelation. Journeys produced natural opportunities for vision, bringing the austerity of fasting, night watches, and extremes of temperature to all but the wealthiest pilgrims and travelers. They also enjoyed freedom from conventional inhibitions (visionary or otherwise). The road where Rabbi Paul experienced God disclosing an unexpected reality within him had been very well prepared. Paul's epiphany—as he made his way to Damascus—came to him as a blow from heaven, but it had been lying in wait for him for centuries, as primordial as the story in Exodus of revelations to Israel in the wilderness.

The Mediterranean sun at noon burned hot that summer day in 32 C.E.; a handful of Pharisaic zealots from the Temple, armed with letters to synagogues in Damascus from the high priest, stopped at midday for their devotions. As they approached their destination, their prayers had focused increasingly on the Temple as the only site of divine epiphany. Their minds ranged back to the Sanctuary they had left behind on a mission to protect its sanctity.

Stephen's vision in the Temple, of Jesus raised from the dead, standing at God's right hand (Acts 7:56), had challenged the unique status of the Temple as the gate of heaven. Stephen claimed that Jesus had become a prophet like Moses, and that his new prophecy spelled the end of the teaching that God dwelt solely in the sanctuary (Acts 7:37–50). "Heaven is my throne, and earth my footstool": These words, originally from the Book of Isaiah, meant for Stephen that "the Most High does not dwell in buildings made with hands." That is what drove Rabbi Paul to side with Caiaphas. His band of Pharisees were shock troops of Caiaphas's opposing stance, grounded in absolute confidence in the sanctuary as God's palace. Visionary messengers who claimed that it needed radical reform were a nuisance at best, and Stephen's claim that his dead rabbi knew what was best to do with the Temple tipped into blasphemy. The Temple, and the Temple alone, disclosed God's glorious power on earth.

The young Pharisees murmured their prayers and chants a few days into their journey, each companion following his own custom within eye- and earshot of the others. Then Rabbi Paul cried out (Acts 26:1–20).[1] Deep in his meditation, he became aware of a strange presence, and light dazzled around him. That was when his companions heard Paul shout out: "Who are you, Lord?" Like seers such as Enoch and Daniel before him, he was afraid of what he believed was an angel. This unknown entity ratcheted up his fear by accusing him in Aramaic (using his Aramaic name), "Saul, Saul: why are you persecuting me?" Rabbi Paul needed to know who the angel was and why it was there.

Divine messengers conveyed God's power, and contact with that sanctity could be dangerous. In Genesis, an angel came to Jacob in order to wrestle with him, and in that contest he changed Jacob's name to "Israel" ("he strives with God"). That angel bent the patriarch's body so violently that he dislocated Jacob's hip (Genesis 32:24–32). Was this the same kind of contest, miraculous but dreadful? Or worse, would the angel offer Rabbi Paul no alternative but punishment for his offense? What had he done wrong? A world of dread is expressed in that question, "Who are you, Lord?" Paul needed to know.

The light that blinded him brought Paul to the revelation that changed his life. Twenty years later he explained the meaning of what had happened (Galatians 1:15–17): "When it pleased the one who separated me from my mother's belly and called me through his grace to uncover his Son in me so that I should announce him triumphant among the Gentiles, I did not confer with flesh and blood. Neither did I go up to Jerusalem to those who were apostles before me; but I departed to Arabia, and again I returned to Damascus."

This revelation was prophetic—like a prophet, Paul felt he had been predestined to this moment from his "mother's belly" (Jeremiah 1:5; Isaiah 49:1–6). The unveiling of God's Son within took priority over any human contact or circumstance.

He puts the deep content of this experience so economically, you might miss its pivotal reference: God determined "to uncover his Son in" Paul. Conventional translations have stood in the way of what he clearly said here. The term "uncover" *(apokalupsai)* in Greek is typically rendered "reveal" in English versions of the Bible. By the same token, the noun *apokalupsis,* our "apocalypse," becomes "revelation." These translations make readers think in terms of external stimuli coming to the seer like ordinary sense perceptions. The basic meaning of this language, however, is that a heavenly mystery has its cover (its *-kalupsis*) taken off *(apo)*: the veil of circumstance is momentarily stripped from spiritual reality. Here the cover is removed from God's Son, who is "in" *(en)* Paul, within his consciousness in an experience uniquely his.

Paul's experience was not of an objective event that other people witnessed with him. He alone was converted that day. His brief reference in Galatians relates to a personal moment of disclosure, an unveiling of the divine. He conceived of his mystical breakthrough in ways rooted in his mixed background, pagan and Jewish. Part of its significance for him was that the risen Jesus represented the fusion of his Tarsan heritage and his Judaic faith.

Many Stoics in Tarsus were taken up with the possibility of people moving beyond knowledge of the divine—and becoming divine themselves. Cicero—the Stoic philosopher who briefly governed Cilicia and was familiar with the teaching of Athenodorus of Tarsus—voiced this hope for exaltation to the status of the gods. Cicero related the Stoic theme of apotheosis in his classic composition, the "Dream of Scipio," his friend.

In the dream, Scipio is taken into heaven, reminded of its superiority to the earth by an angelic guide, and then told he is not limited by his own mortality (*Republic* 6.24):

> Know, then, that you are a god, which lives, feels, remembers, and foresees, indeed rules, governs, and moves the body over which it is set, just as the supreme god does with the universe. And just as this eternal god moves the imperfectly mortal universe, so an everlasting spirit moves a frail body.

Stoics promised immortality, apotheosis forever, and foretastes of that in this world. Knowledge of one's true self mirrored the power of the supreme god of heaven.

The popular source of early Judaism called 1 Enoch reflected a similar longing and shows how the God of Israel could fulfill Stoic aspirations.[2] Precisely because it was a popular, composite work, there were many add-ons through the centuries, but among the most ancient of its visions has Enoch describing his mystical journey into heaven (Enoch 14:8–12):

> And behold I saw the clouds: And they were calling me in a vision; and the fogs were calling me; and the course of the stars and the lightnings were rushing me and causing me to desire; and in the vision, the winds were causing me to fly and rushing me high up into heaven. And I kept coming until I approached a wall which was built of white marble and surrounded by tongues of fire; and it began to frighten me. And I came into the tongues of fire and drew near to a great house which was built of white marble, and the inner walls were like tessallated sheets of white marble, the floor of crystal, the ceiling like the path of the stars and lightnings between which stood fiery cherubim and their heaven of water; and flaming fire surrounded the wall, and its gates were burning with fire.

In this classic from ancient Judaic visions, Enoch then proceeds to the very throne of God that Moses, Isaiah, Ezekiel, and Daniel had also seen.

Enoch relates a vision while Scipio's experience is a dream, but they share a common focus: ascent beyond astral forces into the very presence of God. Paul's vision showed him neither his personal immortality, as in Scipio's case, nor the heavenly court Enoch had described. Rather, in his words, the "Son" of God was disclosed inside him.

Two thousand years of Christianity makes us think instantly of Jesus when we hear of the "Son of God." But the phrase had a life of its own before it was applied to Jesus, referring to angels (Genesis 6:2), the whole people called Israel (Hosea 11:1), and the king in David's line (Psalm 2:7). Direct revelation extends God's favor to people and angels; each is "the Son," "the beloved," as Jesus became[3] in his vision at his baptism.

When Paul felt the divine "Son" uncovered within himself, he encountered the revelation he had known in the Temple, but now it was raging inside him. As angels had once guided Scipio and Enoch, a supernatural guide, a "Son" representing the divine Father, brought Paul to the heaven within himself. That is why the answer to his question, "Who are you, Lord?" came as the most terrifying words he ever heard: "I am Jesus, whom you persecute!" (Acts 26:15) No response could have agonized him more. Profound loyalty to the Temple, not malice, had led Paul to serve Caiaphas, to resist the malcontents from Galilee and the Diaspora who claimed that their dead rabbi's authority trumped the high priest's. Yet now this angelic Son of God was identifying himself as Jesus, risen from the dead.

That ended Paul's commission from Caiaphas and, in his own mind, it also put him irrevocably in the wrong. God revealed his Son in Paul, but as an accuser. Biographers and others have remarked on the guilt that Paul's letters sometimes express, but looking for mysterious psychological causes is superfluous. He openly admitted (1 Corinthians 15:9): "I am the least of the apostles who is not worthy to be called an apostle, since I persecuted the church of God."

He not only acknowledged his guilt in so many words, but also spoke of it while referring to Jesus' Resurrection and his own experience of the divine Son's appearance. While traveling to Damascus, this vision taught Paul that the Galilean rabbi whose movement he had been trying to stamp out was God's Son. There really is no mystery about the source of Paul's sense of guilt.

This painful dissonance, between knowing the divine Son within him and feeling the profound conviction of his unworthiness, never left Paul. This tension powered his ceaseless activity: He might not be worthy to be called an apostle, "but I labored more than all of them" (1 Corinthians 15:10). He strove to work off his unintended blasphemy against God's Son, turning his life over to the guidance of his prophetic vision. This divine Son could become the holy center of God within every person, as Jesus had within Paul: Paul's vision gave him the theme of his thought, and of his life.

· · ·

GOD DISCLOSED the divine Son in Rabbi Paul for a specific purpose: "so that I should announce him triumphant among the Gentiles"

(Galatians 1:16). In Acts as well, the angelic Jesus gives him a new commission to replace the one he had from Caiaphas (Acts 26:18):[4] to go to Gentiles, "To open their eyes, to turn from darkness to light, and from the power of Satan unto God, so they receive forgiveness of sins." By working out divine forgiveness among Gentiles, Paul pursued the forgiveness he needed personally.

Paul's vision was not—and could not have been—one of personal acceptance by God. He had persecuted the same divine Son now unveiled within him. Even toward the end of his life, beset by the machinations of the Roman legal system, he acknowledged that his inner insecurity was greater than any exterior threat. He actively courted suffering in imitation of Jesus (Philippians 3:10–11) "that somehow I might attain to the resurrection from the dead." Paul never doubted the reality of his vision, but—in a way that later influenced Augustine and Calvin—he was never sure he really could be part of such glory. To his mind, his sin against the risen Jesus was so great that he could no more count on salvation than Gentiles could. His struggle for their forgiveness was concurrently a struggle for his own.

The great apocalyptic vision of the prophet Zechariah—embraced by Jesus and at least tolerated by Gamaliel—predicted that the Gentile world would one day come to Mount Zion by means of their worship in the Temple. But in Paul's experience, the divine Son broke through within him like a giant short circuit, arcing over the whole fraught issue of correct sacrifice in Jerusalem. He had been mortally opposed to Jesus' followers, but his own vision proved that they were right and he was dead wrong. Jesus spoke to Rabbi Paul the persecutor, a man as alien to God as a person could be. That showed that God also wanted to uncover the divine Son within Gentiles, whose alienation from God was not the result of their own actions.

Paul says with unmistakable emphasis that God chose "to uncover his Son in me so that I should announce him triumphant among the Gentiles." His visionary realization of the Son within implied that they could be delivered the same way in an outbreak of unprecedented redemption. That is why his conversion involved both a personal conviction of his guilt and a commission to announce Christ to non-Jews. In their forgiveness, their sanctity, he sought the assurance of his own.

Just as the content of his apocalypse pulled Paul back to his Diaspora heritage, so the form of his experience—and the way it is recounted in the Book of Acts—mirrors the vision of Daniel, the classic hero of Israel in exile. Originating during the second century B.C.E. in Judea, the Book of Daniel was quickly translated into Greek in an expanded form and was seen by many Greek-speaking Jews as the climactic last book of their Bible. Daniel provided a model for the belief that seers could be given personal messages by angels that they were to convey to the faithful. These messages could involve detailed timetables of the end of the world, but their tenor conveys encouragement and assurance of divine favor.

In chapter 10 of Daniel, the angel Gabriel provides the seer with the secret of the end of days. Daniel's vision of the angel is much more detailed than any account of Paul's vision, but the emphasis on light is a common element, as Gabriel is described as clothed in linen and girdled with gold, "his body like gold stone of Tarshish, and his face as the appearance of lightning, and his eyes as lamps of fire, and his arms and his feet like dazzling polished brass, and the sound of his words like the sound of a roar" (Daniel 10:6). Like Rabbi Paul's, this vision was fearsome.

As compared to Acts' narrative about what happened on the road to Damascus, the very next sentence in Daniel is truly striking (Daniel 10:7): "And I, Daniel, alone saw the vision, and the men that were with me did not see the vision. But a great quaking fell upon them, so that they fled to hide themselves." That corresponds to what Acts narrates about Paul's companions (Acts 9:7), so frightened they are "speechless, hearing a voice, but seeing no one."

This description directly contradicts a speech Acts attributes to Paul later in the book (22:9): This speech agrees that Paul's companions were frightened, but that they *saw the light* and *did not hear* the voice.

How can a book, edited with considerable sophistication, say one thing about an experience and then its opposite? Obviously, Acts is more comfortable about the subjectivity of Paul's revelation than are some literally minded Christians in the modern period. The point of both Acts and Daniel is that the companions do not fully share the experience, although they recognize an apocalypse is going on.

As a matter of fact, Acts provides a *third* description of Paul's apocalypse (26:13–18), attributed to Paul in a speech before King Herod Agrippa II. Here, Paul addresses a fellow Jew as well as a ruler designated directly by Rome. We might expect this to be the most accurate account of the three, and the fact is that it is closest to Daniel 10, because Rabbi Paul refers to what he personally saw and heard while his fellow travelers simply collapsed in a heap on the ground.

His companions must have been completely outside the loop of his experience. If they really did hear a heavenly voice that identified itself as Jesus (Acts 9:7), or if they literally saw the light (Acts 22:9), where is their reaction? It seems much more likely that, as Galatians 1:16 states and Acts 26:13–14 corroborates, Paul's experience in itself had nothing to do with "flesh and blood." Like Daniel (10:7), he had an experience that no doubt frightened the companions who witnessed his behavior, but part of their fright involved not knowing what was going on.

As he called out to Jesus as to an angel, Paul could no longer see. His vision blinded him, and this sudden incapacity added to his colleagues' confusion. They guided their stricken, now renegade friend by the hand into Damascus, left him there, and went their way, no doubt strengthened in the conviction that the strange new movement centered on Jesus could bring no good. Their final kindness was to leave him with Judas (Acts 9:8–11), a Jew bearing a very popular name who believed in Jesus. Paul commanded enough respect from his Pharisaic colleagues for them to let him follow his new vision even though it contradicted Caiaphas. They did not understand him and he was no longer their colleague, but the Torah's requirement of compassion still guided their actions.

. . .

WHAT EXACTLY was the vision that took away Rabbi Paul's sight? A couple of years after he wrote to the Galatians about his conversion, he sent a letter to Christians in the Greek city of Corinth. There, he specifically lists himself as one of the hundreds of people, including apostles and Jesus' kith and kin, by whom Jesus "was seen" after his crucifixion (1 Corinthians 15:5–8). Paul knew the visionary reality that blinded him was Jesus, risen from the dead, and he identified himself as a witness of the Resurrection. What he says about Resurrection in this letter to Corinth sets out the most exact explanation he ever gave of what he saw on his way to Damascus in 32 C.E. It is also the only firsthand written account in the New Testament of what the risen Jesus looked like.

When he posed the question of the *kind of body* the risen Jesus has, Paul was contemptuous of materialist claims. There have always been people, Jews and Muslims as well as Christians, who think that for Resurrection to have any meaning, it must involve resuscitating the physical body that died. That assumption lies at the root of a great deal of literalist thought, whether it is a Fundamentalist's claim that Jesus was raised in just "the same body" in which he died or an atheist's claim that the Gospels are exercises in wishful and nonsensical thinking.

Paul flatly contradicts any suggestion that the dead are resuscitated when God raises them and impugns the intelligence of anyone who would accept that idea (1 Corinthians 15:36–38):

> Fool, what you yourself sow does not become alive unless it dies! And what do you sow? You do not sow the body that shall be, but a bare germ, perhaps of wheat or of another grain. But God gives to it a body exactly as he wants, and to each of the seeds its own body.

Imagine what would have happened had Paul attended a modern seminary, to train to be a priest or pastor. He never showed concern to soften the blow of his contempt when he felt like challenging a received opinion. His professors would no doubt suggest another line of work to him. Had he somehow made it through to a degree, his first sermon in a conventional congregation would certainly have been memorable. His apocalypse burned away any sense of diplomacy he might once have had. And there is no evidence that he started out from Jerusalem with a great deal of diplomacy to begin with.

Paul never compromised with the literalists of his time over the basic principle that being raised from the dead is about a transformation of this world, including our bodies. His attitude produced controversy, contention, hurt feelings, and no little perplexity: results modern clergy naturally avoid. But when you look at the trenchant literalism of much modern Christianity, permitted or encouraged by preachers who should know better, you wonder whether trying to be a good pastor has been confused with being nice. Nice he was not, and Paul would never yield on the issue of Jesus' Resurrection.

God did not reanimate a corpse when he raised Jesus from the dead, but gave his Son a glorious body "exactly as he wants." Paul nowhere refers to Jesus' tomb being empty, because he thought only a "fool" would say the body that was raised was equivalent to the body that was buried. To Paul's mind, as shaped by his experience on the road to Damascus, God had made a new Adam in the case of Jesus. "Adam" in Hebrew means "human being," and Paul saw the risen Jesus as a model for a new humanity. Jesus' flesh had passed away like a seed in the ground, transformed into a "spiritual body" (1 Corinthians 15:42–45). The first Adam had been a living "soul"—a term which means "breath" in Hebrew, Aramaic, and Greek—breathing in response to the animating breath of God. This last Adam, however, of a completely different substance from the first human being, had become "life-giving Spirit"—the dynamic, metaphysical wind that had moved over the face of the waters at the primeval moment of creation.

Sonship, forgiveness, a new Adam imparting Spirit were all visionary realities Paul encountered in Jesus, risen from the dead. They amounted to seeing God make humanity anew. The task his conversion to Jesus gave him was to mediate this same Spirit to all people who were prepared to receive the new Adam in faith. God had started making Paul a new person in the uncovering of the divine Son within him, and he set about making new people in this image, Gentiles included.

. . .

OBEYING THE APOCALYPTIC VOICE meant that Paul had to be baptized in Jesus' name. This practice had been introduced among Jesus' followers in Jerusalem to signal that, just as John had once immersed people in water, so the risen Jesus now drenched believers in the Holy Spirit (Acts 1:5). Among Jesus' first followers, this immersion in Spirit was the indispensable ritual of faith.

Paul never named the man who baptized him. For him baptism was a supernatural event, so its human agency did not matter. From first to last he was a man of ideas, virtually without interest in circumstantial details. Occasionally he lets some historical information slip while making an argument, but that is usually inadvertent. It is as if Paul begrudged the curiosity of historians.

He even says that he "did not confer with flesh and blood" after the uncovering of God's Son within (Galatians 1:16)—but departed to Arabia. Grammatically that could mean he had absolutely no contact with anyone. But that makes no sense: Someone must have baptized him, brought him to the moment when—as he said happens to everyone who believes in Jesus (Galatians 4:6; Romans 8:14–15)—the Spirit of God's Son entered his heart and he called upon God as his own *Abba,* his divine Father.

When Paul says he did not confer with flesh and blood at this point, he means he did not have any human encounter that was important to him. His mind was totally occupied with the vision of Christ that baptism brought to completion. He says nothing about who actually did the baptizing and where. Nonetheless, he also states that, after his baptism and a three-year sojourn in Arabia, he "returned to Damascus" (Galatians 1:17). So we have got him: he admits he had been in Damascus before, which is just where the Book of Acts puts Paul's baptism. Pinning Paul down is difficult, but by cross-examining his letters, paying attention to Acts, and keeping his historical setting in mind, we can pick up the track of Christianity's most mercurial apostle.

This is a case where the puzzle of the relationship between Galatians and Acts can't be escaped. In two of its three tellings of Paul's vision, Acts names Ananias as the disciple who—acting under divine guidance—baptized Paul (9:10–19 and 22:12–16). There is no reason to doubt that, following the crucifixion and Resurrection, Jesus' Galilean followers found their old haunts uncongenial and would gravitate to cities such as Damascus. Ananias knew the city, familiar with "the Way called Straight" between two of the city's famous seven gates (Acts 9:11)—where Paul stayed with Judas just after his vision.

What happened to Paul next suggests that Ananias was a merchant who had contacts in Galilee, Judea, and Jerusalem as well as in Syria and Nabatea.[5] There were hundreds of his kind just after Jesus' Resurrection: people who were convinced that visions of Jesus alive and elevated to his Father's throne fulfilled God's promises to Israel. They didn't think of themselves as "Christians" yet. That word had not even been coined. They persistently called the teaching of their resurrected rabbi "the way" (hodos in Greek; Acts 9:2; 19:9, 23; 22:4; 24:14, 22), the equivalent of the Rabbinic term halakhah. In this time before there was any formal division between Judaism and Christianity, when Jesus' followers saw their master as the fulfillment of Israel's destiny, most of them worked out their peculiar vision in peace with their fellow Jews.

Paul's baptism was also a moment of healing (Acts 9:17–19). Ananias treated his blindness prior to immersing him: "Brother Saul, the Lord has sent me, Jesus who was seen by you on the way in which you were coming, so that you could see again and be filled with Holy Spirit. And at once there fell away from his eyes something like scales, and he saw again and arose to be baptized, and took food to become strong."

Paul suffered periodically from a painful, lifelong complaint he called a "thorn in the flesh" and an "angel of Satan." He repeatedly prayed about his illness, only to be instructed to make do with divine grace (2 Corinthians 12:7–9). Diagnoses of Paul's condition run the gamut between malaria and epilepsy,[6] but a chronic visual disease seems most likely.

The results of an attack were horrible to look at as well as blinding. He speaks of suffering an affliction of the flesh that could disgust those who saw him (Galatians 4:13–15). Paul fondly reminds the Galatians that when they first heard him announce Christ, "if possible you would have dug out your eyes to give me," to replace his own. Bulging, inflamed, and searing, they felt like thorns in his head during acute attacks of his chronic disease.

This description comports well with an ailment produced by a virus that is activated by anxiety. The same microbe that produces "chicken pox" in children often lies dormant, later in life infecting the nervous system and provoking "shingles" as well as the ballooning, scarring condition of the eye known as herpes zoster. When he was baptized Paul was a stress machine—not for the first time or the last—so it is no surprise he had one of his attacks. God intended this condition, Paul even concluded, to stop him from becoming too proud of his apocalyptic experience (2 Corinthians 12:7–10). Gifted in sight where it concerned heavenly vision, he was reminded of his weakness by pain and incapacity in the physical world.

Ananias provided Paul with therapy, not complete healing. He continued Jesus' practice of *touching* those with illness (Acts 9:17), a gesture that offered comfort, signaling that Paul was an Israelite who was accepted as pure within the fellowship of Rabbi Jesus. Paul could take meals with his host, his host's family, and any guests; as they ate, they sanctified God's name and celebrated his coming kingdom—as in Jesus' practice.[7] At those meals, as regularly in their prayers, they prayed—as Jesus also had—for forgiveness. Touching Paul's useless eyes, Ananias persisted in searching out the compassion of God that releases a person from sin, so that the blinded Pharisee might see again.

· · ·

PAUL HAD COME TO KNOW—in a blinding flash and in spite of himself—the gist of the *euanggelion* ("gospel" for English speakers since the

Middle Ages), which in Greek means triumphal message or announcement of victory. ("Good news," fashionable in English as a rendering
since the 1960s, is technically correct in meaning but so light in tone
as to seem trivial.) Or rather, he knew the Aramaic equivalent of the
same term, *besora*, the word a herald would use to announce triumph,
and which Jesus' followers applied to their rabbi's victory over death as
God's Son.

In terms of content, Paul learned nothing about this message on the
road to Damascus. When he said that "I did not receive it from man,
neither was I taught, but through an apocalypse of Christ Jesus"
(Galatians 1:12), he told the simple truth about his religious experience.
Conversion came when Jesus was uncovered within him as the living
Son of God, and he accepted baptism so as to receive the Spirit his vision had disclosed. The *besora* he had despised—learning of it indirectly
from Pharisaic colleagues in Jerusalem—became the revelation of God.
The message of Jesus, confirmed by the experience of him risen from
the dead and alive in God's presence, reversed Paul's deepest convic-
tions with the power of apocalypse.

Mystical and prophetic, Paul's experience of the risen Jesus marked
a profound conversion.[8] Not from "Judaism" to "Christianity," because
those terms did not yet mean anything in contrast to one another. In
any case, during the course of his life, whether as Saul or Paul, the
apostle would insist that he had been sent by Jesus like the other apostles in order to fulfill Israel's purpose, not undermine it. On the road
to Damascus and in Damascus, a new Jeremiah was called, a new disciple saw the risen Jesus and received the Spirit that came from him,
and an apostle was commissioned to proclaim the message that the divine Son brought Israel's privileged relationship to God to those who
had never known the law of Moses or the covenant with Abraham,
Isaac, and Jacob.

After this conversion, Paul's time was forever short. He had experienced the Son's apocalypse within himself; once started, the apocalyptic clock ticked relentlessly to the catastrophe that spelled the end of
the world. As far as Paul was concerned, God was in the process of

sweeping away the entire world he lived in, what he called "the present evil age" (Galatians 1:4) with all its arrangements of status and power and wealth and its conventions of how to live a worthy human life. Time was foreshortened to the briefest moment of opportunity in this eschatological perspective, which Paul shared with other Pharisees of his era.

Even after Paul's time, the seer of 4 Ezra envisioned the Messiah—the agent of divine judgment—as well as "those who are with him" appearing triumphantly and surviving ultimate cataclysm while the rest of humanity perished.[9] The Messiah brought with him his heavenly host as well as human helpers. Where Paul differed from his Pharisaic colleagues was in identifying this Messiah with Jesus as divine Son. His Messiah's very purpose was to throw out a lifeline to those who lived in the midst of this passing corruption (Galatians 1:4), so that he could "save" or "deliver" them. Paul's vision was spume on the wave of an apocalyptic reckoning that was about to engulf everyone.

Salvation for Paul did not mean feeling good about yourself or passing into the afterlife with the assurance that you were going to heaven instead of hell. Those, respectively, are modern and medieval adaptations of Paul's view of salvation. When he spoke of Jesus saving people, he meant something much more tangible. God had decided to judge the earth justly: This implied that divine fire would scour the earth. Paul shared with Pharisees and Stoics the common, ancient sense that the world's time was limited and that its end was fire.

When Paul in 1 Corinthians 3:10–17 spoke of every human work being tested by fire, he echoed the Pharisaic teaching of the furnace of hell, or *gehenna* (4 Ezra 7:36), as well as the Stoic expectation of the final conflagration *(ekpurosis)*. It is frequently said that Jesus and Paul would have been astounded to learn that human history would continue after them for two thousand years. That is undoubtedly true, but the remark applies as well to Cicero, Seneca, and Philo. After all, the Stoics as well as Israelite thinkers conceived of human behavior as being measured by divine justice. What could pass that standard? And why would God long put up with things as they are? Only an idiot would bet on his doing so.

For the Stoics, only a commitment to reason could see you through the *ekpurosis*, while Pharisees taught that the Torah would bring you to paradise rather than *gehenna*. Paul and his new friends had a different view: only those who accepted the Spirit of God's own Son, putting his justice into practice, could survive. The apostolic task, therefore, was urgent to the nth degree: human survival depended directly upon what Paul and his colleagues did. Time was cut short.

. . .

PAUL'S CONVERSION also cut short the prospect of any sojourn in Damascus. Judas and Ananias cared for him, and he recovered at least some of his sight after something like a week (Acts 9:9, 19). He unwisely started right away to announce in synagogues that Jesus was the divine Son, prompting the inevitable skepticism and controversy. People knew about the stoning of Stephen and knew that this budding Pharisee from the Diaspora had traveled to their city to denounce those baptized in Jesus' name. That's what prompted their taunt (Acts 9:21): "Isn't he the one who laid waste in Jerusalem to those calling upon this name, and came here for this purpose?" Why should they accept the word of an interloper who remade himself so readily—a Jerusalem Pharisee one day, a follower of "the way" another day?

Just where Ananias succeeded, Paul could only fail. Most faithful Jews who believed in Jesus continued to live in Damascus and other cities as well as in towns and villages with little problem. As long as they were not involved with the conflict in Jerusalem between Caiaphas and Jesus' movement, there was no particular occasion for friction with other Israelites. Men like Ananias achieved what Paul never could: a peaceable association between believers in Jesus and other Jews. No wonder Paul never mentioned Ananias in his letters. The contrast was painful, because Paul's past as a persecutor of "the way," coupled with his sudden conversion, made his character seem dubious and the movement itself appear unstable.

When Jesus and his followers claimed that the Temple was to be ruled by Zechariah's prophecy rather than the high priestly party, who could expect the high priests to cheer? But there was little reason, except in extreme cases, for opposition to this new movement outside of Jerusalem. The problem was that Paul *was* an extreme case—and remained so all his life, whether as Pharisee or apostle. Once Paul converted, Caiaphas's supporters could see him only as a traitor, and Paul's visionary flip-flop made it easy for them to spread distrust in him personally.

Jesus' followers were wary, too. Paul remembered people shaking their heads in wonder, saying, "The one who once persecuted us now announces the faith that he once laid waste" (Galatians 1:23). He tried to put positive spin on that, but it did not enhance his reputation for integrity. In the full flow of his rhetoric at a much later stage in his life, Paul bragged that he had become all things to all people (1 Corinthians 9:22). At this stage Paul wasn't anything to anybody.

Remaining in Damascus would have produced only increased animosity. A return to Jerusalem immediately after his conversion was out of the question, although Acts naively does have him go back there at this stage (9:26). Even commentators who argue for the general reliability of Acts don't believe that.[10] It would take years before he could enter Jerusalem again, as Paul indicates in his letter to the Galatians. He specifically says he did not go to Jerusalem, but departed for "Arabia," only returning to Jerusalem via Damascus *three years* later (Galatians 1:17–18). The Arabian region—the country southeast of Israel, politically at that time the kingdom of the Nabateans[11]—is where Paul worked out the implications of his vision for himself during three years of self-imposed exile from all the people he knew, whether in Jerusalem or Tarsus.

Nabatea at first seems an unlikely destination for Paul at this time. Although Aramaic was spoken there, it was a different dialect from what he had learned in Tarsus or adapted to in Jerusalem. The religion of the Nabateans consisted of the worship of tribal deities and veneration of their ambitious kings among Arabian peoples who, like the

Jews, practiced circumcision.[12] What pushed Paul into this hive of Semitic idolatry and nationalism, unalloyed with the healthy influence of Greek philosophy?

When it came to departing from Damascus and avoiding Jerusalem, he did not have a great deal of choice. And it is quite in character that he did not return to Tarsus at this juncture, although his native city would have provided him a cosmopolitan, philosophically freewheeling environment. Paul was an ambitious young man. He had already been advanced in his knowledge of Judaism back in Tarsus, and he had left home to achieve the status of an expert in the oral Torah of the Pharisees: to walk in Gamaliel's footsteps, not just sit at his feet. Until he could claim a real advance in *something*, there was little chance of his returning to Tarsus. To go back as a beginner in any new philosophy would mean showing up home as a failure.

In any case, "the way" of Jesus scarcely had the status of a philosophy at this stage. It was only a rustic, apocalyptic version of Judaism that made bizarre claims about its teacher having survived death in some manner. The odds of making anything of such a teaching within Tarsus's free market of ideas were very long indeed.

With the self-confidence of hindsight, Paul later said, "Things that were gain to me I regarded forfeit because of Christ" (Philippians 3:7). He was proud of that exchange—paradoxically, since he claimed the transaction gave him humility. But he could boast of his sacrifice only after he had publicly advanced in the way of the Christians. In the early days and years after his conversion, he avoided public scrutiny and eked out an existence using the only trade he knew: making tents. Ananias and Judas must have provided the contacts for Paul to make his way, but he took a big step down the ladder of status. As the boss's son and something of a grandee in Tarsus, and later as the high priest's Pharisaic recruit in Jerusalem, Paul had ceased working with his hands. This truly was a loss. It meant doing work for hours that he was familiar with, but not as a regular worker. The calluses on his hands were hard to come by—and welcome, because manipulating a needle pushed hard with the heel of the hand is painful work, especially for anyone with bad vision.

Another more profound force moved him to "Arabia"—a pull rather than a push. His letter to the Galatians provides this clue to Paul's experience and reveals his religious motivation for traveling to the kingdom of the Nabateans. Talking about the mount of vision, where Moses was given the Torah, Paul says that Sinai is "in Arabia" (Galatians 4:25). During the modern period, Sinai has been located on the Sinai Peninsula (hence the name), but in antiquity, people venerated Nabatea as the place of Moses' vision. Paul went to Arabia, to the mountain of vision, because only there could he resolve the deepest conflict he ever faced, a conflict that left a permanent mark on his thinking and on the character of Christianity.

· · ·

WHEN PAUL SPEAKS of Sinai in his letter to the Galatians and locates it in Arabia, he does so to disparage it. He compares Sinai to Hagar, the Egyptian slave Abraham took as a surrogate wife (Genesis 16). For him, Sinai represents bondage, Jerusalem as hamstrung by law, while the heavenly Jerusalem is free (see Galatians 4:22–26):

> Because it is written that Abraham had two sons, one from the slave woman and one from the free woman. But the one from the slave woman was born of flesh, while the son of the free woman was born through promise. These things are meant allegorically: they are two covenants, one from Mount Sinai—bearing for slavery—that is Hagar. Hagar—which is Mount Sinai in Arabia—corresponds to Jerusalem now. She serves as a slave with her children. But Jerusalem above is free: that is our mother.

Once he began writing to predominantly non-Jewish communities, this sort of analogy came easily to Paul, yet it must have been very demanding on his Gentile readers. Although the message that they were not required to keep the Torah of Moses came as a relief to some of them, it is difficult to imagine what people only recently exposed to biblical themes and living in the middle of Asia Minor—as the Galatians did—can have made of this convoluted argument.

Indeed, some of his readers wanted to embrace the very rituals Paul wanted to keep them from: these practices gave expression to their faith.

The later Galatian battle—over whether Gentile Christians needed to keep the whole of the Torah—caused Paul to think back to his own struggle to reconcile a basic dichotomy. If the promise of the covenant was for Israel, how could Jesus fulfill that covenant for the whole of humanity? There was a world of torment for Paul in the discovery that the covenant with Moses that he had served and made his ideal, the cornerstone of all he believed, had been superseded. His own maternal metaphor in writing to the Galatians suggests that he learned the heartache of finding your mother is not your true mother, of discovering your most intimate identity in a stranger.

This recognition of a new mother was a result of Paul's vision, but it did not come all at once.[13] At the time of his conversion in Damascus, the apocalyptic vision, the blindness, the therapeutic touch, and baptism—in short, the uncovering of God's Son within Paul— were a hectic mix, and the requirements of physically mastering a trade crowded out intellectual reflection. Yet the question still arose: How could he square his new calling with the revelation of the Torah to Moses?

Paul traveled in one of the caravans that plied a trade between Damascus and the magnificent city of Petra. Commercial journeys were lucrative, sometimes dangerous, but a skilled (even partially blind) maker of tents would be useful when it came to establishing camps and repairing harnesses and ropes. A craftsman could use the tools of making tents for related kinds of work in leather, felt, cord, and fabric. The families that lived off this constant trade, always on the move, came to be called "Arabs," steppe-dwellers, Semitic speakers who spoke Aramaic in Syria and Nabatea, so that Paul found a provisional, constantly shifting domicile with them. The use of spike, needle, knife, and hardened leather palm on the heel of his hand came easily over the course of time as the caravan wended its way from market to market, through the irrigated, prosperous land of Nabatea.

Acts and Paul's letters agree that, when he preached during this period, he spoke of Jesus as God's Son and Messiah (Acts 9:20, 22; Galatians 1:1, 16), as makes sense, given the circumstances of his own conversion. To him, God's Son, uncovered in the believer, opened the font of Spirit, so that the promises to Israel could be fulfilled. But neither Paul nor Acts claims that he had any success in such preaching, whether in Jewish congregations or among Gentile groups. Some of the bitterness of that failure also shines through Paul's rhetoric equating Hagar and slavery.

Jews of the time saw Nabatean Arabs as circumcised descendants of Abraham through Hagar and her son Ishmael (Genesis, chapters 16 and 21). These were the Ishmaelites, next of kin to the Israelites, who had descended from Sarah and her son Isaac. What better place for Paul to start bringing non-Israelites into the fledgling movement centered on Jesus? Yet Paul's letter to the Galatians echoes no affection for the land of Sinai and denigrates Hagar, while Acts expunges any reference to the three years of Paul's Nabatean sojourn. It clearly was a period of isolation and withdrawal.

Nabatea nonetheless gave him the space he needed to come to terms with Moses in his own mind. Without that settlement of accounts, Paul could never have come into his own. Writing to communities of Christians in Corinth more than twenty years later, he referred in a stunning image to the significance of Moses. It is still difficult to believe your eyes as you are reading; you might expect him to compare Jesus to Moses, and even that would have been an extraordinary argument within the Judaism of the period. But he doesn't go that way. Instead, in the kind of move that gives arrogance a bad name, he compares *himself* to Moses.

The Torah says that Moses veiled himself after meeting God on Sinai, to protect the Israelites from the glory that was revealed in his face (Exodus 34:32–35). In Paul's own time, elders in synagogues also veiled themselves, imitating Moses' precaution.[14] In a calculated reversal, Paul makes the veil that is the sign of Moses' glory in the Torah into the proof that Moses conveyed glory only indirectly.

His veil was as approximate and temporary as the tissue of this world. Vision and baptism put believers, as they had put Paul, face to face with God (2 Corinthians 3:14–18): "Until this day the same veil remains over the reading of the old covenant: covered up, because in Christ it is set aside. Yet still today whenever Moses is read, a veil lies on their heart, but whenever one turns to the Lord, the veil is removed. The Lord is Spirit, and where the Lord's Spirit is, there is freedom. And we all with uncovered face, mirroring the Lord's glory—the same image—are transformed from glory to glory. . . ."

Paul claimed that he looked in the same direction that Moses did and saw directly what only glimmered behind the Mosaic gauze—the image of God in Christ, a powerful source of glory that transformed Paul in a way that made him directly comparable to Moses.

From the point of view of received Judaism, whether ancient or modern, to equate oneself to Moses denigrates the Torah to the edge of blasphemy, if not beyond that point. But in Paul's experience, and therefore in his mind, the encounter with the Messiah, the uncovering of the divine Son within, was an immediate confrontation with God. Living with his own visions and revelations (as he called them; 2 Corinthians 12:1), he came to believe that they were tablets of a covenant every bit as binding as the covenant with Moses, but freer and more genuine—after all, they came from heaven.

In the empty tracks of wilderness patrolled by the caravan of Arabs, picking and choosing among the meats they served (no camel for him, but sheep and goat were fine if properly slaughtered), eating as much of their vegetables and grain as he liked, Rabbi Paul mended harnesses and leather and felt and canvas, and puzzled through the implications of the voice that had called him. In his own way he was a new Daniel (see Daniel 1:8–16) who lived among non-Jews while abstaining from their polluted food, and spent his days pondering his own visions of the night for the benefit of his Gentile hosts and the glory of Israel.

Because the Nabateans practiced circumcision and claimed descent from Abraham through Ishmael, they were a living testimony to Paul's characteristic assertion that circumcision alone was not a guarantee of the covenant (Galatians 3:15–26). You had to see past the veil of flesh and through the clouds of Sinai to perceive a glory that would make you completely new.

part two

THE CONTENDER

· 4 ·

THE PETRINE CONNECTION

P AUL FELT LIKE A NEW MOSES, divine Spirit coursing in him and through him; but he was also as lost as Israel in the wilderness, disoriented by his own vision. The divine Son prompted him to bring that Spirit to Gentiles, without the Torah that had been Paul's first loyalty. What could he or anyone do to accomplish that?

The ad hoc discipline of making tents had toughened him physically. But he was living with an inner conflict. The Torah had been paramount to him, and Paul's vision came at the very moment when the young Pharisee had been at the peak of his enthusiasm for the Temple and his zeal against Jesus. So the Torah, he had learned in the wilderness of Nabatea, amounted to a veil between God and humanity. Moses for Paul was no longer the ultimate authority of Judaism. Instead, God invited every person—Jewish and Gentile (2 Corinthians 3:13–18)—to become a Moses-like visionary and realize the gift of the divine Son within.

In his own mind and by his practice he remained a Jew, yet his vision had changed his perception of what Judaism was. When his Jewish center of gravity shifted, the contours of a new religion began to emerge. The gift of Israel endured: As he said, from Israel came "the sonship, the glory, the covenants, the giving of the law, the worship, and the promises" (Romans 9:4). But sonship came first; the Torah, once preeminent in his mind, turned up a poor fourth, just ahead of Temple worship—a very odd switch for any Pharisee.

Just as Rabbi Jesus had pursued a Judaism that put God's kingdom before the Law, so Rabbi Paul struggled to define what it meant to make sonship the first priority. But where Jesus saw no conflict between Kingdom and Law, Paul's vision involved offering sonship to non-Israelites apart from the Law. Judged by the standards of the Pharisees, Paul and even Jesus look deviant. But the first century was an unruly time for Judaism. If you compare Jesus and Paul to other Jews of their time—like Philo and Josephus, the people of Qumran, and the apocalyptic seers who composed the books of Enoch—then you discover the roots of Christianity and see the force of Paul's vision.

Paul himself was forever conflicted about the Torah. He had once converted to a form of Judaism that made the Law indispensably central, and then converted to the divine Son as the center of his faith. He continued to follow the Torah himself, but believed that Gentiles could inherit the sonship that was Israel's gift to the world without accepting the Law. From the point of view of the Pharisees—and of later, Rabbinic Judaism—that was just crazy. His initial forays as an apostle with this position must have confused many people, Jews and Gentiles alike; charges of inconsistency and hypocrisy dogged him until the day he died.

Nabatea was the land of Arabs who were circumcised but non-Israelite: a strategic choice that Paul had made in his first try to convey by word and practice how the God of Israel was extending his promises to humanity as a whole. But Paul does not say what happened in Nabatea, and Acts skips any reference to this three-year stay. There is a simple reason for the silence: Paul's sojourn there was a failure. His proclamation to both Jews and non-Jews ran afoul of the anti-Jewish policies of the Nabatean king, Aretas IV.

Aretas harried the borders of Herod Antipas and went on to defeat Antipas's whole army in a grab for land in 36 C.E.[1] During the run-up to the outbreak of hostilities between Aretas and Herod Antipas, when Paul was in Nabatea until the year 35 C.E., the Nabatean was at the height of his ambition and power. He had absolutely no use for renegade Pharisees like Paul. Paul claimed that the promises of Israel were not limited to those who were Jews by birth. Embroiled in his escalating dispute with a Herodian ruler, the last thing Aretas wanted to hear about was an ideology that sounded like Israelite expansion, just the opposite of his own territorial program. Vagrant Jewish preachers like Paul might be some kind of Jewish fifth column, agitators from Antipas's side of the border.

Vigilant rulers in antiquity saw to it that any subversion was wiped out, no matter how minor. Aretas's officers ran Paul all the way up to Roman Damascus and into the city itself. One of Paul's letters gives details about his being lowered in a basket over the city walls to evade an attempt by Aretas's agents to grab him (2 Corinthians 11:32–33): "In Damascus the ethnarch of Aretas the king guarded the city of the Damascenes with a garrison to grab hold of me, and through a window in a basket I was let down through the wall, and fled from his hands."

Aretas's *ethnarkhes* ("ruler of a people," in this case, Nabateans in Damascus) posed a mortal danger. Paul had to escape in one of the merchants' baskets that disciples such as Ananias plied their trade with; some of them lowered Paul a hundred feet over the wall of Damascus.

That unsteady descent in the closed basket obviously left an impression on him: he speaks about the escape while listing the many punishments inflicted on him without mention of what he had done to incur them. Jesus' sympathizers in the city also remembered this incident (Acts 9:25). It taxed their ingenuity. Concealing this fugitive involved muffling the sounds Paul no doubt made in his panic. Never a happy traveler, he was not a man to suffer in silence.

Acts makes the apologetic claim that "the Jews" rather than Aretas were after Paul in Damascus (Acts 9:23–25). Like other documents in the New Testament, when the Book of Acts is in doubt, it blames the Jews. They were politically safer targets than the Romans themselves

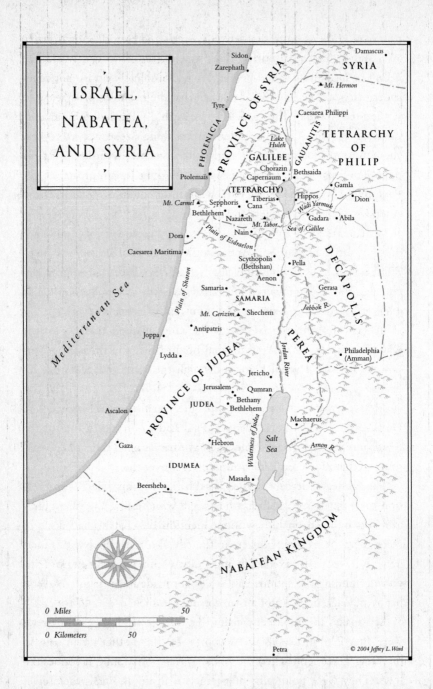

ISRAEL,
NABATEA,
AND SYRIA

Damascus

SYRIA

Sidon

Zarephath

Mt. Hermon

PHOENICIA

PROVINCE OF SYRIA

Tyre

Caesarea Philippi

GAULANITIS

TETRARCHY
OF
PHILIP

Lake
Huleh

Ptolemaïs

GALILEE

Chorazin

Capernaum
Bethsaida

Gamla

(TETRARCHY)

Mt. Carmel

Sepphoris
Bethlehem

Tiberias
Cana

Hippos

Dion

Wadi Yarmuk

Nazareth

Mt. Tabor

Gadara
Abila

Dora

Nain

Sea of Galilee

Plain of Esdraelon

DECAPOLIS

Caesarea Maritima

Scythopolis
(Bethshan)

Pella

Aenon

Gerasa

Plain of Sharon

Samaria

SAMARIA

Mediterranean Sea

Mt. Gerizim

Shechem

Jabbok R.

Joppa

Antipatris

PEREA

Lydda

Jordan River

Philadelphia
(Amman)

Jericho

Jerusalem

Qumran

Bethany

Ascalon

JUDEA

Bethlehem

PROVINCE OF JUDEA

Wilderness of Judea

Machaerus

Gaza

Hebron

Salt
Sea

Arnon R.

IDUMEA

Masada

Beersheba

NABATEAN KINGDOM

0 Miles   50

0 Kilometers   50

Petra

© 2004 Jeffrey L. Ward

or Roman client-kings. Yet Acts' portrait does complement the scene in 2 Corinthians, because Paul confronted pressure on two fronts in Damascus. Aretas wanted to be rid of him as an activist of a greater territorial Israel. But many people who gathered in synagogues were bemused at best—and often offended (Acts 9:21)—that the same young Pharisee who was sent to Damascus to denounce followers of Jesus was now one of them.

Both Aretas and the Jews who opposed Paul in Damascus had a grievance. He did stand for a radical inclusion of Gentiles within Israel, or—what amounts to the same thing—a radical extension of the scope of Israel to include Gentiles. He managed to scandalize both Jews and Gentiles with exactly the same message.

He also put off most disciples of Jesus in Damascus. At this time all of them devout Jews, they could only have been bewildered by this former Pharisee's sudden conversion, as much *away* from the Torah as to God's Son. Later Christianity, deeply influenced by Paul's letters, easily conceived of an opposition between Christ and the Law. When Gentile Christians came to dominate churches, they saw themselves as practicing a religion separate from Judaism, for the most part free from the regulations of the Torah. Most followers of Jesus around the year 35 denied there was any breach with the Law, opposing Paul's view of the Torah as subsidiary to the apocalypse of God's Son. They rejected his vision-induced obsession with Gentiles.

Primitive Christianity was a movement *within* Judaism, directed to Israelites by Israelites, and offering hope to Gentiles only insofar as the Prophets promised that Israel would govern the world. No one had yet said—at this point, not even Paul—that anyone who believed in Jesus as God's Son automatically became an Israelite, no matter what his or her genealogy. All that was yet to be worked out in 35 C.E.

Judaism's attitudes toward Gentiles did not amount to some unusual narrowness of perspective: The fact is that most religions (including Christians at their earliest period and today) and most civilizations see themselves as the best model for humanity, and others as anywhere from second-rate to barely human. When they faced the question of what to do about non-Jews who wished to be baptized in Jesus' name, most of Paul's colleagues believed that they had to submit to the Torah as God-fearers—remaining Gentiles but acknowledging the Law of Moses.

As a matter of fact, most of Jesus' disciples *intensified* their own devotion to the Torah and the Temple when they experienced him as raised from the dead. Paul's vision ran against the grain of that natural loyalty, and there didn't seem much point in his concern for non-Jews. Gentiles had not yet joined the movement in any numbers, and here Paul was saying they could be exempted from the Law of Moses.

His conversion had the look of an about-face and was too much for most people to take. Everyone in Damascus who knew him or knew about him must have wanted him out of the city. Paul himself—seconded by Acts—states that he went up to Jerusalem at this stage. He met over a period of fifteen days with Peter (whom Paul refers to by his Aramaic name, *Kepha*—Cephas in its clumsy English rendering) and James, the brother of Jesus (Galatians 1:18–19). Pressed by his vision, still shy of thirty years old, he went to the heart of Jesus' movement to claim the mantle of an apostle. He made a beginning in 35 C.E. with Peter and James, but it was a rocky start.

· · ·

HIS ONE SOLID ACHIEVEMENT during this first visit to Jerusalem after his conversion was that he came to know Peter—and Peter's wisdom about Jesus. Over the long term Paul could have accomplished nothing more important, because Peter's vision of the risen Jesus shaped Christianity more than any other single factor.

During Jesus' life, Peter had already emerged with the sons of Zebedee, James and John, as one of three Galilean disciples most skilled in their rabbi's mystical practice. These three, whom Jesus had also called to represent him among his delegates (or apostles, from the Greek term *apostoloi*), were experts in visionary discipline. That had enabled them to see Jesus transfigured and speaking on Mount Hebron with Moses and Elijah (Mark 9:2–8). Peter's visionary accomplishment made him the first to see Jesus alive after his crucifixion (as Paul said in 1 Corinthians 15:5, apparently ignoring the role of Mary Magdalene in the Gospels); in his experience Jesus' Resurrection opened the world of Spirit to those who believed in him.

Peter made baptism—until his time strictly a ritual of immersion for the sake of purity within Judaism—into the moment of one's immersion in Spirit. His vision of Jesus raised from the dead, which took place in Galilee (John 21:1–24), pressed him to return to Jerusalem. This was where Rabbi Jesus had promised that God—just as the Prophets predicted—really was making the Temple there into a house of prayer for all the nations of the world (Mark 11:17), the fountain of Spirit for all the earth.[2] With Peter's guidance, other apostles returned to Jerusalem and they joined with him in collective visions of Jesus in their midst.

The disciples worshiped regularly with Peter in the Temple and often "broke bread" in their common home (Acts 2:44–47). Peter's group lived communally in Jerusalem like an extended Galilean family. They also replicated the Galilean custom of living together without money: their possessions were communal. They ate Eucharist together as a domestic meal, beginning with a patriarch's petition for divine blessing spoken over the bread and invoking Jesus' visionary presence.

This visionary Jesus appeared and promised, "John indeed immersed with water, but you will be immersed in Holy Spirit, after not many of these days" (Acts 1:5). And during the Jewish feast of Pentecost, Spirit descended upon them in the shape of flame over their heads (Acts 2:1–4), an emblem of mystical experience in the Judaism of the period.[3] This endowment of Spirit proved to be the pivot of the entire movement of Jesus after his death. Indirectly familiar with this teaching as a result of controversy about it in Jerusalem, Paul the persecutor embraced it as a result of his vision. His move to consult Peter personally made excellent sense.

For Peter and those like him, baptism was more than a good dunking; immersion in Jesus' name brought a rush of Spirit—and the human heart needed serious instruction to be open to this infusion from

God's own throne. The disciples had started to memorize Jesus' teaching, but not yet in an agreed format. Peter's influence—and the influence of teachers like him in the primitive phase of Christianity—was greater than was the norm among a rabbi's disciples in Judaism. A rabbi was usually someone who had ordered his own teaching into a *mishnah* (a memorized "repetition") for his disciples to commit to memory and repeat. Jesus, killed at around the age of thirty, was taken from his followers before he could do that. So Peter was in a position to craft the disciples' memories within his own outline of faith. That is what he instilled in Paul (as Paul says, Galatians 1:18) during just over two weeks of intense meeting.

In his story of Rabbi Jesus being baptized, witnessing to the reality of God's kingdom, suffering for the kingdom, and finally achieving immortal glory (Acts 10:34–43), Peter set out a path of faith for every believer to follow. He spoke of eternal life, not only for Jesus but also for everyone who followed him in a life endowed with Spirit. This was the message, validated on the Damascus road, that Paul made his own.

Yet by temperament, background—and even their visions of Jesus—Peter and Paul were different men. Although Paul deferred to Peter and embraced his teaching, events proved that these two never really understood one another. Paul even had trouble getting to see Peter and James in the first place. Acts bluntly admits that, after his 180-degree conversion (9:26), "everybody feared him, not believing that he was a disciple." Here Acts tells the truth while Paul tries to gild it.

Barnabas, like Paul a Diaspora Jew, broke the logjam of distrust and introduced Paul to the other apostles (Acts 9:27). Why did Barnabas buy Paul's conversion when others were—to say the least—reserved? Barnabas shared with his Tarsan colleague a foreign origin as well as pride in a Judaic heritage that included knowledge of Aramaic. But then Barnabas was a Levite while Paul could boast descent only from Benjamin (the least of the family clans of Israel), so their backgrounds alone do not explain the affinity between these two men or the connection that lasted long beyond this initial encounter in Jerusalem.

Paul's vision of Jesus resonated with Barnabas's personal knowledge of Jesus from the early days of the movement until when Jesus raided the Temple to object to the high priest's installation of vendors there. Barnabas knew from firsthand experience that Jesus' motivation for the last, climactic protest was to realize the prophecy of Zechariah.[4] At the end of days, Zechariah had forecast, the Gentiles would stream into Jerusalem with Israelites in order to offer sacrifice in the Temple without any commercial middlemen.

"My house shall be called a house of prayer for all the nations," Jesus had said (Mark 11:17), quoting Isaiah's promise that the blessings of Israel would be for the whole world. And that word "nations"—in Hebrew, Aramaic, and Greek as well as in Latin—means Gentiles. Paul's vision compelled him to announce Jesus to the Gentiles as God's Son—to take this message directly to them without converting them to Judaism or making them God-fearers. When Barnabas brought Paul to Peter, he introduced Jesus' movement to the possibility of a completely new understanding of what their rabbi stood for. Rabbi Jesus had never taught this way, but Paul claimed that the risen Jesus mandated this special mission.

All the while he learned from Peter, the issue of how his commission to the Gentiles could be fulfilled consumed Paul's heart and mind. Getting at that was tough—precisely because Rabbi Jesus never had spoken of deliberately including non-Jews in his movement. Neither could Peter offer direct guidance on the basis of his Pentecost vision. That had prophesied an outpouring of Spirit on Jews and converts to Judaism all over the world, not the direct approach to Gentiles without conversion to Judaism that Paul's vision demanded.

That is why something strange happened next. Strange, that is, if you expect that earliest Christianity was a harmonious movement in which disagreements were muted. After merely fifteen days with Peter, Paul left Jerusalem completely, going to "Syria and Cilicia" (Galatians 1:21), the Roman province that included Tarsus. Acts states more specifically (9:30) that "the brothers brought him down to Caesarea and sent him off to Tarsus"—no doubt with considerable relief. After just over two weeks, the man Acts dearly wishes to celebrate as the great and universally acclaimed apostle to the Gentiles was shipped unceremoniously out of Jerusalem. What went on?

Acts blames this unexpected departure on the same Diaspora Jews who turned on Stephen (Acts 9:29). Yet later in Acts, a flashback appears in a speech by Paul in which he says another vision, in the Temple, made him leave (Acts 22:17–21). In that sacred place he fell into "ecstasy" and Jesus told him, "I will delegate you to Gentiles afar." Repeating such ecstatic messages in the Temple could not have made for a hearty welcome among those who worshiped there in deliberate separation from the Gentiles.

At this point Paul was a pretty anomalous Jew, quite aside from his belief in Jesus. His mind filled with his visions in the Nabatean wilderness, he insisted in the Temple that Gentiles should be offered the realization of God's promises to humanity *without accepting the Law of Judaism*. If they tried to do so, he said that would only make them children of Hagar (Galatians 4:22–26): slaves to obedience rather than brothers and sisters of the beloved Son of God. He did not actually say the Jews should stop keeping the Torah, although anyone who listened to him must have at least flirted with the idea that this was his real meaning.

Writing twenty years later to communities in Greece, he said, "From Jews five times I took the forty lashes less one" (2 Corinthians 11:24). This refers to a punishment mentioned in the Bible (Deuteronomy 25:1–3) and fine-tuned in the Mishnah (see Makkot 3:10–13). The culprit had his hands tied on either side of a pillar and his clothing ripped from his torso. Then an expert in the lash flogged him from behind so that one-third of the blows landed on his chest and two-thirds on his back. The total number of blows was limited to thirty-nine—Paul's "forty lashes less one."

Although such flogging was nothing compared to the Roman version, which went on and on with steel-tipped whips and could kill a man, it remained a painful disgrace (see Josephus *Antiquities* 4.238–39). Just the thing for a Diaspora interloper who thought he could compare himself to Moses: the Mishnah says the punishment is for failing to observe the Torah (Makkot 3:14). The synagogues of both Damascus and Jerusalem had the means and the will to administer the thirty-nine lashes, and it's likely Paul received a couple of his five floggings in those cities. Whatever he said about Gentiles and the Torah, he was an Israelite, and he accepted the authority of synagogues and its physical cost.

Peter and his colleagues were themselves sometimes harassed by the high priest and his sympathizers, who arrested and beat them (Acts 4:1–21; 5:17–42) in an attempt at intimidation. The apostles had every reason to bundle Paul out of the country to reduce tensions in the city. They were concerned with living inside Jerusalem, not with some outlandish outreach to Gentiles who denied Judaism.

Daily life posed challenges enough without Paul's presence. In their little community, in a neighborhood of small houses between the Pharisaic neighborhood and the Essenes' settlement, the apostles and their adherents lived expectantly, free to hope that this Temple and this world would indeed be transformed according to the golden promise that Zechariah had prophesied and Rabbi Jesus had put into action. The demands of sacrifice as well as survival depleted their meager resources. Barnabas, always loyal to Peter, saw his prestige increase when he sold his property in Jerusalem and gave the proceeds to Peter's apostolic group (Acts 4:32–37): a wealthy child of the Diaspora became a son of Galilee for the sake of Jesus.

Peter's group was ferocious when it came to the ideal of communal wealth. Once a man and his wife both claimed to have given the full value of a property they sold to the apostles, but in fact held some money back for themselves. Peter interrogated them one after the other (Acts 5:1–11). He accused them of lying to God, and supernatural violence broke out immediately—they both literally dropped dead, according to Acts.

Assessing the accuracy of this account isn't at issue here. The point is that the story was told, insisting that lying about wealth in this commune brought the retribution of the Holy Spirit. The same Spirit that had descended on Jesus at his baptism was poured out on those who believed in his Resurrection and transformed the apostles in the Temple into prophets of the new prophetic order. That order, that Spirit, included the power of death itself.

Barnabas was implicitly bringing a question about this new age of prophecy to Peter when he introduced Paul to the Jerusalem movement. Did Paul's vision on the road to Damascus provide divine guidance? Were non-Jews now, *without* the obligation to observe the Torah, without making pilgrimage to the Temple, to be included in the outpouring of God's Spirit? Could there be for them a Law-free version of the message of Jesus? All these questions were bundled together in the person of Paul, aspiring Pharisee turned grubby tent-maker and wannabe apostle.

Peter gave no recorded verbal answer to that basic question. But his action—or lack of action—was as eloquent as a papal encyclical. Nothing changed after Paul's visit, and he was sent off to Tarsus (Acts 9:30). His idea was so revolutionary, there was no way to put it into action. At best Peter would have seen it as remotely plausible, at the very edge of prophetic possibility. The Jewish practice of Peter and the vast majority of Jews in his time focused on the Torah as the guide for true worship in the Temple. What conceivable sense was there in announcing in Jerusalem that the Torah was not the ultimate revelation of God for Gentiles as well as Jews? The time for Paul's idea had not come, and he tried it out in exactly the wrong place.

Acts and Paul both sugarcoat the decision to send the newly converted Pharisee packing. Acts portrays the same Hellenistic Jews who had instigated the stoning of Stephen as wishing to kill Paul (Acts 9:28–29); Paul talks about going back to his home territory as if it were his own decision (Galatians 1:21). Some commentators have accepted one or another of these spins, but Günther Bornkamm speaks for sound scholarship when he concludes that when Peter and Paul first met, "that cannot have led to full agreement."[5] Peter answered the question represented by Paul's presence in Jerusalem with an implicit but clear "no." Only time would turn that into a "not yet." Paul found no welcome in Jerusalem beyond fifteen days. He had to make his own way back to his native Tarsus.

· · ·

PAUL RETURNED TO HIS FAMILY with practical skills that made him valuable to them. He had mastered the craft of making tents with his own hands in Nabatea, had traveled to Jerusalem and Damascus, and his years of study and debate had made him into a garrulous speaker, a "word-scat" *(spermologos)*[6] as people called him. Those qualities made him a good boss in a hard trade as he approached his thirtieth year; as his parents aged, he came into his own.

He could demonstrate by example how work should be done and encourage long hours of efficient labor by showing up and talking—about tents, about Torah, about Christ. He had the entrepreneur's habit of skipping from one topic to another as if they were connected, the busy brain of a man who juggled one task with another while tumbling from one pet idea to the next. For such people, even quiet meditation occasions a storm of interconnected ideas and plans.

Paul prospered in Tarsus between 35 and 40 C.E. Commercial contacts in Asia Minor served him well for the rest of his life. The entrepreneurial side of Paul's character is often overlooked because it is of no interest in the New Testament, but it comes out in a variety of ways.

Business involves selling, and salesmen the world over were vehicles of surprising new ideas as well as conventional wisdom. They traveled more than almost any other class of people and talked more, wandering from subject to subject before homing in on the little matter of price. Of such gambits bargains and profits were made—and sometimes minds were changed. A salesman's apparently aimless airing of views is not beholden to the orthodoxies that a priest or a teacher or a philosopher might feel bound by. A salesman can say anything he likes, and often he likes to say a lot.

Overselling is not a fault, if it gets results, and some of the themes of Paul's letters are explained and explained again, illustrated by references to the Scriptures of Israel that seem repetitive because they are—oversold until you buy them. When a *spermologos* is also a boss in an enterprise, his staff quickly gets to know his favorite subjects; they brace themselves for his patter. In the case of Paul, his employees and slaves had a lot of bracing to do.

His views at this stage were, to say the least, idiosyncratic. Belief in Jesus characterized a tiny movement inside Judaism, what the French call a *groupuscule*: a fragment within a sect. The spectacle in provincial Tarsus of an aspiring Pharisee returning after seven years in Jerusalem, Syria, and—of all places—Nabatea, not as a Pharisee at all but with weird claims about seeing a Galilean rabbi raised from the dead, had to seem strange. This wasn't even heresy in Tarsus, because the local synagogue did not have enough experience of Jesus' disciples to consider them any threat. It was simply bizarre.

Paul didn't make many converts in that synagogue, not even according to Acts, which tends to exaggerate his impact. Instead, his letters and Acts both ignore this period, which Jerome Murphy-O'Connor has called "The Missing Years."[7] His only regular audience at this stage was probably of the captive kind, those obligated to him for their livelihood. When the boss's son talked—outside under a tent where workers gathered for big contracts, or inside in oil-lit darkness to finish work during the night—there wasn't much to do but listen and go along.

Working guilds in antiquity were not just bunches of workers, but trained men and women who had profound connections with one another. They often lived in close proximity to each other, devoted themselves to common gods, and developed long-standing relations by marriage; the boss was a patriarch. As the boss's son, Paul could command a hearing, yet the guild as a whole, his family as a whole, evidently did not devote themselves to the worship of Jesus. Paul was a commercial success, a religious failure, and that taxed his inner resources.

. . .

SOME OF HIS FAVORITE THEMES during his impromptu discourses in Tarsus are probably reflected in his letters, all of which come from a later period. They reflect set pieces of rhetoric that he launched into, pretty much unsolicited. Just as they intrude into his letters whatever the topic at hand might be, he had no doubt tried them out on his captive audience in Tarsus.

How can a person receive the Spirit of God? Spirit refers to the vast, unfathomable ocean of divine creation—making, unmaking, reshaping our world. How can that power touch the fragile human form without destroying it? That's possible only when people have learned the art of "listening with faith," he replied to his own question. Faith is the act of God within the human heart, and for that reason faith alone is durable enough to survive contact with divine power. That question, that response, came out of the blue to Paul's hearers in Tarsus, which was how it came to the congregations he later wrote to in Galatia (Galatians 3:3–5). He fixated on this question, because it was embedded in his own conversion, the disclosure of Spirit that came when God's Son was uncovered within.

He raised the matter whether or not anyone was interested. And having raised it, he pursued how divine Spirit could come only in this way, by believing in Jesus, not by means of the Torah. Paul thought he was the paradigm of everyone.

Take the example of Abraham, he says: before Moses or the Torah ever came on the scene, the Bible says Abraham believed in God, and that this faith made him righteous in God's eyes. So everybody who believes—with or without the Torah—is really a child of Abraham! That became one of Paul's signature themes (Galatians 3:6–7)—the conviction that belief in God alone, without any recourse to the Torah or to the genealogy of the patriarchs or circumcision, makes a person into Abraham's child.

Venturing into uncharted territory, he felt compelled to prove his point from Scripture. Following his detailed references to texts (Galatians 3:8–14), you can easily see why pagan listeners had trouble following him. Unless you are familiar with these Scriptures (or consult an annotated Bible) it is unlikely you will get his point. But then, of course, if you were that familiar with the Bible of Israel, that was probably because you believed God gave Moses the Torah on Sinai as a complete revelation of his will.

If you had taken the trouble to learn enough Torah to follow Paul, the chances were you would *not* agree that the Torah was only a side issue compared to Abraham and Christ. For these years in Tarsus, Paul lived in the rhetorical catch-22 that his own conversion had produced. He threaded his way through and around texts to free himself from that trap—how successfully is a matter of opinion.

The promise of Israel was intended for Abraham's "seed"—note the use of that singular (in Genesis 12:7), says Paul. That means Christ, not many generations of genealogical descendants (Galatians 3:15–20). So the Torah is a guide, not to how everyone should live, but to how they should come to Christ (Galatians 3:21–25), because, he concludes (Galatians 3:26–29): "For you are all God's Sons through faith in Jesus Christ. Because as you were immersed in Christ, you clothed yourselves with Christ. There is not a single Jew or Greek, not a single slave or freedman, not a single male or female, because you are all one in Jesus Christ. And if you are of Christ, then you are Abraham's seed, inheritors by promise." Christ in Paul's experience and thought became the primal human being that healed all the world's divisions.

No argument could be more simply stated, more clearly argued—or be more likely to bewilder the burghers of Tarsus. A commercial tentmaker's son is telling the staff—and countless later generations of Christians—that the most basic divisions of societies (ethnic, religious, social, and sexual) do not really matter? Easy for him to say, a man who lives near the top of the status ladder. And all this oneness—this common inheritance of a single, human promise that realizes primal unity—comes how? Because we are all like Abraham? Why make this case through such a convoluted argument? Why not say that Tarku unites us?—a pagan might wonder. Or Moses, any Jew might think.

Paul seemed inconsistent to people throughout his life, and that can't have helped him find a hearing in Tarsus. His famous brag that he became all things to all people, to Jews a Jew and to Greeks a Greek (1 Corinthians 9:19–23), could easily be turned against him. For all his argument that the Torah is ancillary to Christ, he never abandoned his personal practice of Judaism. So what about being "one" in Christ? His listeners must have wondered, and the question must have crossed Paul's mind, too.

By the mid-50s C.E., Paul had worked out an answer, but during this period in Tarsus after 35, he perplexed those around him by keeping the Torah while insisting that it didn't matter too much. He attended synagogue, kept kosher, observed the Sabbath and the festivals of Israel. A typical Tarsan, he also heard lectures in the halls of the city, and no doubt tried to enter into debate. Once he became famous, synagogues and lecture halls were among his favorite venues. But in Tarsus he found a hearing in neither. In a city of ambitious philosophers, wily tradesmen, devout pagans, dedicated Jews, and loyal Romans, he was an intellectual manqué, a gabby man of business with no forum to sell the ideas that mattered to him most of all.

· · ·

IN HIS INTELLECTUAL ISOLATION, Paul developed another of his signature ideas for his little audience. A few sympathizers came to the point of being immersed in Jesus' name and of joining Paul in practicing the holy meal of Jesus. When Paul speaks of the Eucharist, he does so as a long-standing, personal discipline handed on to him by Peter (1 Corinthians 11:23–26).[8] It was the heart of his own spirituality from those fifteen days in Jerusalem onward, and it is probable that a small group gathered with him in Tarsus.

From this practice of the Eucharist, limited though it was, Paul developed his second great, innovative idea alongside his teaching about faith and the Law. Although a great deal of what he taught remains controversial to this day, in his conception of "the body of Christ" he provided ecumenical Christianity with one of its most enduring beliefs. In his time, as today, many different meanings were attached to Jesus'

Eucharistic words, "This is my blood," "This is my flesh." In Tarsus around the year 37, Paul repeated those words, drank wine, and ate bread with whatever little group of believers or experimenters he could convince to join him and gave the ritual a significance that made sense in the Greco-Roman world.

Paul saw that the bread of the Eucharist had the magical quality of sacrifice. Any act of offering in the ancient world was understood to become sacred when the deity took part in the ritual. God was pleased and joined the worshipers in their sacrifice. So here, the Eucharist did not merely repeat what Jesus had done, but invoked the presence of God and joined participants with all who worshiped God in heaven and on earth—including Jesus himself.

In the Greco-Roman world this was an easy idea to grasp because religious meals were already understood to bring people into contact with their ancestors as well as with their gods. In one of the most detailed stories of his Resurrection in the New Testament, Jesus joins with disciples in their breaking of bread and then disappears from their sight (Luke 24:13–35). He was a risen presence in every act of eating Eucharist. So, Paul concluded, when believers eat the bread as Christ's "body," they actually *become* Christ's body.

He insisted that anyone who ate the bread "not discerning the body *(soma)*" that connected all believers was unworthy and subject to God's judgment (1 Corinthians 11:27–29).[9] The "body of Christ" for Paul was both the offering of bread as a sacrifice in the manner of Jesus *and* the awareness of Jesus' presence in the community as risen from the dead.

However pathetic the little Eucharistic group was in Tarsus, Jesus joined them together in his spiritual body when they broke the bread that was his sacrifice. This assurance of a sustaining, divine presence in the Eucharist was buttressed by Paul's own creative addition to the theme. This "body" not only connected those who made the offering with the risen Jesus but linked all believers in an organic whole. "The body of Christ," a reference to the collective of all disciples in their sacrifice and their awareness of the risen Jesus, derives from Paul's practice, so that, as he said (1 Corinthians 10:17), "Although many, we are one bread, one body, because we all partake of the one bread."

This is classic Pauline chutzpah. The leaders of this movement had sent him into practical exile, yet he told his few odd sympathizers that they were part of a seamless whole in solidarity with Jesus' practice. Every day he said his prayers, remembering that the God of Israel is One, and now at Eucharist he claimed that all believers were One, articulated into a single body by the Spirit of Christ.

How did he get from a little group gathering for a meal to this vast, encompassing, social definition of the body of Christ such that it mirrored God's oneness? Paul's native Tarsus provides the key to his thought in this case. The Stoic philosophy that had prepared him for his apocalyptic vision on the road to Damascus also readied him to see unity where others saw chaos. The Stoics, with their rational mysticism, could conceive of the entire cosmos and the Roman Empire as a single body animated by reason. Their expression could take on a distinctly patriotic turn, as when Seneca—Paul's contemporary—called the emperor the spirit that animates the body politic (*De Clementia* 1.3.5). Paul's inventive synthesis took the social cohesion envisioned by the Stoics and married it with the sacrificial solidarity of Eucharist, so that all disciples everywhere were marshaled into a single body.

· · ·

WITHOUT HIS RELATIVE ISOLATION in Tarsus, it is unlikely that Paul could have worked out these ideas. Their originality is rooted in persistent reflection, bold idiosyncrasy, and a deliberately non-Pharisaic embrace of Stoic thought. In another aspect as well, the course of his life marks a deliberate step away from commitment to the synagogue community that had sidelined him.

In all probability he never married. Constant travel later made marriage impracticable for him, because a husband had to maintain his wife in an area she was accustomed to (see Ketubot 13:10 in the Mishnah). But his celibacy was also intentional and has fed the negative assessment of sexuality in much Christian teaching. It would make life easier for

Jesus' followers now, and make Paul more like other rabbis of his time, if he had been married.[10] In Tarsus he had the opportunity, the contacts, and the encouragement from his family to find a wife. But instead, Paul held himself up as an example of celibacy (1 Corinthians 7:25–40) and should be taken at his word.

When Paul refers to his sexual continence, it is to stress that an unmarried person can be better devoted to the Lord, free of the care of marriage.[11] This is consistent with his conception of the "body of Christ" that believers form. For him, devotion to that body precluded devotion to a wife. He understood that a man sexually becomes "one body" (1 Corinthians 6:16, see Genesis 2:24) with a woman—and for that very reason, Paul thought marriage was a bad idea. Consorting with a prostitute, which also made you "one body" with her, was even worse.

Paul's decision did not reflect merely misogynist or antisexual attitudes. He felt that the global "body of Christ" demanded the commitment of his own body. At the same time, nature was pulling him in different directions. In an exquisite passage of his letter to the Romans, he was to write, "The good I will, this I do not; but the evil I do not want, this I commit" (Romans 7:19). A plain statement of a psychological principle Dostoyevsky would later make a career exploring, this reflects a period of deep introspection and struggle—just what Paul went through in Tarsus during the years between 35 and 40 C.E. He never identified the "evil" he had in mind, but his vehement warning about staying away from prostitutes does make you wonder.

Paul was headed only for deeper introspection, further idiosyncrasy, and struggle against the forces of his own nature. But fellow visionaries in Israel intervened: A breakthrough there put Paul and the movement of Jesus on an entirely new course.

. . .

WHEN PAUL HAD VISITED Jerusalem in 35 C.E., Peter and James couldn't see what to do with him. They were committed to the prophetic prediction endorsed by Jesus that all peoples were to join in sacrifice on Mount Zion, but in their minds that was to occur through the gate of the Torah, not by relegating Moses to some secondary status. For them the best place for Paul was Tarsus, or any city far from Jerusalem where his strange ideas would not cause trouble.

Even with Paul out of the way, trouble came to visit Peter, in visionary form. Just as Paul's vision is referenced three times in the Book of Acts (chapters 9, 22, and 26), so is Peter's (chapters 10, 11, and 15). That repetition signals that what Peter saw is as pivotal as any event after the Resurrection of Jesus. Unlike the appearance of the risen Jesus to Paul on the road to Damascus, Peter's vision resulted in an immediate change in the emphasis and direction of primitive Christian practice, according to Acts. Peter exerted an influence Paul could only dream of having at this point. And unlike Paul's vision, Acts relates specifics of Peter's in detail.

Peter went to pray at noon on the roof of a house where he was staying (Acts 9:36–10:9). As food was being prepared downstairs, he felt hungry and "ecstasy *(ekstasis)* happened upon him" in the words of Acts (10:10). In this state, which literally means "standing *(stasis)* outside *(ek)*" oneself, he saw the heavens open, as Jesus did at his baptism. Like rabbis who practiced the mystical vision of Ezekiel's chariot, such as Ben Zoma (Chagigah 15a) and Jesus (Mark 3:21), Peter was "beside himself." In Peter's case, as in Jesus', the world of the chariot was opening up to him and a heavenly mystery was about to be disclosed. What Peter saw, however, was not the empowering dove that descended on Jesus when he practiced John's baptism, nor did he hear the reassuring message that he was embraced as God's Son. Instead, he saw a vast linen cloth descending upon the earth, four-cornered like the world itself (Acts 10:11). It was at first an all-embracing cosmic vision, the linen as pure as heaven itself was holy.

What filled the linen bewildered Peter: all the four-footed beasts of the world, the reptiles of the earth, and the birds of the air (10:12). In this vision of cosmic purity, clean and unclean mixed together indiscriminately. The voice that spoke (Acts 10:13) compounded the horror: "Arise, Peter, slaughter and eat!"

This must be a test, he thought. He had been on Mount Hebron with Jesus at the Transfiguration (Mark 9:2–8) and knew that visions could be instruments of ultimate insight. But he also knew from Jesus' story of his own Temptation (Matthew 4:1–11) that Satan could work his deceit in vision as much as in life. So Peter answered boldly, "By no means, Lord, because I have never eaten anything profane and unclean" (Acts 10:14). Spoken like the good Israelite he was, and with words echoing Scripture: Ezekiel (Ezekiel 4:14) had said much the same thing centuries before.

But God had contradicted Ezekiel, telling him that the siege of Jerusalem would force its inhabitants to eat impurities. Now a voice contradicted Peter as well: "What God cleansed, don't you profane!" (Acts 10:15) Yet there was no prediction of a siege, no explanation of how God cleansed the beasts teeming in the cosmic cloth, or why. Peter was at a loss to explain what he saw and heard, although his vision came three times (Acts 10:16–17). He understood the meaning of the vision only later, as a result of the circumstances surrounding him and the events that followed the vision.

His experience took place not in Jerusalem proper, but in Joppa, which served as a port city for the landlocked capital of the Jewish world. He stayed by the sea in the house of a sympathizer who bore the common name Simon, as he did: Simon "the Tanner" hosted Simon "the Rock" (Acts 10:5–6). Using nicknames was one of the habits Rabbi Jesus' disciples continued and developed after his death. In its expansion among Jewish adherents, the movement radiated from Jerusalem and included people in professions (such as tanning) that many people regarded as undesirable. In location, in proximity to the stench of animal hides dipped in tannic acid and stretched in the sun, with the sounds of proper food being prepared below, Peter was indeed on the boundary of uncleanness.

Near to Joppa was an imposing metropolis whose extravagant expanse has recently been opened up by archaeology. This was Rome's seat of power, ensconced in the midst of harbor facilities, a garrison, theaters, stadia, odeons, and baths, decorated by Greek and Latin inscriptions, richly ornamented with the emblems and treasures of em-

Antioch who were baptized in Jesus' name—but these Gentiles became a local curiosity. Like Cornelius, they were God-fearers, no ordinary pagans, but the fact remained that they were Gentiles.

Barnabas sought out Paul in Tarsus (Acts 11:25). The very feature of his thought that had made him an anomaly in Jerusalem five years earlier—God's inclusion of the Gentiles in the revelation of God's Son—now made Paul a potential asset in Antioch. At long last he was called to be an apostle, if not in Jerusalem, then at least by the church of a major city as well as by his own vision of Christ. That vision had called him, but Peter's vision as interpreted by Barnabas gave him a job.

· 5 ·

ANTIOCH

WITH A TOTAL POPULATION topping a quarter million[1]—
third largest city in the Roman Empire—Antioch housed
differing factions of Judaism the way nineteenth-century
Paris accommodated variants of socialism. One such mix involved
non-Jews believing in Jesus and as a result claiming that the hope of
Resurrection, the promise of Israel's Scriptures, belonged to them. In
its time this claim appeared bizarre and represented only a tiny minority of Jesus' movement, which was overwhelmingly Jewish. But by the
end of the first century this once marginal group defined the mainstream of Christianity. That change started in Antioch. Paul of Tarsus
played the role of a catalyst in this reaction and, in the way of catalysts,
he disappeared from the scene once the process was well and truly under way.

The character of Antioch was as important to the emergence of
Christianity as the character of any of Jesus' disciples. Without the particular situation that emerged in Antioch when it did, and without the
influence of Barnabas, Paul would in all probability have died in idiosyncratic anonymity in Tarsus. Set back from the heavily trafficked but
dangerous Mediterranean coast on the Orontes River, Antioch joined

East and West in commerce. The Persians founded the city around 300 B.C.E. and Antiochus the Great made it a pivotal center in his Seleucid Empire. But the Romans annexed the place in 64 B.C.E. in their superpower seesaw match with the Persians and co-opted Antioch's civic architecture for their own propaganda; they played out their usual gambits of replacing the images in vast Persian temples to honor the emperor as well as building their own temples.

Alongside honor, the Romans reaped the rewards of rich trade by land and sea that included Chinese porcelain. Where a city such as Tarsus brought the empire the benefits of a provincial economy, Antioch provided Rome a cultural and military hub that assured the defense of the East. With that development came the baths, aqueducts, theaters, and amphitheaters that were emblems of Roman prosperity and dominance. Spice manufacture, a vigorous trade in wine and oil, tent-making, metal foundry, jewelry and idol-crafting, masonry, pottery, weaving, dying, and silk-making, the haute couture of dozens of different cultures were all pursued here with the vigor of industrial cities in the West during the nineteenth century.

Above the thousands of shops in the city, tens of thousands of workers resided in multistoried tenements. Artisans could claim the living space of ample apartments, but slaves and the working poor—the vast majority of the populace—lived out their lives in cramped quarters, doing their best to group in families, edged in on every side by colleagues and competitors, some friendly, some threatening, some from the same parts of the world, many from regions so barbaric they spoke barely intelligible Greek. Entertainment in the hippodrome or the circus only intensified contact with strangers, bizarre tongues, and a bewildering array of customs.

People of wealth enjoyed lavish accommodations. The richest and best established of them owned freestanding homes with courtyards and separate rooms for entertaining, eating, lounging, studying, and sleeping. A family of the nouveaux riches could afford a mansionlike complex of rooms inside an enormous *insula,* the ancient equivalent of a condominium. An up-market apartment boasted an atrium and fountain; the owner stamped his identity on the place with furnishings in the Roman or Greek or Syrian or Persian manner and with magnificent mosaics. Privilege feasted on the wealth of a teeming city and its cheap, readily available labor force. The rich had access to baths and theaters and odeons for music, philosophical debates in a world-class university, and symposial entertainments at home ranging from learned discourse to frank pornography, all well lubricated with Antioch's heady wine.

Faithful coteries of enthusiasts, hangers-on, and priests devoted themselves to virtually every god in the Mediterranean world, Israel's included. Households and homogeneous guilds often claimed common loyalty to one god or another, and Jewish families in Antioch comparable to Paul's back in Tarsus made good livings despite occasional—sometimes violent—outbreaks of local prejudice. Preferential policies toward Jews under Antiochus the Great and Antiochus Epiphanes established thriving Jewish communities—more than twenty-five thousand people in all—that grew and diversified under Roman hegemony. During the second century B.C.E., a high priest of the Temple, Onias III, had even sought refuge near Antioch when a competitor usurped his position in Jerusalem.

This polyglot, multireligious city with its proud Jewish communities was a natural contact for Barnabas, a Levite from Cyprus, and the Jerusalem apostles sent him there (Acts 11:19–24). When conditions are right you can actually see Cyprus from Antioch. With his wealth and Levitical descent, Barnabas had good contacts with well-placed Jews in the city. His family had invested in land as far abroad as Jerusalem, and Antioch—nearer by and easily accessible by sea—was a lucrative market for Cypriot wares. God-fearing Gentiles attended dozens of synagogues representing various factions of Judaism. One of them was Nicolas of Antioch, a circumcised convert to Judaism who later came to Jerusalem and was numbered with Stephen among the first Greek-speaking leaders of Jesus' movement (Acts 6:5). These were just the kind of people that Peter's vision in Joppa had announced could be baptized in Jesus' name and receive his Spirit.

But Antioch also brought Barnabas contacts that did not come at all naturally to him. God-fearers in Antioch for the most part lived and worked among ordinary Gentiles. Ordinarily, Gentiles were what we call pagans: idol-worshiping, sometimes pig-eating subjects of Rome who had views of Judaism that ranged from incomprehension to outright prejudice. What should happen if some of these *idolaters* presented themselves for baptism in Jesus' name?

Peter's vision and his visit to the house of Cornelius did not cover that. He acted on the basis of visionary experience, not systematic theology; what he saw in Joppa empowered him to baptize God-fearers, not pagans. Yet vision or no vision, Barnabas could not get away from this issue. Antioch precluded any neat separation between God-fearing Gentiles and the rest of the non-Jewish world. In any case, how exactly would you know whether a given Gentile acknowledged the God of Israel? Attendance in the synagogue was a matter of reputation; no one kept complete records. In a mixed community, the practice of baptizing God-fearers was bound to splash over onto pagans.

So the inevitable happened in Antioch before it happened anywhere else: Pagan Gentiles were immersed in Jesus' name for eternal life. The story of Paul's baptism at the hands of Ananias makes it quite clear that any disciple could conduct immersion in Jesus' name; the hierarchy of clergy that later monopolized the ritual had not yet emerged. It was perfectly natural for some God-fearing Gentiles, living in a tenement with hundreds of other workers representing dozens of different ancestral religions, to speak of Jesus to their pagan colleagues. When they believed in the risen Jesus, the natural response was to celebrate and confirm this fresh outburst of God's Spirit by means of immersion in Jesus' name. After all, if Peter—who was sensitive to issues of impurity—could overcome his scruples about cleanness to baptize Cornelius, how could a God-fearer deny baptism to a fellow Gentile?

Antioch pressed the logic of Peter's vision to its limit—and beyond. The simple fact is, he did not authorize baptizing pagans. Questions and problems emerged immediately from what happened in Antioch. If Gentiles were to be immersed in Jesus' name, how much did they have to know about him, and what aspects of Israelite religion were they to acknowledge and practice? Teachers such as Barnabas shared Peter's vision and accepted its authority, but they had no policy to deal with the situation in Antioch.

The intelligentsia of Antioch was bemused at the spectacle of Gentiles devoting themselves to some dead rabbi as if he were a god. They were neither Jews nor God-fearers, so how should they refer to these people? They made up the name "Christ-groupies," or *Christiani* (Acts 11:26), because they were as loyal to this teacher as the "Caesar-groupies," *Caesariani,* were to the emperor.[2] Only this was no emperor. In the first century, as now, conventional opinion had no idea how to deal with the first stirrings of a religious movement, and it seems easy to dismiss new cults as subversive excesses of devotion to some guru or another. Little did the chattering class of Antioch realize that they were inventing a name for what would become a global religion.

Barnabas's position was particularly delicate because he was a Levite. What would regular contact with pagans do to him? If they did not abstain from blood, for example, they were contagious sources of impurity. And many of them just ate whatever was sold in the local market, without any idea whether there was blood in their meat or their sausage, or whether some butcher had killed it in sacrifice to an idol.

Barnabas—as savvy a leader as Christianity has ever known—knew Paul's vision of Christ exactly suited the conditions in Antioch. Paul understood the uncovering of God's Son within him as a model of what was to happen for humanity at large, with or without their embracing the covenant with Moses. Now Barnabas had found a use for him, because Paul's apocalyptic vision on the road to Damascus had directed him to the pagans, just the people who had begun sporadically converting to Christ in Antioch.

. . .

THE SHORT JOURNEY from Tarsus was like no other in Paul's life. He didn't travel to Antioch for safety's sake, as he had once fled back to Tarsus, or to fulfill a purely personal ambition, as he had once made his way to Jerusalem, but to answer the invitation of Barnabas. Barnabas came personally to Tarsus, seeking Paul out (Acts 11:23–26). That was no small honor for Paul's family. Here a wealthy son of the Diaspora, a Levite as well as an apostle, wanted Paul to help teach and guide communities in Antioch that believed in Jesus.

Paul's relatives must have been bewildered. Jesus' movement was an oddity to them; they could not have known in 40 C.E. that the communities their son served would one day constitute a religion separate from Judaism. At the time, Barnabas's visit seemed to vindicate Paul's longing for a rabbi's standing, albeit in offbeat congregations. With his family's blessing, he left the comfort and prosperity of Tarsus behind to make his way as an apostle.

Eager pagan "Christians"—as they were now openly called—traveled with him. During the decades between 40 C.E. and the end of the first century, that name caught on, and believers embraced it, too. But Paul himself *never* used the term: He knew where it came from and the kind of distance from the heritage of Israel it implied. The pagan Christians of Antioch already knew they were unlike God-fearers and Jews: They still wanted an apostle for themselves. Paul was their golden boy. He had seen the risen Jesus—that is what made him an apostle— and his vision directed him toward pagans just as Peter's pointed him toward God-fearers. They fussed over Paul, offering him scented oil and fresh food during the voyage.

Pagans who met Barnabas and Paul for the first time were known to compare Barnabas to Zeus, with his bearded, strong, and reserved presence, and Paul to Hermes (Acts 14:12)—largely because he never stopped talking. That comparison must have crossed the minds of the pagan Christians from Antioch as Paul basked in the importance of his first real commission as an apostle.

With that commission came tough questions. How would he put into effect his revelation that Gentiles became Sons of God by immersion in Jesus' name, just as Jews did? Would he have them baptized as soon as they professed faith in the risen Jesus—while they still believed in other gods? After all, people in Antioch celebrated the revival from the kingdom of death of the gods Dionysos and Osiris and Tammuz; why not Jesus, too? Maybe they would simply add his image to the many deities venerated on the oil lamps of the period that have been excavated.

Paul developed an unequivocal response to this most basic of issues. The uncovering of the divine Son within every believer meant that, like Jesus, they received God's Spirit at baptism. The one God became their Father as he had become Jesus' Father, and God alone was the living source of creation. Even baptized Greek-speakers cried out the Aramaic word for "Father" and committed themselves to the monotheism it implied (Galatians 4:6): "Because you are Sons, God sent out the Spirit of his Son into our hearts, crying: *Abba,* Father!" Just as God sent this Spirit, so (in his own proud phrase; Galatians 2:8) Paul represented God's "sending" or apostolate *(apostole)*—"for the Gentiles." When they accepted baptism, they embraced the *one* God.

A "father" in Aramaic refers not only to a parent but also to a source, an underlying principle—in the case of the divine world of angels, prophets, patriarchs, visions, and mediators, the "Father" is the sole power that animates the whole. Every other so-called god was, in the prophetic critique of Israel's Scriptures, a lifeless idol without reality or power. Paul brought new believers to appreciate this new divine fatherhood. At the same time, he bragged that he became a father to them (1 Corinthians 4:15), begetting them in the gospel of the Father and the interior disclosure of the Son.

Paul's principal purpose from his apostolic beginning in Antioch to its end was, as he specified, "not to immerse, but to announce triumph" (1 Corinthians 1:17). By means of his preaching, Paul intended to guide would-be Christians who had been pagans to see what it meant to live with the revelation of the divine Son within. He targeted Gentiles fresh from baptism, or catechumens in the process of preparing to be baptized.

His aggressive, abrupt style in addressing them has put off some readers (Galatians 4:8–9): "But once—not knowing God—you slaved for things that by nature are not gods. Now knowing God, or rather—

being known by God—how can you turn again to the weak and impoverished deities that you want to slave for again all over?" Paul put
himself right up into the faces of the idols, just as they were in his face.
It was easy enough for the Scriptural prophets of Israel to mock the
statues of metal and wood that other people worshiped, precisely because they were foreign deities. Paul had to walk into tenements filled
with idols—sculptures at the entrance downstairs, oil lamps with gods
whose images flaunted their power or allure, wall paintings daubed by
amateurs or beautifully completed by craftspeople in off hours.

His torrent of words excoriated idolatry. Those who gathered
around him, listening out of conviction or curiosity, learned very
quickly to leave the grossest ornaments of their world behind them. A
lamp with a Priapus in full erection—a common enough motif during
the time—must have elicited a cataract of syllables from him. He felt
no compunction at all about telling people what to do. Many of them
had to make the choice between baptism and prosperity. If the more
wealthy among them made a show about bringing meat that had been
sacrificed to an idol to a meal with believers, he told them to eat their
food at home (1 Corinthians 8:9–13; 11:20–22)—and to stop drinking
themselves drunk, to boot!

"If you have myriads of guides in Christ, you don't have many fathers—for in Jesus Christ I spawned you through the message of triumph" (1 Corinthians 4:15): That thought he repeated in a variety of
ways. He reveled in this role, crossing thresholds of houses that a
Barnabas or a Peter would never enter, delivering his revelation that
pagans could know the divine Son within them at baptism without
obeying the Torah, despite the real sacrifices he demanded. He loved
the rabbinic title "father" and would allow it to no one else once he
was in charge of a gathering of believers. If other teachers insisted that
they should be circumcised in the way the Torah demanded of
Israelites, Paul responded that these interlopers should cut off their own
genitals (Galatians 5:12). Fatherly care brought with it an unblinking
assertion of authority.

His patriarchal pride put him in conflict with another school of thought in the New Testament. Matthew's Gospel, written around 80 C.E., clearly states (Matthew 23:8–9) that no person should be called "father" and that only Jesus can be named as "rabbi." (Roman Catholic practice today falls in line with Paul, while Protestants try on the whole and with many variations to uphold the injunction in Matthew.) How could Paul just ignore that command? This is a case where his understanding of Jesus' teaching differed sharply from what later came to be written in the Gospels. He represents the view that principal teachers can and should be seen as "fathers," just as prominent rabbis were. In Antioch, even as he articulated his message to Gentiles, he realized much of the ambition that had made him train as a rabbi.

As compared to the Gospels, Paul says little about Jesus himself. To some extent that is because he writes to people who have already heard and embraced the message about Jesus and accepted immersion in his name. He had learned that message as Peter had crafted it and passed it on. But Paul announced Jesus as the risen Son of God, not as a person who once lived in Galilee and died in Jerusalem. He conveyed that eternal presence as much by his attitudes as by information.

Not content with addressing idolatry, Paul also insisted that Gentiles seeking baptism should also clean up their sex lives. In Tarsus, Paul had developed his idea of "the body of Christ," which involved believers belonging to Christ and Christ disclosing himself within them. The Son of God was revealed in each believer at baptism, and therefore the Holy Spirit made the body of every Christian into a temple. Paul often expressed the ethical implications of that infusion of Spirit in negative terms, because his Hellenistic environment was filled with opportunities to treat one's body otherwise (1 Corinthians 6:15–20):

Don't you know that your bodies are Christ's members? So: shall I make the members of Christ members of a whore? No way! Or don't you know that the one who joins himself to a whore becomes one body? For the two, it states, shall be one flesh [Genesis 2:24]. But the one who joins himself to the Lord becomes one Spirit. Flee fornication. Every sin that a person does is outside the body, but the fornicator sins against his own body. Or don't you know that your body becomes a temple of the Holy Spirit in you that you have from God? And you are not just your own, because you were bought at a price—so glorify God in your body!

Joined to Christ, infused with Spirit, your body became sacred. He did not say that subtly, nor did he flinch from spelling out the change of behavior his attitude implied. But at the same time, he was telling his audience of slaves and underlings that their bodies mattered to God.

Paul often expressed his views rudely; you have to wonder why his original readers put up with his "fatherly" rebukes. They are ingrained in his letters, derived from long-standing habit. His congregations at first were made up of people from classes lower than his, slaves and servants, occasional workers and craftspeople rather than owners or managers. (As time went on, the socioeconomic level of Christianity drifted up, and Paul's letters take on a different tone with people of higher classes.) These first believing pagans in Antioch—gathered in a dozen or so groups of no more than forty per meeting—were accustomed to taking orders from the boss. You listened to your professional master during the day, barking commands and showing a patriarchal interest in only the best of cases, and at night had a mind-set prepared to hear out the effusive orator who announced he was your boss in Christ.

In a city teeming with gods and goddesses, deities, demons, and competing philosophies, slaves and servants were at the beck and call of supernatural masters as well as earthly ones. Disease and bad luck came by the whim of a thousand divinities; Greco-Roman paganism brought not only the imperative to worship many gods but also the fear of what they could do to people who did not reverence them properly. Votive inscriptions and prayers as well as literary texts make it clear that people in the ancient world covered their theological bets quite widely. The religious problem of antiquity was unlike the modern world's—people suffered from too much divinity, not from its absence. Slaves and servants were not in a good position to choose their own divinities because their household and commercial functions often involved them in their masters' worship. Even craftspeople and managers operated within severe constraints.

Christianity offered to liberate them from the gods of this world, and it is a telling fact that one motivation for persecuting Christians in antiquity was for "atheism." With their liberation from other gods and their relationship to a single heavenly father, they embraced the hope that, with the uncovering of the divine Son within them, they could share in the ongoing spiritual life of Jesus, God's Son raised from the dead. And with that life, they got their own bodies back from the world around them, whatever the demands of their worldly masters during the day. That drew them to the Christian meeting at night called an *ekklesia*,[3] a gathering or "church," a term deliberately different from "synagogue."

These pagan Christians longed for comprehensive deliverance from the theological tyranny of gods as well as the physical tyranny of their masters. For Christianity the term "salvation" *(soteria)* came into its own in Antioch. *Soteria* had long been used to express a hope for rescue,[4] but Paul and his colleagues gave it such an edge that it marks one of the greatest and most successful innovations of the Antiochene churches. Being "saved" meant dumping the false gods of this world and becoming aware of a spiritual life shared with God's Son, and offered the prospect of resurrection in God's kingdom. Every servant and slave who turned to Christ believed he was to be a king. The abuse that might come their way for their faith was a small price to pay for such a treasure.

· · ·

PAUL'S ACHIEVEMENT proved vital in Christian history and theology, but there is an irony in his success. He had once left the Diaspora to seek the purity of Pharisaic teaching in Jerusalem: now his triumph in the Diaspora was based on his visionary conviction that the Spirit of God's Son could be realized as salvation for Gentiles apart from the Torah. There is something comic about imagining him ensconced in a tenement of tent-makers, his head filled with sacred texts, his mouth caressing the rhetorical devices of his schooling in Tarsus, his squeaky voice exhorting workers who dozed after the labors of the day or worked by the light of oil lamps to make a little money from piece-work.

Yet the scale and profundity of his success cannot be doubted. Antioch did see an influx of pagans into Jesus' movement. Nothing like a majority of any single socioeconomic group accepted baptism, but the appeal of Paul's offer of the Spirit of God's own Son reached at least marginally into several classes.

Slaves famously formed the single largest group of these new believers. Most of them were not even the household servants of prominent families, but the indentured employees of the countless crafts of Antioch. Their tenements teemed with idols and incest, trade in favors for status, competition for space and rank and the best form of work they could get. Usually they saw the light of day only to work and coveted what room they could find in their dark quarters. These were men and women who could not even dream of freedom or leisure. Their lives were bought and paid for.

Such pleasures as they enjoyed were either the easy debaucheries of a cosmopolitan city or the shadowy domestic arrangements they managed to scrape together. By means of Paul, they were promised a new kind of life in the midst of their weary existence. By baptism, their bodies no longer belonged to the owner in the shop or the bullying fellow slave in the loft. Uncovering the Son of God within meant that a new power inhabited them, over which no claim on earth could assert precedence. Even if they made a living making idols or working the metals and jewels and paints and cloth that went into them, they belonged to the single, living God alone.

Paul envisaged a world transformed by divine judgment, and saw the tensions between believers and the world around them as a sign of transformation. The promise of justice—not only long delayed in the experience of slaves, but unimaginable in their conditions—drew hundreds of men and women to the strange new teaching of a rabbi who had been raised from the dead. Very often it drew them in as families, and living in a family became a symbol that a Gentile, although not a God-fearer, had left a life of debauchery behind. This movement, which during Rabbi Jesus' life had separated families,[5] found its domestic values in the rough and tumble of crowded tenements.

Underclasses inevitably mixed. Slaves talked with one another and with their owners. Learned slaves taught the children of their households. Words traveled freely throughout the ancient Mediterranean, offering serious entertainment. Intermittently but with increasing persistence, the message of Jesus made its way up the social ladder, boosted by strangers of relatively high standing like Paul. He was far from the only one. Even a friend of Herod Antipas, named Menachem (or Manaen as Acts 13:1 spells it), had converted to Christianity and lived in Antioch.

The family wealth and contacts of Menachem, Barnabas, and Paul were considerable, and two Africans—Simeon, called "Niger," and Lucius from Cyrene—filled out a diverse corps of leaders so effective and powerful they were called "prophets and teachers." Antioch became a prominent base of operations for the movement because it had real resources at its disposal.

Some of these congregations met in the houses of wealthy people; scholars today call them house churches. Others met as guilds, professional groups that accepted common worship along with their shared craft; others gathered in tenements. But synagogues still claimed the biggest groups of Christians. What these assemblies did not do naturally was mix with one another. Pagans, God-fearers, and Jews formed up into discrete groups as readily as slaves, freedmen, Roman citizens, and the occasional aristocrats who expressed sympathy. By class, temperament, cultural bias, and religious custom, Christianity was a fractured movement from the moment people started using the term "Christian."

This segregation struck no one as odd at the time. Yet Acts does provide a clear indication that the leaders of these diverse congregations worried that the pagan component was becoming too big, too fast. The extent of this growth posed a basic question of identity: Who

was this movement basically for? Was it to serve Israel using coopera-
tive Gentiles, or were Gentiles the aim for which Israel had been created? Should Paul's radical claim that you did not need the Torah to
make your way to salvation govern the way the loose association of
congregations that believed in Jesus conducted themselves? Could you
have Christ without Moses? Those questions were deeper and more
divisive than anyone could handle at the time. Paul had catalyzed a new
kind of church, but—like a true catalyst—he had to disappear from the
new mix he had produced.

· · ·

HIS LEAVING ANTIOCH was unlike his ignominious departure from
Jerusalem seven years earlier. In the spring of 42 C.E. he belonged to
the leadership of a marginal but growing cluster of congregations in
Antioch that believed in Jesus. Barnabas and his colleagues needed to
address what to do about pagans who believed in Jesus without any association with a synagogue. To tolerate such assemblies was one thing;
the prospect that they might come to predominate quite another. The
vector of Gentile belief needed to be controlled.

Barnabas had introduced Paul to Antioch, and he was pivotal in es-
corting him out. In traditional scholarship this departure has been
called Paul's First Missionary Journey, as if it were a well-organized
campaign of spreading the faith. But Barnabas took Paul out of
Antioch both to relieve growing tensions there and to experiment
with Paul's approach elsewhere; at this stage they did not even move
into completely new territory. Instead, they traveled to Barnabas's native Cyprus.

There, Barnabas could continue to attend to Jews and God-fearers
associated with synagogues, honoring his own Levitical concerns in
those contacts while Paul concentrated on his special venture with pagans who could be contacted outside of synagogues.[6] But the decision
that Barnabas and his junior colleague should go to Cyprus was not
theirs alone. The leaders in Antioch, called "prophets," sent them there
as a deliberate, prophetic act.

Simeon Niger, Lucius from Cyrene, Menachem, Barnabas, and Paul himself (Acts 13:1–3) guided individual congregations, each gathering a given community for the common meals Jesus pioneered. They also joined with one another privately to address issues of how their diverse churches should relate to one another and outsiders. The decision to bring Paul to Antioch, for example, and to tolerate what in any other community at the time would have been seen as his aberrant venture, was made by Barnabas in consultation with his prophetic colleagues.

Now it was time for Barnabas and Paul to leave the city. The prophets—as Acts explicitly calls them (13:1)—did not come to this view by majority vote. Their private prophetic enclaves were intensified by periods of fasting, communal meditation, and withdrawal from routine contact with congregations in the city (Acts 13:2–3). The prophets in Antioch perpetuated the practice of Rabbi Jesus on Mount Hermon, when he appeared transfigured before his disciples with Moses and Elijah (Mark 9:2–9). Apostles learned from one another how to devote themselves to the communal practice of God's presence.

Fasting constituted a particular focus of the prophets' discipline, and they prayed, not for themselves and the welfare of their people, but in order to be of service to their Lord: What should they do on behalf of the risen Jesus who endowed them with Spirit? That same Spirit interrupted their devotion (Acts 13:2): "While they were devoting themselves to the Lord and fasting, the Holy Spirit said, Now separate to me Barnabas and Paul for the work to which I have called them."

Paul knew that his companions all heard what he heard. This was unlike his conversion and represented a new, communal confirmation of his own sense of purpose, as well as an important step in his spiritual experience.

Acts says remarkably little about this prophetic session (especially as compared to its repetitive references to Paul's conversion and Peter's vision). But writing in 2 Corinthians 12:2–4, Paul details his religious experience in Antioch and even dates it for us: "I know a person in Christ, fourteen years ago, whether in body I don't know, whether out of the body, I don't know—God knows—someone carried away to the third heaven. I also know that this someone—whether in body or apart from the body I don't know—God knows—was carried away into Paradise and heard unutterable expressions that it is not appropriate for a person to speak."

Within the prophetic assembly, Paul shared in the mystical ascent to the third heaven, the place where the Merkabah tradition of the time located the heavenly banquet prepared for the rabbinic sages. He entered Paradise, the mystical Garden of Eden restored next to the divine chariot, as sages of Israel near in time to Paul also had done. He did not know whether he was in his body or outside it. He was "beside" himself, like Jesus (in Mark 3:21) and the Merkabah mystic Ben Zoma (Chagigah 15a in the Talmud) and Peter (Acts 10:10). In the ecstasy of the chariot, one's body was forgotten.

The prophets of Antioch introduced Paul to the practice and experience he had not been able to cultivate in Jerusalem as a Pharisee. In that regard, ironically, his rabbinic formation was completed after his conversion: he had developed a personal discipline he could share with others who joined in the mystical ascent to the divine Throne. But just as his strange teaching, that the Torah was secondary to the revelation of the divine Son within humanity, set him apart from other rabbis, so he heard something in the midst of his ecstasy that he said no one should repeat, and he did not speak of it at the time.

In the communal, prophetic practice of the Merkabah in Antioch, the Spirit openly spoke of sending Barnabas and Paul to Cyprus, but Paul himself heard something that was too painful to say out loud. He would speak of it only later, finally compelled to utter a blinding revelation that he preferred to keep to himself. Even his brief description of his vision is dragged out of him in 2 Corinthians, to answer challenges to his apostolic authority fourteen years after the prophets of Antioch had sent him to Cyprus. And then he spoke of it only in that strange, third-person narrative that attests his desire to keep his spiritual discipline under wraps.

What he heard in the third heaven would separate him from some of his closest colleagues, including Barnabas, and break his heart with a conflict he never resolved. Never a comfortable practitioner of the communal Merkabah, he kept his revelation to himself until events forced it out of him.

. . .

BARNABAS AND PAUL made land at Salamis in Cyprus accompanied by John Mark (Acts 13:4–5), Barnabas's cousin from Jerusalem (Acts 12:12; 12:25; Colossians 4:10). They made their way across the island, addressing synagogues where Jesus' disciples regularly found a hearing while Paul followed up with Gentiles who wished to learn of Jesus' way but did not attend a synagogue. But when they had crossed to the west of the island and came to Paphos, the emphasis of their journey changed (Acts 13:6–13). Contact with the Roman proconsul, Sergius Paulus, made that change permanent, at least as far as Paul's activity was concerned.

The Book of Acts signals that change dramatically by having Paul adopt a new name. Until this moment, Acts consistently calls him Saul, the Aramaic cognomen he had taken as a Pharisee in Jerusalem. Then from Paphos on, Paul is always called Paul, making him the namesake of Sergius Paulus. That presentation is too schematic to be plausible; Greek-speakers had probably called him Paul, his name in his native Tarsus, long before the trip to Paphos. Had he really insisted on being called *Saulos* until then, the puns that would have come his way would have been unbearable (recall that the Greek word *saulos* was the equivalent of "swisher"). But Acts does accurately signal by this device that from his time in Paphos, Paul deliberately chose to emphasize his Hellenistic connections.

The proconsul eagerly gave Barnabas, Paul, and John Mark a hearing. But another Jewish teacher—styled a magus and false prophet—resisted their claims. Acts relates a prophetic battle (Acts 13:9–12): "Saul—who is Paul, too—filled with the Holy Spirit, glared at him and said, Full of all deceit and all fraud, devil's son, enemy of all righteousness, will you not stop perverting the straight ways of the Lord? And now look: the Lord's hand is upon you and you will be blind, not seeing the sun for a time. Immediately, mist and darkness fell on him and he went around seeking people to lead him by the hand."

Paul took pride in announcing Christ with "the signs of an apostle"—miracles breaking in from heaven through the hands of a man delegated by the risen Jesus (2 Corinthians 12:12). However cruel, the blinding of his prophetic opponent—like the sudden deaths of Ananias and Saphira at the hands of Peter (Acts 5:1–11)—signaled Paul's supernatural authority, mirroring his experience on the road to Damascus.

Paul and Peter both saw the power flowing through their hands as capable of harm, not only healing. Neither of these stories features prominently in the passages of the Scripture Christians like to read in church today, but ancient Christians—no doubt exaggerating events in the telling—proudly cited these displays of force that proved the truth of what they believed. The Antiochene apostles, sent by the prophetic Spirit, contended with differing strands of Judaism in prophetic terms with signs that could wound or comfort.

As proconsul, Sergius Paulus was in no position to accept baptism, whatever his sympathy with Jesus' teaching (Acts 13:12).[7] Fulfilling high civic duties inevitably involved idolatry—arranging for the divine honors due the emperor as God's Son and customary sacrifices to the local pantheon, for example. But Sergius Paulus supported Paul tangibly, providing him with resources to travel and with an introduction to a new field of mission. With this generous gift, the proconsul both encouraged Paul and put an end to the prophetic contention in Paphos.

Paul's benefactor had him leave Cyprus altogether to travel to an obscure spot deep in Turkey. Excavation near the modern city Yalvach has uncovered a small but wealthy center—really a glorified Roman garrison, veterans colony, and caravan site—named Antioch, *much* smaller than the great city on the Orontes.[8] The local museum houses inscriptions found at Antioch, where local worthies saw to it that their names were inscribed in memory of their good deeds, sponsorships of sacrifices and fetes, and endowments of buildings. These inscriptions establish Sergius Paulus's connection with the city, and in the correct period. Paul had become Sergius Paulus's man, and he went to the site of his benefactor's provincial estate.

What Paul did in Antioch of Asia Minor—and where he did it—raised critical problems for many of Jesus' disciples. Jesus himself had directed his activity to Israel, in a territorial and an ethnic sense. In the manner of the Hebrew Bible, he predicted the inclusion of non-Jews within God's kingdom, but that was to occur by their being incorporated within an all-powerful Israel. Subsequent to the Resurrection, teachers such as Peter put into practice the idea that non-Jews, by fearing God and accepting baptism, could enjoy the benefits that came to Israel by means of Jesus. But in Antioch of Asia Minor, Paul crafted a radical claim that startled even Barnabas, his closest colleague, and went beyond his teaching in Antioch on the Orontes.

When he sailed to Asia Minor and trekked inland, Paul crossed a fateful line. He made land at the port of Antalya on the coast of Asia Minor[9] and journeyed north along the Aksu River. On this rough climb of some 120 miles, he and Barnabas avoided his native Tarsus, where he seems never to have enjoyed success as an apostle. They passed through Perga, a little jewel of a city, but only to make their way to the garrison of Antioch deep inland from the coast (Acts 13:13–14). Perga's beauty as compared to Antioch's official ostentation makes you see how far Paul's loyalty to the proconsul in Paphos went, especially when you consider that Perga is better placed for travel and has a more agreeable climate.

As recent scholarship has shown, Paul's hard journey was unprecedented as well as onerous. His benefactor had sent him into explicitly Gentile territory. This was a region without tangible connection with Jerusalem, and he went there without any guidance from the prophets back in Antioch on the Orontes. As a matter of fact, John Mark showed his displeasure by returning to Jerusalem (Acts 13:13), where the scandal of this excursion would stir up trouble for Paul. Why enter the world of a Hellenistic town built by the Persians and garrisoned by the Romans?

Before he came to Antioch in Asia Minor, Paul kept a secret revelation locked up inside himself, those "unutterable expressions" (2 Corinthians 12:4) he had heard during his prophetic trance in Antioch on the Orontes. When his benefactor sent him into a new land in 43 C.E., for the first time he spoke his esoteric knowledge openly. He had come to a strange land because he had something strange to say.

Paul's letter to the Galatians, addressed to believers living in this region of Asia Minor, reveals what Paul's message was and explains what scandalized John Mark, troubling even Barnabas to the point that the two companions went their separate ways after this foray into Asia Minor. The unutterable now came to open expression.

. . .

SINCE HIS TIME IN NABATEA, Paul had asserted that for non-Jews the Torah was secondary to the truth of God's Son, uncovered within the believer at baptism. That was too much for the Church in Jerusalem, although Antioch on the Orontes had found a use for this strange perspective. But beginning among the Galatian communities, in Antioch in Asia Minor first of all, Paul also insisted that faith in Jesus at the moment of immersion in his name totally redefined who the people of God were.

Every single person who believed in Jesus—whether Jew or Greek, male or female, slave or free, everyone without distinction—was a child of Abraham; he loved to say that and had been saying it for a while (Galatians 3:28–29). In Asia Minor, however, he went public with the apocalyptic consequences of that claim. Those who believed and were baptized were actually "the Israel of God" (Galatians 6:16): Being an Israelite had nothing to do with who your parents were or whether you kept the Torah. It came down only to the issue of whether you received God's Spirit by realizing the Son uncovered within. Paul wanted to redefine what Israel really was, and to do that in a categorically Gentile land.

John Mark had no trouble getting Paul in trouble back in Jerusalem. Plunging into the backwoods of Asia Minor, Paul the converted Pharisee told idolatrous pagans that, if they believed in Jesus, they were really Israelites. This claim could only seem bizarre by all conventional definitions of what made Israel truly Israel.

The Book of Acts provides the only account there is of what happened in Antioch. Paul—as his letter to the Galatians shows—was using the credit of Sergius Paulus's benefaction to proclaim a completely new view of Israel. Acts says, "the Jews, seeing the crowds, were filled with zeal and spoke against the things spoken by Paul, blaspheming" (Acts 13:45).[10] No doubt. Imagine going to a Knights of Columbus meeting and announcing that everyone who thinks the way you do is really an Italian. And Paul wasn't speaking of just an ethnic group when he said that pagans became Israelites: He meant they were the direct inheritors of Abraham, Isaac, and Jacob—the people of God.

Hearing both the message about Jesus and Paul's revelation about the true Israel for the first time, leaders in the local synagogue could only have been bewildered. The one constituency in Antioch that was crucial to Paul, in political and financial terms, was made up of the Roman ladies of the Sergius Paulus family who frequented the synagogue, "worshipful and prominent women" (Acts 13:50). Upper-class ladies in the Greco-Roman world showed sympathy for Judaism (and later, Christianity) more easily than their husbands, because they were less involved in idolatrous civic duties, and the issue of circumcision was obviously beside the point. But Paul's prophetic stridency was just too much for them as well. He wore out the cover of Sergius Paulus (Acts 13:50), and the synagogue leadership with the backing of his family and their associates "threw Paul and Barnabas out of their districts."

This was not just a matter of wearing out an invitation: Paul and Barnabas were physically forced out of the synagogue and out of Antioch. Paul's bright idea would have better remained unuttered because speaking it was a disaster for him and his colleague. He had so alienated the leadership of the synagogue that they let loose the young thugs who in any congregation are always ready to punch their way into orthodoxy. Acts does not specify the means of expulsion—but counting up to thirty-nine might well have been involved.

No wonder Paul and his companion were driven out of Antioch.

Why should anyone maintain that believing in Jesus and receiving the Spirit of God made you an Israelite? That kind of thinking was a seditious confusion of ethnic difference from the perspective of the Roman Empire, and a blasphemous denial of the Torah from the point of view of Judaism.

Paul and Barnabas fled to Iconium, nearly a hundred miles southeast of Antioch. That took them well away from the ire of local Roman dignitaries, because Iconium's peasants, carpet-makers, miners, and traders boasted little more than a market, some extra accommodations for travelers and traders, and a small contingent of Roman colonists. But there was a synagogue (in the sense of a congregation, with or without a building), whose loyal participants had no doubt in their minds about the true Israel—and no patience with Paul's revisionism. Fiercely loyal to their heritage, they cherished the local tradition that survives to this day,[11] that Iconium was the first city built after Noah's flood.

Local Gentiles were no less fierce in their pride: they boasted that this was the place where Perseus had beheaded the Medusa. Neither Jews nor Greeks were ready for Paul's message that there was no real difference between them. Acting together, they threatened him with stoning (Acts 14:1–5)—the ultimate punishment for blasphemy.

Acts can be so apologetic, commentators have been tempted to regard such reports as exaggerations. But Paul himself once catalogued his apostolic woes (2 Corinthians 11:24–27). Even before the final conflicts of his life, he had faced up to mortal threats: "From Jews five times I got the forty lashes less one; three times I was beaten, I was stoned one time, three times I was shipwrecked—a night and day I spent at sea. With frequent journeys, in dangers of rivers, in dangers of thugs, in dangers from my race, in dangers from Gentiles, in dangers in city, in dangers in wilderness, in dangers at sea, in dangers from false brothers, in toil and hardship during frequent sleepless nights, in famine and thirst, in frequent fastings, in cold and nakedness. . . ."

He could not resist voicing radical ideas that had not been heard before, and he often did so at the risk of his life. The threat of stoning at

Iconium was very real. He had left the urbane Judaism of Tarsus and Antioch on the Orontes: the Israelites who eked out their existence in the sticks of Asia Minor were not about to play with someone who denied their identity as Israel with his fancy talk.

The pressure of his own thought and his busy mouth drove Paul further and further from synagogues. Barnabas is still put on the scene with Paul in the Book of Acts at this stage, but he must have felt completely out of his element. How far Paul strayed from Jewish culture is shown by Acts' report (14:6–18) of his time in Lystra, twenty-four miles south-southwest of Iconium. There wasn't even a synagogue there: Paul and Barnabas were on virgin Gentile terrain. How virgin, events would prove.

The two apostles prayed for the healing of a man, who was released from his paralysis. The people of the city cried out in their own language (Lycaonian), "The gods have come down to us, formed as men!" They called Paul Hermes (or Mercury), that insufferably communicative god, and referred to the impassive Barnabas as Zeus (Acts 14:8–12). The apostles could not have understood their Lycaonian acclamations, but everything became all too clear when the local priest of Zeus made preparations to sacrifice to them. According to Acts, the apostles barely managed to dissuade the locals from this idolatry in their honor (Acts 14:13–18). Who knows whether they really prevented everyone from offering this sort of sacrifice? Old customs adapt but rarely die.

Paul's vision in the third heaven had brought him to the limit of blasphemy. Speaking as he did to idolaters, Paul knew very well that they could easily turn back to their idolatrous understanding while worshiping Christ (Galatians 4:8–11). In his judgment, that risk was worth running.

An intuitive, brilliant thinker, he was a dreadful judge of people and situations. What he said undermined the identity of the Israelite communities of the Galatian region. If they were not real Israelites, what were they? If *any* believer in Jesus was Abraham's son, what was the point of circumcision, keeping Sabbath and kashrut, enduring Gentile insults for refusing to engage in idolatry? Paul was a blasphemer, and the punishment for that was stoning.

He had misjudged the peasant vehemence of these Jews and their capacity for swift, coordinated action. He was in the wilderness now, not Tarsus or Antioch or Jerusalem or Damascus: there was no civic authority to appeal to in the village of Lystra, because here the Roman colonists were mostly retired soldiers who kept to themselves. So when Jews arrived from outlying places (Acts 14:19 names Antioch in Asia Minor and Iconium, but there were no doubt others), they and their local collaborators seized Paul from the house he was staying in and took him to a cliff. Stripping him naked, they threw him off and crushed him with a huge stone, following the practice given in the Mishnah (Sanhedrin 6:4).[12] A few smaller rocks gashed his inert flesh. In Lystra, his enemies left Paul for dead.

· 6 ·

ON PROBATION

FROM JERUSALEM

T HE STONING IN LYSTRA left Paul bloody, bruised, broken-
boned. He paid the price of contradicting home truths, Jewish
and Gentile. Whatever his insistence that God wiped away the
difference between Israel and the nations with the force of divine
Spirit, the scars on his body told a different story.

Yet this message touched some of those in Lystra; sympathizers cir-
cled around him (Acts 14:20), crying prayers and lamentations as they
lifted his broken body from the ground. A circle of healing answered
the executioners' circle of stoning. Among the enslaved, dispossessed,
and socially dislocated people of the region, some people longed to
hear Paul's kind of message, wished it to be true.

Their sparse land had been overrun by a succession of Greek,
Persian, and Roman conquerors, pillaged sporadically by local war-
lords.[1] In Paul's day, Roman control of trade meant that the little the
people of Lystra had, the privation and disease they faced, looked all
the more miserable compared to the wealth their new lords enjoyed.
They were not citizens; the empire was not designed for them; they

had no rights as we understand rights. Paul spoke of rebirth in this world and the next, and that quickened their desire for release from oppression. For many onlookers, these nascent aspirations seemed dashed with his body.

They brought him to Derbe (Acts 14:20), east of Lystra, in proximity to the Taurus Mountains and the Cilician Gates. Had he died there, it would have been near his home. But he did not die. He revived under care—treatment, rest, and nutrition as well as prayer.

But Paul was not in any shape to travel. In an interlude that would be comic were it intentional, Acts has him just pick himself up after the stoning to retrace his steps with Barnabas through the same places where people had all but killed him (Acts 14:20–21). That strains credibility to the breaking point and betrays the strong tendency toward legendary embellishment in Acts. Barnabas could return by that route, confining his activities—as was his Levitical habit—to Jews and God-fearers in synagogues.[2] But we have to contradict Acts and leave Paul enough time in Derbe to heal in relative safety, well away from the kind of zealots who had tried to kill him.

Paul remained the lone apostle in the area of Derbe, and his letter to the Galatians shows that. Although this letter provides many details about Paul's first meeting with the people in the Galatian region around Derbe, it nowhere mentions Barnabas as being with him when he preached in his wounded condition to the people of Galatia. When Paul *did* work with Barnabas, he was proud of the fact; his famous companion gave weight to his own idiosyncratic positions and mixed reputation. So Galatians confirms what the romantic presentation in Acts might already make you suspect: Barnabas had gone his own way back to Antioch by the time Paul began preaching in Galatia.

He remembered what a ghastly sight he was to those who first saw him near Derbe (Galatians 4:13–15):

> You know that because of debility of the flesh I first announced the gospel to you, and—this was your testing in my flesh—you did not despise or spit but accepted me as God's angel, as Jesus Christ. . . . I

warrant to you that, if possible, you would have dug your eyes out and given them to me!

That appalling image, expressed with characteristic lack of taste, indicates what a mess his face was, and especially his eye.

The damage he sustained in Lystra inflamed the chronic condition that had already caused temporary blindness on the road to Damascus and often gave Paul pain so bad he compared it to having a thorn in his flesh (2 Corinthians 12:7). With each attack herpes zoster can swell, inflame, blind, and permanently damage the eye. Stress and injury exacerbate the problem, and Paul suffered from both of those amply—and brought them on himself throughout his life.

Paul used his own injuries, most visible in his face, to drive home the message he announced in Derbe. He portrayed Christ Jesus as crucified before the Galatians' very eyes (Galatians 3:1), because—as they could see and he insisted (Galatians 6:17)—he bore the marks of Jesus (the stigmata, he said) on his own body.

Deformity made him all the more "God's angel" to them, and this strange, hyperbolic claim—capped by his direct comparison of himself to Jesus—is no flight of egotism. Paul believed that in his trials, his witness to the message about Jesus, those who listened to him discovered a new reality (Galatians 4:19): "My children, with whom I am again in labor until Christ is formed among you!" He was the birth mother of the little communities he had visited in Galatian villages; his damaged body attested the pain of his travail. Just as God had revealed his Son in him a dozen years earlier, so he shaped that divine reality in the hearts of his listeners.

He made his way painfully and secretly from group to group, using the cover of night to evade a further attack, which might easily have killed him at this stage. Now age thirty-seven, he was young enough to heal well, but his injuries and illness made him frail and horrible to look at for months. The drama of his own shattered but gradually healing face mirrored the hope of his audience, that they might be restored in their brokenness.

An extraordinary capacity to bring his experience of Christ into the hearts of others was the keystone of Paul's achievement as an apostle. Praying about his "thorn in the flesh," he once said that God told him personally, "My power is completed in weakness" (2 Corinthians 12:9); that was a plain statement of what had happened in his own case. It is exactly from the time just after his stoning in Lystra that Paul enjoyed unequivocal success among the ordinary Gentiles that Antioch had sent him out to deal with.

From this moment, although he refers to various other ways of realizing Christ for his congregations—exorcisms and healings, for example—Paul's preferred approach became his own narrative of Jesus' impact on him. He engaged his listeners with his hypnotic account of how the Spirit of Christ totally transformed his understanding of himself, the Torah, and Israel, and of how that same transformation could change any person on earth forever.

This was the source of Paul's charisma: the resonance of his experience with his hearers' aspirations, a faculty for translating his own vision into their experience of transformation. The Galatians truly felt Christ formed within them; they heard Paul's message, and their "listening with faith" (Galatians 3:2–5) brought an experience of God's Spirit. The divine Son he had seen on the road to Damascus formed afresh in them. He conveyed the vision of Christ risen from the dead, converting that into an individual's personal conviction of having a new life emerging within, filled with the possibilities of a clean start now and an enduring place in God's eternity. Paul propagated the actual experience of salvation, not just a hope in its possibility.

In modern history, Jonathan Edwards and John Wesley demonstrated this capacity—and largely learned it from their reading of Paul's letters, as did Augustine and Martin Luther before them. The testimonies of millions today who speak of how they have been "born again" despite the predations of a secular world echo this deeply Pauline experience and the desire to replicate it in others. Paul founded the most durable, effective, and enduring means of propagating faith in Jesus that has ever been known, and for that reason—for all his oddities, inconsistencies, failures, and setbacks—he stands as the most successful religious teacher history as ever seen. Broken-bodied and nearly blind, he saw the first stirrings of his personal triumph in Derbe.

Paul's impact on Christianity is second to none; his successful focus on salvation through Christ has resulted in the frequent assertion that it was really he rather than Jesus who founded Christianity. But here, during his period of recovery and preaching among the Galatians, Paul shows us both how vital his contribution was and—by comparison with Jesus'—how circumscribed it was. Jesus provided the content of Paul's message, and every element in that message derived directly from Galilean Judaism. Paul did not invent the conception of God's kingdom or divine Sonship; his apostolic signs and healings and exorcisms reflected the practice of Jesus' Galilean apostles before him; what he said about resurrection from the dead and the role of suffering in preparing for a life of Spirit derived directly from Jesus' teaching. Even his extension of the message of Jesus to Gentiles had a precedent in Peter's visionary endorsement of the baptism of God-fearers in Jesus' name.

Where Paul broke free of the other apostles intellectually was in claiming that this baptism made these Gentiles, and any Gentiles who believed in Christ, Israelites. That idea, the product of his prophetic vision in Antioch on the Orontes, certainly made him unique, but by itself it also subjected him to fierce persecution and almost deadly stoning.

In pushing back against his opponents, however, in flaunting the wounds and scars of stoning while he preached, Paul became the model of Christ for his hearers, bearing the marks of Christ in his body, speaking as God's angel, as Jesus himself. All of Paul's ideas would never fully prevail, but his technique of conveying the experience of the divine Son within became the most powerful instrument of Christian success in the Greco-Roman world.

In the environs of Derbe, Paul rejoiced to have found the means by which his vision of God's Son could be conveyed to others as the sav-

ing experience of the formation of Christ within them, so that they became Israelites, one with the people of God's eternal choosing. Paul's
suffering, his near death, had revealed the glory of God in Christ.

. . .

PAUL ENJOYED personal care and sympathy in Derbe; his sympathizers—a mixed group of peasants, slaves, and petty entrepreneurs—
nursed him back to his usual rude health. Most important—his
rhetorical gifts had at last found the focus that gave them genuine
power. He had mastered a dynamic, persuasive technique of propagating Spirit, discovering a theme and an approach that would resonate
with disaffected denizens of the Roman Empire everywhere—and he
knew it.

The people of Galatia had no prospect of being in charge of their
own lives; they did not have recourse to the solace of a universally recognized religious tradition, as did the Jews of Galilee. Slaves did not
rule their own bodies, their own sexuality. Any hopes they had for a
real life, for control over their own bodies, for intimacy—freedom
from the pain and debilitation of daily existence—found expression in
religious poetry rather than in political thought or action. Paul made
the message of Jesus into that kind of poetry.

Festivals of gods of rebirth—Dionysos, Osiris, and Attis for example,
as well as Tarku from across the Taurus Mountains—excited the
Galatians. These gods returned from death in the spring, and rituals
called Mysteries[3] permitted people to join them in becoming divine.
Springtime revival brought them the prospect of rebirth into a different life in another world. In our time, oppression typically results in
movements of political liberation. In antiquity, amid an empire whose
apparatus of terror permitted no politics, the Mysteries offered freedom.

Paul promised the dispossessed of Derbe and surrounding villages
that they could be drenched with the Spirit of God that poured out
through Jesus, the divine Son who was raised from the dead in the
spring. Every baptism meant a new way of life could be lived imme-

diately that would be consummated when heaven's kingdom supplanted every other power. Especially among serving classes, Paul's take
on Christianity offered the prospect of unprecedented equality and fulfillment.

Departing from Derbe can't have been easy for him. But he needed
to return to Antioch on the Orontes if he expected anything like his
interpretation of the message to have a chance. His success could not
last and could never be extended if he moldered in the Taurus highlands.

In any case, he could not continue his clandestine meetings in the
Galatian region indefinitely: sooner or later his enemies would strike as
they had before. By staying clear of synagogues, Paul had avoided open
confrontation, but his security was tenuous. His wounds must have
taken some eighteen months to heal, because he did not return to
Antioch until 45 C.E. That was long enough for him to develop a deep
emotional attachment to the region that saw him as God's angel, as
Jesus Christ.

This time his trip toward Antioch was overland; he had no way to
book passage on a ship. Stripped for stoning and left for dead by his enemies and by Barnabas in Lystra, Paul had no resources, no finances,
nothing to barter with. He was now fit enough to walk, but vigorous
walking would have been hard, and he probably never recovered his
sight completely.[4] A single traveler was too easy a target for crime in
any case. His enemies forced him to avoid retracing his steps. The old
route he took with Barnabas, which would have brought him to
Antalya, went exactly the wrong way for an overland transit toward
Antioch. So he was lucky to have old connections in the region, and
sympathizers in Derbe—however impoverished—could help him contact people. A tent-maker's network found him a caravan to pass
through the Cilician Gates with so he could return to his native Tarsus.

He returned to Tarsus a convalescent during 44 C.E. Both Paul and
Acts are silent about this homecoming; they also pass over his visit to
Tarsus after his conversion in silence, although they put him in the
right vicinity. Paul's family offered him crucial support. In his stubborn

insistence on his independence, Paul did not acknowledge that himself, while Acts was so taken up with the dewy-eyed belief that Christians can fully take care of one another that it also ignored what Paul's family did for him. But much later, in a letter written in Paul's name by one of his followers, the apostle conceded his continuing debt to the family traditions of his home city (see 2 Timothy 1:3). Those traditions included help for pilgrims, help they extended to their broken son, still scarred from his near execution; he stayed with them several months before he made his way to Antioch.

With fresh sets of clothing, a staff, sandals, a newly bought cloak, and money from his family, Paul the traveler and apostle was on his way by ship to Antioch again in 45 c.e. He was not dressed as Jesus' apostles had been back in Galilee during the 30s. His linen tunic was expensive and decorated on the border in the Greco-Roman manner. His hair was close-cropped, following imperial fashion; his staff had been carefully carved and smoothed, his sandals were thick and of high quality, his woolen cloak was finely woven and fitted with an ornamented clasp. His traveler's bag, slung over his shoulder, contained changes of clothing and even a few tools. Not for him the mandate to travel barefoot, without staff or extra tunic or staff or bag. That was advice for a different time and place, when Jesus' followers were commanded to treat all of Galilee as if it were part of their own household.[5] This was no local foray, but real travel; and that made being an apostle different. He intended to reenter Antioch on the Orontes with the same kind of confident preparedness he had left with. This was to be a triumphal return, as if from the dead.

·   ·   ·

SURPRISE DID GREET PAUL in Antioch, but without triumph. Conflict had been brewing in the city between Jewish and God-fearing believers during his three-year absence. He did not cause this argument, but his return certainly did nothing to settle it. Some disciples from Judea—Pharisees by background and continuing practice at the same time they were Christians—arrived in Antioch and insisted that all believers including Gentiles had to accept the covenant of circumcision when they were to be baptized in Jesus' name (Acts 15:1, 5). The argument for their case was strong, simple, and obvious: the Book of Genesis, in a divine commandment to Abraham (17:10–14), makes circumcision *the* unconditional seal of the covenant.

These Christian Pharisees—like the Pharisees generally—are often portrayed in scholarship as if they were narrow-minded. That is just silly. The commandment of circumcision in the Bible is explicit, there for anyone to read, whether in Hebrew or Greek. The commandment applied to everyone in Israel, even foreigners bought as slaves: "A foreskinned[6] male who is not circumcised in the flesh of his foreskin, that life is cut off from his people; he has violated my covenant" (Genesis 17:14). Anyone who can read and takes the Torah seriously will understand that the Christian Pharisees had a compelling case. Theirs was not the only way to deal with Gentiles who believed in Jesus, but it was a cogent way.

Peter's vision and his contact with Cornelius the centurion had taken those in his circle of teaching and practice in a different direction. He baptized God-fearers, righteous Gentiles who acknowledged the God of Israel and the Torah but did not keep the requirements specifically directed to Israelites. They avoided idolatry and consuming blood and unclean animals, for example, but did not circumcise their males or give any tax for the Temple, as Israelites did. They could be compared to Noah: righteous in their own way (Genesis 6:9), although not Israelites. The Christian Pharisees no doubt had their hands full arguing in Antioch with the supporters of Cephas,[7] or—as they called him in Greek-speaking circles—Peter. Barnabas headed up these partisans in Antioch, and he was much more concerned with defending Peter's position than with dealing with the newly returned Paul.

Paul's unexpected reappearance in the midst of a raging argument over what made a disciple truly a disciple only made matters worse over the next year. In a strange way, his whole position strengthened the hand of the Pharisaic disciples. He was willing to enter into direct contact with idolaters, without the prior requirement that they live as righteous Gentiles, and proudly spoke of his encounters with them in Galatia completely apart from meetings in synagogues. Paul's great triumph in his wounded condition, his nurture of a profound and personal Christ-experience among those who longed to transcend conventions such as "Jew" and "Greek," represented exactly the kind of activity that worried Christian Pharisees. However understandable his avoidance of synagogues when he lived among the Galatians, they had to ask: How could this serve the Torah of Moses?

The quarrel in Antioch became so severe, the leaders of the various communities of believers decided to send a delegation to Jerusalem (Acts 15:2) to determine whether circumcision really did need to be required of believers. The same group called the "prophets" that had sent Paul out in 42 C.E. (Acts 13:1) to preach to Gentiles now acknowledged that they might have to change their practice. The controversy went too deep to be adjudicated by these local prophets and teachers. The very direction of Jesus' movement was at stake. All sides acknowledged that the apostles and senior rabbis of the movement in Jerusalem (Acts 15:2)[8] should ascertain the true range and requirements of salvation. Even Paul admitted that he submitted his program to them (Galatians 2:2) "in case somehow I was running or had run in vain." That uncharacteristic modesty reflects his high regard for the leadership in Jerusalem as well as the widespread concern in Antioch to have a poisonous quarrel settled.

Everyone was ready for resolution, even if that meant being overruled. A situation in which one group of Christians (those who accepted circumcision) denied the legitimacy—and therefore the salvation—of other groups (uncircumcised God-fearers and ordinary Gentiles) meant that people were being excluded from meetings for worship and told they had no part in Christ. For the small, marginal community of believers in Antioch—probably only several thousand people at this point—that kind of internecine battle could easily mean self-destruction.

Paul traveled with Barnabas to Jerusalem fourteen years after his conversion (and so, in the year 46 C.E.); the old partners made their way south and brought along with them Titus, a God-fearing, uncircumcised believer (Galatians 2:1–3). He was to be the litmus test of whether the Christian Pharisees or those who followed Peter's vision would prevail. Paul had risked his life in Galatia for the sake of Gentile baptism; in Jerusalem, Titus put his foreskin on the line.

The apostles, senior rabbis, prophets, and teachers of Jerusalem and Antioch convened in a synagogue in the Essene quarter of Jerusalem. It was possible to meet there because, under the leadership of James, the brother of Jesus, Christianity had become a movement respected by many if not most pious Jews in Jerusalem, and James had adopted some of the practices of the Essenes,[9] including the refusal to use oil and to clothe himself in any material but linen.

When Paul refers to the leaders of this meeting—and therefore the leaders of Jesus' movement, insofar as a movement of tiny fragments has leaders—he names James first (Galatians 2:9), before Peter. The oldest son in Jesus' family had become the linchpin of the community that lived near the Temple. For James the Sanctuary was the epicenter of Israel's worship, of Jesus' original vision, of continuing sacrifice and revelation. Peter's vision by contrast had pushed him away from Jerusalem proper, toward congregations of Jews and God-fearers in Judea, Galilee, and along the eastern coast of the Mediterranean. As was natural for a native of Bethsaida and resident of Capernaum, Peter could speak enough Greek to get along with centurions such as Cornelius. This natural extension of his contacts outside Jerusalem diminished his authority in the city itself as compared to James, who became the community's residential leader, the first "bishop" of Jerusalem.

Paul had met James back in 32 C.E. (Galatians 1:19) and knew of his dedication to the Temple then. But by the year 46 C.E., James had emerged as a dominant figure in Jerusalem with an intense focus on the Temple and the purity required by the divine presence there. James stood for the integration of Jesus' visionary movement within the Temple, whose worship Jesus himself had died to reform.

Thousands of people in Jerusalem—many more than Christians

there—revered James, a holy man of genuine grandeur. Jesus' dispute with the high priests carried over to him as well and broke out in a mortal attack on James in 62 C.E. But although the priestly elite in the city posed a threat, they did not prevent him from earning popular respect.

Yet James' pivotal importance in Jesus' movement has only recently been recognized in scholarship.[10] His reputation fell victim first to the Gentile Christianity that emerged during the second century, and later to the Reformation. Gentile believers then and now have focused on Paul to the exclusion or marginalization of other teachers. For dogmatic reasons, you will still find Christians (a few of them claiming to be scholars) who deny that Jesus had a brother and that, even if he did, no teacher of the Church ever attained Paul's stature. When you add to that Peter's preeminence in Roman Catholicism, it is easy to see why James has been ignored.

All such claims are examples of Gentile Christians projecting their image of themselves back onto Paul and Peter (as they have done for centuries onto Jesus) and manipulating the straightforward evidence of ancient texts. (It makes you wonder when people who claim to be literalists do this, blithely ignoring or distorting the plain meaning of words and phrases.) In his own time, James' stature was dominant; the Book of Acts says so plainly and Paul openly admits the fact.

No wonder people admired him. James was the eldest son of Jesus' family who—after years of reserve and antagonism while Jesus was active in Galilee—joined his brother's quest in Jerusalem to make worship in the Temple conform to the visions of Israel's prophets. He was among those who saw the risen Jesus, confirming that, one day, these prophecies would come true and that the Temple would indeed become what both Isaiah and Jesus had called "a house of prayer for all nations" (Isaiah 56:7; Mark 11:17). Following his vision of his brother after the crucifixion, he dedicated himself to worship in that Temple in a way that drew widespread admiration in Jerusalem, from Jesus' followers and many, many others.

Like Peter and Paul, James pursued his apostolic leadership on the basis of his vision of the risen Jesus. Vision is what made Christianity a vital religious movement: the impetus of the living Christ more than the memory of what Rabbi Jesus had taught provided the dynamism of these teachers. But those same visions also produced deep disagreements. Just as Peter was sent by a vision to baptize God-fearers, Paul's voice told him to seek out ordinary Gentiles, and James' epiphany brought him to worship in the Temple. All three of them agreed with Rabbi Jesus' vision, that the Temple would one day draw all humanity to the God of Israel, but each followed a different trajectory to achieve that prophetic aim. Rabbi Jesus had endorsed none of these practices: baptizing in his name, approaching Gentiles, residing permanently in Jerusalem were all visionary strategies that evolved *after* his death. And James' strategy was, in its time, the most successful visionary strategy of all.

. . .

WE KNOW ABOUT JAMES, not so much from the New Testament (which gives scant attention to Jewish sympathy toward Jesus and his movement), but from the Jewish historian Josephus and the ancient Christian historian Hegesippus.[11] The source of James' reputation for sanctity was his dedication to the practice of the Nazirite vow, a dedication also reflected in the Book of Acts (21:18–24). James' Nazirite practice made him an outstanding figure within the Judaism of his day, and he made this ritual characteristic among Jesus' followers. James welded Judaism and Christianity seamlessly within one of the most ancient Israelite sacrifices.

A man or a woman became "consecrated" by this vow; that is what the word *nazir* means in Hebrew. The Bible of Israel provides precise instructions (Numbers, chapter 6) for becoming holy in this way: the *nazir* undertakes to live in a state of particular purity for a set time (say a month). During that period you drink no wine or distillate, eat no grapes, exercise care not to approach any dead person or animal, and cut no hair on your head. At the close of the agreed period you shave all your hair off your head—and offer the locks at the altar of burnt sacrifice in Jerusalem together with sacrificial beasts and produce. This sacrifice is the key to the entire vow: your body becomes pure enough to produce hair that can be made holy in immolation before Israel's God. The Nazirite vow was in effect a sacrifice of oneself.[12] It is as bizarre and beautiful a practice as the Hebrew Bible attests, rooted in the primordial rituals of Israel, and it was the focus of James and many Jews in his time.

When James experienced Jesus speaking to him from beyond the grave, it was during a period of fasting such as Nazirites observed.[13] Every breath he breathed after that was dedicated to this practice and to bringing others to this practice. To him, Jesus was the "gate" of heaven, the entry point into the path toward Israel's God. His Nazirite dedication gave him access to the Temple despite the continuing antagonism of many in the high priestly class to him and to Jesus' movement as a whole.

Special disciplines featured in James' devotion. He ate only vegetables because meat is the product of a carcass; he declined to use the ordinary immersion pools in Jerusalem because natural, "living" water alone—as used by John the Baptist and Jesus during his time with John—was universally agreed to be pure; he avoided smearing his body with oil because everyone recognized that olives were especially susceptible to inadvertent uncleanness. Everything he did was geared to make the offering in the Temple so pure that Jesus' vision for the apocalyptic, all-inclusive feast on Mount Zion could come to pass.

Within the circle of James' practice, Jesus was even called *Nazarenos*[14]—"the Nazirite"—rather than *Nazoraios*, "the Nazorean," meaning the rabbi from Nazareth. This serious play with words enabled James' disciples to insist that the significance of Jesus' teaching—when viewed in the light of his Resurrection—turned on the true purity of Israel. However much Rabbi Jesus during his life might have consorted with sinners, eaten meat, drunk wine, and smeared his body with oil, James insisted that the inner meaning of his teaching was the purity God required in the Temple. James' vision of his risen brother carried an imperative to go beyond the letter of Jesus' teaching, just as

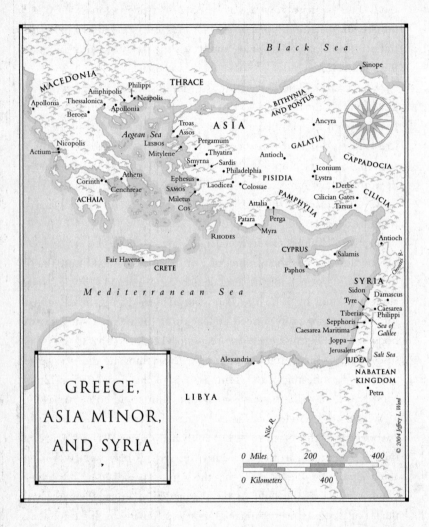

Black Sea

Sinope

MACEDONIA   THRACE   BITHYNIA
Philippi   AND PONTUS
Amphipolis Neapolis
Apollonia Thessalonica   Ancyra
Apollonia Beroea   ASIA
                    Troas   GALATIA
Actium Nicopolis   Assos   Pergamum   CAPPADOCIA
            Aegean Sea LESBOS   Antioch
                    Mitylene Thyatira   Iconium
                    Smyrna Sardis   Lystra
            Athens   Philadelphia PISIDIA Derbe
Corinth   Ephesus   Cilician Gates CILICIA
        Cenchreae SAMOS Laodicea Colossae   Tarsus
ACHAIA   Miletus   PAMPHYLIA
            Cos   Attalia
                    Patara   Perga   Antioch
                        Myra
                RHODES   Opontis R.
                        CYPRUS Salamis
        Fair Havens   Paphos   SYRIA
            CRETE   Sidon Damascus
                                        Tyre Caesarea
        Mediterranean Sea   Tiberias Philippi
                                    Sepphoris Sea of
                                Caesarea Maritima Galilee
                                        Joppa
            Alexandria   Jerusalem Salt Sea
                                    JUDEA
                                NABATEAN
                                KINGDOM
                    LIBYA   Petra
GREECE,
ASIA MINOR,
AND SYRIA
                        Nile R.
                    0 Miles   200   400

                    0 Kilometers   400

© 2004 Jeffrey L. Ward

Peter's and Paul's did. The visionary experience of Jesus' Resurrection was not just a matter of Rabbi Jesus saying "hello" *(shelama)* again, but also a commanding disclosure of where he was leading his followers. Those revelations did not agree, and primitive Christianity was a fragmented movement of vision that threatened to vaporize at any moment in its ceaseless controversy.

. . .

PAUL—A RABBI whose vision of Christ had taken him away from the Temple to the godless circumcised of Nabatea and the wild Celts of Asia Minor—must have despaired of finding acceptance for his unique activity among ordinary Gentiles. Why would James have anything to do with him? But events brought Paul, if not vindication, then at least a fighting chance to pursue his strange quest. He was not the only apostle or prophet or rabbi to be amazed by what James decided.

The meeting in Jerusalem in 46 C.E. was the most vital that has ever occurred in Christian history. Paul was more an observer than a participant, but the bold and wise resolution of the dispute about circumcision by James permitted Paul to continue his course as an apostle. The description of Acts refers to "much controversy" (Acts 15:7)—as close as that book ever comes to acknowledging the deep divisions that threatened the existence of the new, visionary movement. Circumcision was the sign of the Abrahamic covenant (Genesis 17:11)—this meeting had to decide whether or not all believers belonged to that covenant and would separate themselves from the uncleanness that foreskin epitomized. While the visiting prophets from Antioch tried to hold their ground on behalf of the God-fearers, the believing Pharisees made out their devastating case on the basis of Scripture itself (Acts 15:4–5). Only Peter's intervention, telling about his vision in Joppa (Acts 15:7–12)—the third and final time that story is invoked in the Book of Acts—kept the position of Barnabas and the delegation from Antioch alive.

Peter was after all the second most prominent leader in Jerusalem after James, as Paul indicates (Galatians 2:9): Peter's long intimacy with

Jesus (when James was still at odds with him), his visions after Jesus' death, could not easily be discounted. And James did not discount them. He brought the meeting to its verdict and silenced the stormy session when he spoke (Acts 15:14–17):

> Symeon has related how God first visited, to take from Gentiles a people in his name. And the oracles of the prophets agree with this, just as is written [in the Book of Amos]: After this I will come back and restore the tent of David which has fallen, and restore its ruins and set it up anew, that the rest of men may seek the Lord, and all the Gentiles upon whom my name is called. . . .

James' finding is unequivocal, precise, and closes all discussion.[15] He accepts Cephas's vision (calling him Symeon rather than Simon, because he was speaking Aramaic) and therefore allows that God indeed desires "to take from Gentiles a people in his name." But those people are not the same as Israel: Israel—defined as the family of the patriarch Jacob[16]—was always the focus of salvation for James.

Gentiles were to be part of restoring the "tent of David," in the words of the prophet (Amos 9:11–12), but they were not actually *in* the tent. They could be baptized; they did not have to be circumcised, but neither were they Israel. Israel alone was the chosen people, and Gentiles were added on to them in a subordinate position, fulfilling prophecy and Jesus' own vision—as James understood his brother's vision in light of the Resurrection.

James delivered his judgment with magnificent autonomy. "I decide not to make trouble for those from the Gentiles who have turned to God" (Acts 15:19). After all the controversy, it all comes down to James' saying, "I decide." He wielded the kind of personal authority that Gamaliel did among the Pharisees, as must have been obvious to Paul. In addition, James sees his judgment as a matter of verbal agreement with the prophets, which is characteristic of the Essenes he lived near. They devoted one of their books (among the scrolls discovered near Qumran) to explaining how the prophet Habakkuk predicted the life and history of their group. They called their autonomous leader the "supervisor" *(mebaqqer)*, and Christian historians attributed that same title to James in Greek: he was the first *episkopos* in Jerusalem, occupying the office known as "bishop" in English. Within the community in Jerusalem, James welded together Pharisaic and Essene models of leadership along with his visionary authority as one who had seen the risen Jesus. On his say-so, circumcision would not be required of Gentiles. James made the most important decision ever handed down in Christian history.

. . .

JAMES' VERDICT gave believing Gentiles a status clearly secondary to Israelites, although because they remained Gentiles he obviated any requirement of circumcision. To that extent James vindicated the vision of Peter and the practice of Barnabas and the prophets from Antioch. But two sides really were left out of this judgment.

The Christian Pharisees might take some comfort in seeing the priority of Israel maintained, but their insistence on circumcision was refuted. James' focus on the Temple was designed to realize the feast for all nations that Jesus and the prophets of Israel (especially Isaiah and Zechariah) had predicted there, so his judgment did not require that Gentiles become Israelites. But these Pharisaic disciples did not just wither away in the face of this decision or change their policy, however great James' prestige was in Jerusalem. They made their way for centuries,[17] practicing their faith in Jesus together with their loyalty to the covenant and its commandments, requiring that observance of their adherents—including circumcision. They thrived despite all the controversy about them (involving both Jews and Christians), especially in territorial Israel, Syria, and Mesopotamia, at least until the rise of Islam.

The other side that found itself left out of James' agenda was Paul's perspective. His opinions were not even discussed. In all likelihood he was the only person who held them. For him, this meeting was a tutorial in spiritual power and a lesson in humility. In a magnificent stroke, James trumped the commandment of Genesis championed by the Pharisees with the prophecy of Amos, silencing all discussion with a patriarchal finesse worthy of Gamaliel. The catch for Paul was that he was one of those silenced.

His position had never been discussed, whether according to his own account (in Galatians 2) or according to Acts. For such unity as Jesus' movement was able to find by means of James' intervention, that was just as well. Paul's take on the whole matter would rapidly have turned the Christian Pharisees into some other kind of Pharisees.

Had he spoken, Paul's answer to the Pharisees—the product of his years in Nabatea—would have been that for Gentiles, Moses' law was only window dressing around the promise to Abraham. The Torah was not binding on them as it was on Israelites. If you tried to impose any of it on people it was not intended for, that would be—as he explicitly said (Galatians 5:1)—a form of enslavement. This was *not* the view of Peter and Barnabas and their colleagues, who felt that, as good God-fearers, believing Gentiles had to accept those commandments that righteous non-Jews such as Noah had observed. They had a case they could make on the basis of biblical interpretation as well as vision. Not Paul. He had only his vision to go by. And not even Paul claims he dared make this argument about "enslaving" Gentiles directly to the Pharisaic disciples, or to James.

James had never heard of the idea that Gentiles actually became Israelites by baptism—that was one of the "unutterable expressions" of Paul's revelation in Antioch in 42 C.E. (2 Corinthians 12:4). Neither did James hear any such thing during this meeting: the first and only recorded case of Paul maintaining a diplomatic silence. That's how much he was in awe of Jesus' brother.

If Paul were going to make his way with his new, charismatic method of promulgating the experience of Christ within his Gentile hearers, he needed to support Barnabas against the Christian Pharisees and then use that as a basis to continue his own approach. That is exactly what he did, as his own account of what happened in Jerusalem goes on to show.

Once James had made up his mind for everyone about circumcision, the large gathering in the synagogue broke up. The results were exalting, disappointing, or troubling, depending on a participant's point of view. One thing we can say unequivocally is that Titus was relieved (Galatians 2:3); he got to keep his foreskin.

James and the next apostles in the informal seniority system of Jerusalem—Cephas and John (the son of Zebedee)[18]—met with Barnabas and Paul (Galatians 2:2, 6–10) privately. They all had to deal with the obvious difference between God-fearing Gentiles and ordinary pagans, who had not put aside their idolatry or acknowledged the God of Israel prior to baptism. Here, as in the treatment of the issue of circumcision, the resolution is astute, pragmatic, and upholds the priority of Israel: James' thinking at its best.

The prophets in Antioch had already made a distinction between the territory of the circumcised and the territory of the uncircumcised. The Jerusalem triumvirate confirmed that distinction and established differing spheres of interest. Peter, Barnabas, and those like them would direct their attention to Jews and God-fearers in the synagogues of Israel and lands contiguous with Israel. Paul calls this "the apostolate of circumcision" (Galatians 2:7, 8). Paul could make his way *outside* that large region (into Asia Minor, for example) with what he calls the apostolate "of foreskin"—that is, for Gentiles. James of Jerusalem together with his colleagues endorsed Paul's work with ordinary Gentiles, assuming he did not interfere with the priority accorded Israelites.

It was an endorsement Paul could barely have hoped for. He does not usually refer to physical contact with people. But here, just after he speaks of James and Cephas and John accepting his apostolic venture to ordinary Gentiles, he says that they extended "the right hand of fellowship" to him (Galatians 2:9). This was more than a handshake: it was the embrace of Jerusalem itself.

Still, by his own testimony Paul had said nothing about his most original idea: that Israel could be defined in a completely new way by baptism into Christ. His silence earlier—during the argument with the Christian Pharisees—can be defended as diplomatic. Adding his "unutterable expressions" to Peter's vision and Barnabas's outreach to God-fearers in synagogues would have only added a confusing new dimension of strife to an already roiling controversy. But this private meeting was a different matter, and here Paul's behavior is disappointing.

James and Cephas and John could have had no idea that Paul would be telling Gentiles that their belief in Jesus made them Israelites as well as Christians. These three apostles were Galilean Jews, and not even Cephas's vision caused him to say anything like Paul was saying. The whole basis of carving up territory between the "apostleship of circumcision" and the "apostleship of foreskin" was that Israel was different from the other nations, a people apart in the definition of the Hebrew Bible. This was a moment to speak, if Paul really wanted authorization for his view, and he said nothing.

Human factors—his slow recovery from stoning, the perennial difficulties of travel, the emotional roller coaster of the big meeting with apostles from far afield, his manifest awe in his personal meeting with James—help explain why Paul hid the pivotal element of his own theology. But it is difficult to defend his silence. Subsequent events prove that Barnabas could not.

James invoked a condition for his acceptance of Paul's activity that made his own absolute dedication to historic Israel explicit. He required Paul, in Paul's words, to "remember the poor, which was the very thing I was eager to do" (Galatians 2:10). A famine in Judea during the year 46 (cf. *Antiquities* 20.97–104)[19] occasioned this insistence to a large extent, but a much deeper issue of principle was at stake: James wanted assurance that he and his Nazirites could persist in their worship even in conditions of poverty, and that Gentile believers would prove their subservience to the house of David by providing resources for that purpose.

"The poor" is a designation for devout Israelites in the Book of Psalms, those who attend with joy, devotion, and humility to the Temple. The term for "poor people" in Hebrew *(evyonim)* was in fact applied in the early centuries to Christians who continued the practices of Judaism. In the time of Paul, the term referred to those like James and the Christian Pharisees, who lived in Jerusalem and worshiped in the Temple.

Remembering these poor meant acknowledging not only the Temple itself but the importance of dedicated Christian sacrifice in the Temple. Paul was indeed eager to do just that. By collecting funds among ordinary Gentiles, he could support sacrifice in the Temple: the collection would amount to what he called "the offering of the Gentiles" (Romans 15:16). By his own work, the prophecy of Isaiah and Zechariah—that Gentiles will enter into the worship of Israel—would cycle into completion. "Eager" is probably putting his enthusiasm mildly.

But in that enthusiasm, he "forgot" to say something. "Forgot" to mention that these Gentiles were Israelites in his mind, while for James they represented only support for the Israelite core of the movement. James was ready to see God-fearers baptized and ordinary Gentiles turn from their idolatry for the sake of baptism. But that clearly implied encouragement for them to get nearer and nearer to Israel, not any claim that they suddenly *became* Israel.

James was powerful, and he was no fool. Although there is no indication that Paul or anyone told him that bizarre new definitions of Israel were about, James saw to it that someone he trusted would monitor Paul's activity. His appointee, Silas, became Paul's new companion (Acts 15:22, 37–41). Paul and Barnabas would never work together again.

Barnabas was committed to Peter's mission as defined in Galatians—to Jews and God-fearers—not Paul's. He would henceforth work in Antioch on the assumption that God-fearers were to be the recipients of baptism, not Gentiles fresh from the raw state of their natural idolatry.[20] And he would never again put himself in the position of hearing Paul say that they were the same as Israelites.

Through Silas, James could know that Paul was in fact adhering to the conditions of his acceptance by the Jerusalem triumvirate. This new partnership with Silas was much shorter lived, its eventual rupture less deeply felt, than the deep friendship with Barnabas, but it resulted in Paul putting his words on papyrus for the first time. Silas—in effect James' mole as well as Paul's minder—began Paul's literary career as the single most important contributor to what would eventually be called the New Testament. In the fraught politics of differing visions of Jesus, James wound up giving Paul, through Silas, the means he needed to speak beyond his own time and shape the identity of Jesus' movement forever.

EXCOMMUNICANT

THE MEETING WITH JAMES, Peter, and John gave Paul new authority; working with Silas assured that he would not exceed that authorization. Antioch no longer had to take responsibility for its most contentious apostle. He departed that city with Silas (Acts 15:40). Paul was now Jerusalem's man, and Silas's problem.

His handshake with the movement's three most famous apostles—along with the constant surveillance of Silas—put Paul on a new track. In Jerusalem he had privately agreed to move west, farther west than he had before. He had to steer clear of lands traditionally associated with Judaism, agreeing in his own words to leave the territory of "circumcision" to Peter and to stick to uncircumcised lands himself (Galatians 2:7–9).

Silas and Paul made their way toward the north of Asia Minor—until this time untrammeled Gentile territory from the point of view of Jesus' message. The quick-paced transit across Asia Minor (Acts 15:41–16:8) suggests that Paul again used his contacts to travel with a caravan of traders. They could use his skills and commercial experience, and to cross unfamiliar territory he needed speed and protection for himself and for Silas.

This journey took the two apostles through Galatia, the scene of Paul's near death by stoning and of his breakthrough to contact with non-Jews. Yet what Paul did there this time around completely contradicts the widespread idea that Paul believed the Torah of Moses didn't matter. He publicly and unmistakably affirmed his personal loyalty to the Jewish Law, puzzling readers of the New Testament ever since.

Paul met a young man named Timothy who was a hybrid, born "of a Jewish woman believer, but a Greek father" (Acts 16:1). Did that make Timothy a Jewish disciple like Ananias, or a Gentile believer like Titus?[1] Circumcision cut to the core of Israelite identity, and therefore Christian identity.

Paul had preached that all believers were "the Israel of God" (Galatians 6:16), so you could easily imagine him dispensing with the surgery in Timothy's case. That is what many people do imagine. But that is just where Paul surprises you: "he took and circumcised him" (Acts 16:3). As descriptions go, this one is about as bare as you can get: Paul himself wielded the knife that cut off Timothy's foreskin.

This was no little ritual snip for Timothy or Paul. Timothy was not a child: he underwent a painful operation in front of witnesses (male only in this case, since he was an adult) that risked complications in the case of a mature male. Timothy's flesh was marked with the sign of the covenant, and this act put Paul indelibly on record as endorsing Israelite circumcision. In the very region where Paul had been stoned for saying that Gentile believers really were Israelites, his deed acknowledged circumcision as the mark of the covenant for Jews. James and his man Silas had triumphed.

In the years after this event, Paul justified both of his positions, passionately arguing that all believers—Jews and Gentiles—really were children of Abraham *and nonetheless* that circumcision as practiced by Jews honored the covenant. But when he circumcised Timothy, his action must have looked like a reversal to many, many people at the time. To this day various commentators, including some who usually insist that the Book of Acts is historically accurate, have just refused to believe that Paul "took and circumcised" Timothy.[2] Scholars have used earnest arguments about the relationship between faith and law in Paul's thought to support this convenient answer, but that is an implausible maneuver. Paul himself says in his letter to the Galatians that people said "I still preach circumcision," alluding to what he did to Timothy (Galatians 5:11). He adamantly denies that he required circumcision of Gentiles, but Timothy presented a different case.

By a stroke, Paul seemed to many Galatians to be honoring just the distinction between Jew and Greek he had once denied. Paul himself set the trap that would later catch him time and again: some people thought he was keener to please men than to please God (Galatians 1:10), changing too rapidly for a man of integrity.

Right after this account, Acts breaks into a geographically accurate, detailed description of Paul's journeying with his companions, written in the form of what "we" went on to do. (Such passages appear sporadically in Acts, and are called the "we-sections.") The author of the travel diary is not identified, but a leading candidate is Timothy himself. If he could get such matters as the itinerary of cities and the direction of winds straight, I should think any man in his teens would also remember who lopped off his foreskin, why, when, and where. Acts is right in this case, and Paul's apologists are wrong.

. . .

WITH SILAS effectively in charge, Paul's little company—including Timothy (limping slightly)—made their way north and west across Asia Minor. Acts speaks of the group being "forbidden by the Holy Spirit to speak the word" in Asia Minor (Acts 16:6).[3] The agent of this interdict was Silas, who claimed this whole region for a mission like Peter's. Silas wanted Paul to go farther west, into ever more obviously Gentile territory.

Silas's motivation was visionary. Like James, he expected Jesus to return from heaven as the "one like a person" (or "son of man"; Daniel 7:9–18). He wove a scenario of that final judgment out of Daniel and other prophetic visions, which would influence Paul for the rest of his life.

The final chapter of the Book of Isaiah speaks of the end of days, when God will send out messengers among the Gentiles, specifically, far to the west of Israel: "to Tarshish, Pul, and Lud, who draw the bow, to Tubal and Javan, to the coastlands afar off, that have not heard my reputation or seen my glory" (Isaiah 66:19). The name "Tarshish" must have pricked up Paul's ears when Silas quoted this prophecy; it was the biblical equivalent of Tarsus. Alongside his commitment to collecting for the poor in Jerusalem, Paul received a permanent aspect of his program from his contact with Silas:[4] he moved west, always west—the direction of all the lands mentioned here—in fulfillment of this part of Isaiah's prophecy.

None of this new activity—not even circumcising Timothy—came as an imposition to Paul. He willingly circumcised Timothy in Galatia, willingly arranged to travel west by means of his own contacts and resources. He made Silas's vision his own; after all, it empowered him to implant Christ in the hearts of Gentiles with the support of the apostles in Jerusalem. The promptings Paul experienced in his own discipline of prayer confirmed what Silas was saying.

Paul brought a deep sense of the impermanence of this world to his relationship with Silas. That attitude was embedded in the apocalyptic milieu of Diaspora Judaism, in Pharisaic eschatology, and in Stoicism as well. Stoics expected the *ekpurosis*, a fiery conflagration that would consume the cosmos. Philosophers such as Seneca, Paul's contemporary, taught that the power of reason alone would survive[5] that scarifying inferno.

The real world for Paul was not the society of people or the physical universe, but the Spirit's revelation of how everything was going to change. One night in Troas, the coastal city on the west of Asia Minor, Paul saw a Greek man in a vision (Acts 16:9) who pleaded with the apostle, "Come across to Macedonia: help us!" One of the places mentioned by Isaiah, Javan, was identified as Macedonia in Paul's time: this visionary man Paul saw in Troas was confirming the prophecy of Isaiah as conveyed to Paul by Silas. So with his own Greek skills and Timothy's, Paul sailed to the Greek cities of Samothrace, Neapolis, and Philippi (Act 16:11–12), the prosperous Roman colony where he made his first real contact.[6] His message came to Europe as part of the dedicated westward expansion of Christianity that was part and parcel of Silas's vision.

. . .

PAUL COULD BE a different man in Greece. At least, he behaved as if he thought so. That was the beginning of his trouble there.

His initial connection in Philippi was with Lydia, a God-fearing woman from Asia Minor who sold dyed cloth (Acts 16:13–15). She and some like-minded women had been gathering on the Sabbath by a river. Silas and Paul seized the opportunity to engage with women who already worshiped the God of Israel. Baptizing them presented no problem to any party in the dispute that had broken out in Antioch: because the congregation was all female, not even a ghost of the old controversy about circumcision could emerge. Besides, the bulk of the Jewish population of the city was inside its gates, meeting in the synagogue buildings whose construction Roman colonies such as Philippi encouraged. For the mainstream of Judaism, what a few God-fearing females did outside the city and away from established synagogues scarcely mattered.

Silas and Paul had found an ideal congregation, ready-made. The women put cash at his disposal, not just food and lodging, so Paul made a good start at collecting funds for poor Nazirites like James in Jerusalem. Everything about Philippi was propitious. For years to come (Philippians 4:15–16), Paul would refer to the warm generosity of the Christian community there, and to their continuing support after he left their city.

Philippi might well have provided a permanent base of operation for Macedonia (the northern part of Greece) and Achaia (the southern part). But Paul was not content to speak to the God-fearing congregation by the river alone. Paul was Paul. If there was a step too far, he had to take it in the name of his vision.

Over the course of months, Silas, Paul, and Timothy became familiar figures in the city. As they walked Sabbath by Sabbath to the river

meeting, a female slave—a pagan girl with pagan masters—liked to follow them. She was especially valuable to her owners because what was
called a python deity possessed her, the emblem of the Delphic oracle.
The python endowed her with gifts of divination. She tagged along behind the apostolic group, shouting out, "These men are slaves of God
Most High, who announce the way of salvation to you!"

Some people might have been happy with the advertising, but it
bothered Paul: he knew that publicity of this kind redounded more to
Delphi's benefit than to Jesus' (Acts 16:16–18). So he did what he had
learned to do with any spirit that was not the Holy Spirit, any deceptive, partial, idolatrous distraction from salvation. He exorcised the girl,
and her python departed from her.

Paul's letters give us his own theory of how exorcism worked, and
what he says provides some support for the examples that Acts gives.[7]
Exorcism for Paul was a deeply personal encounter, involving first
what he called "discernments of spirits" (1 Corinthians 12:10). Discernment meant identifying those fragments of personality within a
person that can take over behavior. Paul understood obsession, self-
abuse, flights of egomania—all traits of what modern convention thinks
of as mental illness—to be incursions of foreign spirits that displaced
and fragmented human personality. Only a correct diagnosis of invading spirits could enable him to command them to depart with the authority that came from the Spirit of the risen Jesus.

Paul must have been proud, not only of the exorcism itself, but of
his strict adherence to the terms of his agreement with James. The
slave girl was a pagan whom he had turned from the idolatry of
Delphic divination in a way that honored Israel's God, and he had done
that without any interference whatever in the life of any synagogue in
Philippi.

Paul was right in one respect. Trouble did not come to him from
Silas or any community of Jews or God-fearers. Trouble did come
nonetheless, quickly and violently.

From Paul's perspective the python spirit prevented the slave girl
from seeing the truth of her own words. She might say that he and Silas

and Timothy served the true God, but she needed to be free of the Delphic python in order to see the wisdom of what she said. Her masters, predictably, did not share this perspective.

Faced with losing the income they had earned from displaying their slave's power of divination, they dragged Paul and Silas in front of the Roman magistrates (Acts 16:19–22). The trouble went well beyond a spot of legal action: a mob quickly formed up around the apostles.

Who could have foreseen all this? Countless people during and after Paul's time have wished for more tact from him than he typically showed, but for an ancient holy man of acknowledged attainment, his behavior as described in Acts is hardly scandalous. Healing and exorcism were among the recognized therapeutic arts of antiquity. In a metropolis like Antioch on the Orontes, owners of divining slaves had the prudence not to parade their skills in public. You never knew when an exorcist—Jewish, Christian, Egyptian, Pythagorean, or whatever— might take it into his head to clear out the possessing spirit. What made the girl's owners flaunt her python deity? Why the explosion of hostility from the local populace, not just the girl's owners, when Paul exorcised her?

In this case, Paul was not courting disaster. He just walked into it unaware. The late forties brought a change in the religious policy of the emperor Claudius, and Philippi—an insular Roman colony—reflected that change more quickly and vociferously than most cities.[8] Claudius insisted on strong support for ancestral Roman religion.

In Rome proper, Claudius extended the range of the *pomerium* (the district in which *only* Roman gods could be worshiped), resuscitated several ancient practices of Roman divination, and banished aristocrats who dabbled with oriental cults. His vigorous pursuit of the old-time religion of Rome encouraged colonists elsewhere to insist upon their ancestral prerogatives. Without meaning to, Paul brought a grievous punishment on himself and on Silas, this time at Gentile hands.

The charge of the crowd against Paul and Silas makes perfect sense in the atmosphere that Claudius's reforms had produced (Acts 16:20–21): "These men, being Jews, are agitating our city and promulgate customs that are not permissible for us Romans to accept or practice." There is nothing like contempt for foreigners to whip up displays of what passes for patriotism. The mob knew very well that "Jews" had to be tolerated—that was long-established Roman law—but they charged that these men in particular had used their Judaism to introduce new practices that were antithetical to ancestral religion. Paul's exorcism of a pagan slave owned by pagans had stopped ancestral divination of the kind Claudius was encouraging. It was an outrage.

Paul's treatment by the Roman magistrates in Philippi was less violent than his stoning in Lystra, but it was painful and humiliating (Acts 16:22–24). Armed guards stripped Silas and Paul of their clothing, beat them, and threw them into a prison where they were kept in stocks. This beating with short rods, administered by officials called lictors, was designed as a quick, corporal blast of Roman authority against mischief-makers. Later, Paul would say that lictors had laid into his scarred back on a total of three occasions (2 Corinthians 11:25). This was the first, a ghastly start to bringing Jesus' message to Gentile Europe.

As Acts describes the scene, the companions were spared further detainment because an earthquake collapsed their prison. The jail-keeper converted on the spot (16:25–34).[9] The breathless pace of the narrative makes it seem implausible, and the literary trope of a sage's miraculous escape from imprisonment is well known in ancient literature. Yet Philippi was periodically damaged by seismic activity during this period, and Paul himself refers to imprisonment as an opportunity to talk with his jailers (see Philippians 1:12–14). A longer time frame than Acts allows would permit Paul to insist on an apology from the authorities (Acts 16:35–40), although he never got one. Silas and Paul needed a new plan and a new city in order to avoid rough treatment, and they departed Philippi.

. . .

FROM PHILIPPI they traveled overland by a coastal road through Amphipolis and Apollonia to Thessalonica (Acts 17:1–4), a metropolitan city with a big, well-established Jewish population.[10] Here they gave up the strategy they had followed in Philippi. Through with seeking out groups of God-fearers marginal to the Jewish community, they headed straight for the protection of a prosperous synagogue. At this stage Silas was still very much in control of what he and Paul and Timothy were doing, whatever results Paul's occasional forays into freelance apostleship might bring.

The new approach, which followed Peter's vision, began auspiciously. Contact with the synagogue brought an invitation to preach on successive Sabbaths, and God-fearers—including prominent women in the city—liked to listen to Paul and Silas. Paul's announcement of salvation and of freedom from social conventions in a new, divine order appealed especially to women who knew that their capacities far outstripped what their society would let them achieve. Acts may overplay the appeal of his message to women of upper classes all the way through Paul's Greek sojourn, but there is some truth in its exaggeration. Naturally, however, not everyone in the congregation agreed with this challenge to the status quo.

Paul leaned heavily on the theme that Jesus fulfilled the messianic predictions of the prophets of Israel, that "it was necessary for the Christ to suffer and to arise from the dead" (Acts 17:3). That contradicted the view of many Jews who thought that the messiah was to be a glorious ruler, not a figure of suffering. They resisted the claim that an obscure rabbi from Galilee (who had, after all, been put to death by Roman crucifixion) was the agent by whom the God of Israel would change the world. This strange, powerless messiah was disturbing or ridiculous, depending on how seriously you took the idea. These times were difficult for Jesus' followers throughout the Roman Empire. The messianic controversy they awakened often gave them grief from Jews and Romans alike.

On the Jewish side, the denial that the coming messiah was a mighty king could obviously seem defeatist, and in Rome itself running battles between partisans of Jesus and other members of synagogues had broken out in the year 49 C.E. Stone-throwing, beatings, street gangs of rival factions stripping the odd matron or pummeling a Levite—these are the kinds of activities the Roman historian Suetonius has in mind when he talks about crowds of Jews engaging in "tumult" in Rome.[11] All this because the "Christ incitement"—as Suetonius calls it— sparked violence among competing synagogue-factions, and Claudius banned groups of Jews from meeting inside Rome altogether.

From the Roman side, talk of Jesus being the anointed ruler proph- esied by Scripture could of course seem seditious and revolutionary. The same kind of partisanship that blazed out against Paul and Silas in Philippi could strike them in any city of loyal Romans.

In Thessalonica it did strike again. Two potentially antagonistic groups—members of the synagogue who opposed Paul's messianism and Romans who feared sedition—made common cause against Paul and Silas. By drawing together in opposition to a weak opponent, they avoided conflict with one another and strengthened their respective positions. For that to happen, of course, they needed an incentive, and Paul provided that for them—without really trying.

One of Paul's prominent new converts, a Gentile named after the mythic hero Jason, had given the apostles hospitality in his home (Acts 17:5–9). By taking up residence with a Gentile, Paul and his companions were making a claim not only on Jason and his house- hold, but establishing a foothold in a part of the city that was tradi- tionally non-Jewish. They broke with the customs of both synagogue and city. In Thessalonica, as in every metropolis of the Mediterranean world, where you lived expressed your religious identity as much as what you ate, when you worshiped, who you married. The very fact of success among people known to be Gentiles, whatever the numbers involved, made the locals suspicious of Paul. Their reaction shows that, contrary to the surmise of some scholars, Jason was known to be a non-Jew.

His opponents recruited a mob of thugs—both Jews and pagans— from the vast marketplaces of the city. Heedless of Jason's status, they stormed into his house, demanding that he hand over Paul and Silas. When they discovered the apostles were not there, they dragged Jason himself and a few other Christians before their local leaders. The charge? That Jason supported men who "all act against Caesar's edicts, saying that there is another king—Jesus!" (Acts 17:7) There is no getting away from the political nature of this charge in Roman law. Only Jason's wealth and status—accompanied by a handsome bribe (Acts 17:9)—saved him from mob violence and a lictor's rod.

The only safe course was for Paul, Silas, and Timothy to clear out of Thessalonica. Their sympathizers sent them by night to Berea (Acts 17:10–12). In this town southwest of Thessalonica, a synagogue of people Acts calls "better bred than those of Thessalonica" gave the three companions a hearing, and they enjoyed their usual success among prominent God-fearing women and men.

That success was short-lived. Some antagonists came from Thessalonica to renew the old charge against Paul—that he was inciting Gentiles to disloyalty to Caesar by invoking the kingdom of Christ (Acts 17:13). Although Paul had managed not to transgress into pagan domains in Berea—as he had clearly done in Philippi and Thessalonica—there was no denying the likelihood that sooner or later he would. That was his vocation, empowered by his vision and authorized by James of Jerusalem.

Silas and Timothy reacted decisively when their Thessalonian opponents arrived. They got Paul out of Berea and shipped him off in an Aegean coaster (Acts 17:14).[12] Silas and Timothy remained and had no further trouble from the Thessalonians or the Bereans. They understood all too clearly what Acts does not openly admit: the cause of their troubles was Paul. By venturing outside of synagogues and into the pagan populace of patriotic cities in Macedonia, he ran into the charge of sedition from Jews and Gentiles alike.

Neither Silas nor Timothy had any reason to run this risk with Paul. Their experience in Berea proved that by concentrating on Jews and God-fearers in synagogues, the message of Jesus could be conveyed without fearing repercussions from the Roman authorities and without inflaming the local Jews. Timothy, after all, had been prepared to concentrate on synagogues by a painful operation at the hands of Paul himself, and Silas's natural affinity was with the historic heritage of Israel.

Silas and Timothy knew the kind of person they were dealing with. They had seen Paul's disruptive activity firsthand and concluded that they could not work in the same town with him. They had learned what Barnabas knew: it was much easier to follow Peter's lead than Paul's, and leave Paul to his own devices. They shipped him not only out of Berea, but also out of Macedonia altogether, to Athens in Achaia, the south of Greece (Acts 17:14–15). Paul was the persecuted odd man out; his companions cut him loose, and he went to Athens alone.

. . .

ONLY A MAN OBSESSED would continue to pursue a program that he knew would get him into trouble. Acts tries to gloss over the split that had opened up between Paul and his companions, stating that Paul wrote that Silas and Timothy should come as "quickly as possible" (Acts 17:15) to meet him in Athens. Whatever he might have hoped, that never happened. His companions never came to Paul in Athens, as Acts admits. He was strictly on his own.

Athens was a different city from Philippi, Thessalonica, or little Berea. With the rise of Rome, it had long since ceased to be the center of power it once had been, but that historic change in no sense dampened the Athenians' belief in their own intellectual superiority. Wealthy, diverse philosophical schools set up shop around marketplaces in sight of ancient monuments to empire; speakers hawked the wares of Epicureans, Stoics, and a host of other fashionable ideologies and exotic imports from foreign lands. This was the London of its time. Acts explains very well why this was an opportune place for Paul (17:21, and see vv. 16–20): "All Athenians and the foreigners who stay there occupy their time with nothing other than speaking and hearing about whatever the latest is." This is obviously not meant as a compliment, but the itchy ears and readiness for discussion of people in Athens gave Paul the chance he desperately needed to pursue his quest. Cultural ar-

A Roman road (photo courtesy of the author). South of Troas, near Assos, this passage of coastal road represents the feat of engineering that facilitated commerce and travel within the Roman Empire. At the same time, the growth of briar on the sides of the road, and between stones, makes it obvious why any traveler who wanted to complain of an acute pain would speak of a "thorn in the flesh" (2 Corinthians 12:7).

rogance can breed tolerance, and Athenian tolerance was in Paul's case a window of opportunity.

There were synagogues in Athens, of course, and Paul happily entered into argument in several of them. In these debates his training as a rabbi was useful, but it didn't really win him much support. Athenian marketplaces, however, gave him a new kind of forum. Here, freed from the constraint of having Silas looking over his shoulder, he bypassed a Jewish audience altogether and overtly disputed with philosophers. They gathered to hear what this "word-scat" (the *spermologos*; Acts 17:18) had to say.

Paul's favorite venue became the Hill of Mars (17:19–31), where he crafted an attractive appeal to leave idols (such as Mars himself, the god of war) and discover the single, living God. God is the one in whom we live and move and have our being, he argued (Acts 17:28), quoting the poet Aratus: he cannot be made with human hands.

Paul made out a similar case in his letter to the Romans, written a few years later. He argues in a practiced set piece that God's imprint is manifest in the creation that He made, and that only human folly changed the truth of God into the lie of idols (Romans 1:20–25): "Because his invisible qualities, his eternal power and divinity, have been demonstrated perceptibly from the creation of the world by the things that have been made . . . therefore knowing God they did not give God glory or thanks, but became futile in their thoughts and their senseless hearts were darkened. Claiming to be wise, they became fools, even changing the glory of the incorruptible God into the likeness of a corruptible image—of man or birds or animals or reptiles!" Worship a frog? Please. Dress up war as the naked Mars, his gleaming skin without a scar? Give me a break. This was the ancient prophetic critique of idols, expressed with the barbed rhetoric of a native of Tarsus. The sense of divinity, Paul told his pagan audiences again and again, cannot be captured in dead, dumb stone, but only in the living presence of Spirit.

This was the kind of vehement, rigorous criticism that pagan philosophers liked to engage in themselves. Intellectuals at this stage in the history of the Roman Empire had long been wary of the libidinous, violent, manipulative gods their ancestors had bequeathed to them. Divine debauchery could lead to the human kind, and frequently did. Paul also links the sin of idolatry with sexual impurity of all kinds: by making God's image into the false reflections of animals, Greek mythology inflamed its hearers with the bestial sex of its gods (Romans 1:23–32). Lust after false gods went together with the lust by which people pervert their own sexual responses, in Paul's mind.

By the time Paul left Athens, Acts can name only two converts to his credit, both of them Greek—a man (Dionysios) and a woman (Damaris)—although anonymous "others" are also mentioned (Acts 17:34). His message rejected ancestral customs and ancient sexual mores. On the other hand, he had also found a venue of philosophical debate—the kind of setting that many budding rhetors from Tarsus longed for. Paul, once a Pharisee, became a public intellectual in Athens.

The forum of the marketplace was limited. You could get a fair hearing, but not an audience who shared your mystical vision or embraced your spiritual practice. In fact, Athenians ridiculed Paul when he preached on resurrection (Acts 17:32–33). The experience of Christ as a living, divine presence within your being—precisely the experience he had translated so successfully in Galatia—fell flat in the free market of Athenian ideas. Intellectual concepts could take him only so far. They did not convey his vision of the divine Son. Debate was fine, but worship was where the Christ within could reveal himself. Paul responded to this realization by seeking another setting, a different city.

. . .

PAUL HIMSELF CHOSE his next destination—Corinth. This time his instinct served him well. In Corinth he met two fellow tent-makers, a Jew who believed in Jesus named Aquila and his wife Priscilla (Acts 18:1–4). In them, Paul at last found fully sympathetic coworkers. And the city proved to be a fertile field of endeavor. For a little while it seemed he had left behind the controversies of Antioch, Galatia, and Macedonia forever.

Aquila had also grown up in Asia Minor (in the province of Pontus, near the Black Sea), but had most recently come from Rome, expelled like many Jews in 49 C.E. by Claudius. He and Priscilla came to Corinth already Christians: their acceptance of God-fearers and their hospitality for Paul reflects that they had been influenced by Peter's vision. Trade between Rome and Joppa—where Peter's vision guided him to the house of Cornelius—brought the visionary as well as commercial products of Palestine to the center of the empire.

Priscilla and Aquila managed at least as well as Silas and Timothy to develop a Jewish and God-fearing community of Christians from their contacts with local synagogues. These gifted craftspeople understood how to make contacts not only in the tenements of the city, but also with the shop owners downstairs. They pointed Paul in the direction of purely Gentile congregations where his approach was appreciated—and kept him away from meetings of Jews and God-fearers where his talk of all believers as "the Israel of God" could only have caused trouble.

When he met them, Priscilla and Aquila were already well on their way to becoming among the most influential agents of Jesus' message in the Greco-Roman world. Part of the reason the couple was so successful is that they were in exactly the right place. Corinth was nowhere near as large as Antioch on the Orontes, but its diversity was legendary, even in its own time. As a port city it attracted seafarers, ships, and trade, and had the dynamic mobility of a city with a constantly changing populace. It was as free, loose, and uncontrollable a place as existed in the Mediterranean during the Roman Empire. If Athens was the London of Greece, Corinth was its Los Angeles.

New cults flourished alongside old practices. It was impossible for a local magistrate to keep track of all the fresh sects among the hundreds of religions that travelers brought with them from foreign lands. The Roman lords of Corinth evolved a policy of live and let live, provided civic order was maintained. It was in this environment that Priscilla and Aquila were able to become two of the most innovative and inclusive Christian teachers of their time.

News of their accomplishment probably motivated Paul to depart Athens and link up with them. In the free atmosphere of Corinth, he could meet with little congregations of pagans—in shops, in tenements, or on a ship. At the same time the many congregations of Jews and God-fearers who had already been contacted by Priscilla and Aquila offered Paul an occasional forum. Their success brushed off on him. At long last Paul was striking the right balance between Jewish and pagan believers. It is no surprise that he spent the better part of two years in Corinth before finally departing in 52 C.E.

The seal of his success was that Silas and Timothy finally joined him again, eventually making their way from Macedonia (Acts 18:5). The cooperation of the three companions in the same city proved that Jews, God-fearers, and pagans could coexist within the same movement, although they did so in separate congregations, Paul serving his people, Silas and Timothy theirs, Priscilla and Aquila theirs. They had at last worked out a way to make James' vision of his brother's movement viable on the ground.

From this active but comparatively peaceful period comes the first of Paul's letters, which he wrote with Silas and Timothy—1 Thessalonians. Their confidence at this stage is reflected in the very fact that they wrote the letter. The concept of an authoritative missive from one community to another came from Silas and his experience with James in Jerusalem, and it resonated with Paul's service under Caiaphas. Despite all the difficulties Paul had faced (and stirred up!) in Thessalonica and Macedonia as a whole, 1 Thessalonians sets out the attitude toward Gentile believers on which James had insisted.

Paul takes the lead in 1 Thessalonians because it was addressed principally to Gentile Christians in the city. In the way of first efforts, there is a tentative quality here compared to Paul's later letters. The three teachers nonetheless declare unequivocally that their message comes from God's own Spirit (1:5) and focuses on Jesus as divine Son, who alone can deliver humanity from the rapidly approaching end of the ages (1:10).

This eschatological tenor is typical of primitive Christianity and characterizes Paul's letters. Time is truly short, because the day of the Lord comes as a thief in the night (5:2) at a time that cannot be reckoned. In view of this upcoming judgment, the Thessalonian Gentiles had put their idols aside (1:9), and that also meant (as Paul is never slow to point out) that sexual sanctification had to follow. Lust was a reflex of idolatry: now was the time for "every one of you to keep one's own vessel in sanctification and honor, and not in the passion of lust just like the Gentiles who do not know God" (4:4–5). The three teachers agreed that turning from idolatry and perversion to serve the living God was the only means of human salvation in the short time before the Day of Judgment.

They also fiercely stated that the Pharisaic teachers from Judea who had tried to prevent contact with Gentiles formed an obstacle to the gospel (2:14): "For you, brothers, became imitators of the churches of God that are in Judea in Jesus Christ, because you also suffered the same things from your kinspeople as they did from the Jews."

This refers back to the deep contention in Jerusalem. Paul, Silas, and Timothy are using the word "Jews" (*Ioudaioi* in Greek) to mean the people back in Judea who wished to "forbid us to speak to the Gentiles" (2:16). But the same term could also be used during the first century (and later, of course) to mean practitioners of Judaism generally, and that is the sense of the term "Jew" in common usage. So the three companions, writing to Thessalonica and dealing with local issues and recent history, spoke in a way that has encouraged anti-Semitism. Had they known they were writing for something called the New Testament, and how their words would be used to justify the persecution of Jews, they obviously would have spoken differently.

The community in Jerusalem, and especially James, Peter, and John, had authorized their work to enhance God's promise to Israel, not to deny it. Paul, Silas, and Timothy also refer to working night and day in Thessalonica (2:9)—in Paul's case, as a tent-maker—so as not to burden the community there. Such funds as they could scrape together were to go toward the offering for "the poor" in Jerusalem that was also a vital part of the agreement with James. Paul had desired to visit the Thessalonians himself, but he claimed that "Satan prevented us" (1 Thessalonians 2:18). His emissary Timothy and this letter had to take his place, because the satanic rods of the lictor remained a threat. In his apocalyptic fervor, Paul's reference to his Roman masters was no kinder than what he said about his Jewish opponents.

This first letter Paul wrote was the last effort of the three companions to present a common front. Corinth's fluid diversity—together with the acumen of Priscilla and Aquila—had enabled them to work together. Their agreement to the terms James had set forth permitted them to write to Macedonia with a common theology of revelation. But Paul was Paul. Never able to leave well enough alone, he was about to spark the forces of diversity in Corinth into a violent confrontation.

. . .

WHERE IT CONCERNED his definition of what Israel was, Paul usually said what was on his mind—except when he had met James in Jerusalem in 46 C.E. Other than that, despite the threats of stoning from a mob or a lictor's rod, he sooner or later insisted on the revelation that all who believe in Jesus were children of Abraham, regardless of whether they were Jews. Part of the practical genius of Priscilla and Aquila was that they had found safe venues for Paul to expound his radical theology.

Something in Paul's temperament distrusted safety. Once Silas and Timothy were with him again, he found his way back into a local synagogue (Acts 18:5). Why? Did the fact that he had once been a persecutor make him court persecution himself? Was it the native love of Tarsans for the rhetorical clash of sword upon sword? Did his past standing in the Pharisaic and priestly establishments in Jerusalem prompt him to make arguments in synagogues with the passionate, systematic rigor he had honed years before? Perhaps he just had a collegial desire to worship in the same place with Silas and Timothy. Whatever we are to make of such suggestions, it is plain that Paul insisted on his Israelite identity (Philippians 2:5). Sooner or later he was bound to worship with other Jews.

Whatever the precise mix of emotions that brought him there, he was in a synagogue again, his mouth was open—and his most difficult idea poured forth in exactly the setting where it was most likely to cause offense. Paul being Paul, he did not take objections well. They only ratcheted up his rhetoric into fierce, Tarsan polemic. Faced with disagreement in a synagogue in Corinth, Acts has him saying, "Your blood is upon your head! I am pure! From this moment I will proceed to the Gentiles!" (Acts 18:6)[13] It is interesting that similarly violent language is directed against "the Jews" in 1 Thessalonians, where Paul says—writing from Corinth—"Wrath has come upon them to the last" (2:16). His bit of success as well as his apocalyptic visions had made him immoderate; to his mind, if Jews would not see that their inheritance was for all humanity, then *only* pagan believers were the real Israel.

Having been pressed by his own revelation beyond a conventional view of who the people of God were, he then turned around and persistently *excluded* from his definition of Israel everyone who did not agree with him. Of all of Paul's emotional reflexes, this proved over time to be the most destructive. During his life he suffered from it more than anyone else, but through the centuries it has made his letters a trove for heresy-hunters. The man pursued as heretical by both synagogues and magistrates reacted so vehemently that his own words fed the kind of persecution he suffered from himself.

Paul's words in Corinth hastened an inevitable ruckus. Rome had seen street fighting among Jews over the issue of belief in Jesus; exporting Rome's problems to Corinth was destined to bring trouble in some shape or another, sooner or later. But Paul made the inevitable happen faster than it had to, his zeal fueled by a fresh vision of Jesus (Acts 18:9–11). He did have some God-fearers on his side, including Titius Justus, and a couple of prominent Jews in the synagogue, named as Crispus and Sosthenes (Acts 18:7, 8, 17). An open breach divided them from other synagogue members and (as earlier in Philippi and Thessalonica) both pious Jews and loyal Romans denounced Paul's heresy to the local authorities. A mob even beat Sosthenes in front of the building where the Roman proconsul, Gallio, held court (Acts 18:17). Gallio left a dated inscription in Corinth,[14] enabling us to place this incident in the year 52 C.E.

Gallio heard the complaint against Paul but refused to take action. Absent evidence of actual sedition, he knew better than to get mixed up with the myriad cults of Corinth. He showed an intellectual detachment that was outside the ken of the magistrates in Philippi, Thessalonica, and Berea. But then Corinth was different from those Macedonian cities, and Gallio was a different kind of ruler. Gallio was an aristocrat, appointed directly from Rome, and lavishly educated: his brother was none other than Seneca, the Stoic philosopher. Secure in his standing, he had nothing to prove by persecuting pathetically small religious groups.

No harm came to Paul from an official quarter (Acts 18:12–17). On another front, however, this incident put all his work in jeopardy. The beating of Sosthenes showed the danger posed by local feeling, however benign the proconsul's neglect might seem. Acts does not mention where Paul's second and third beatings (2 Corinthians 11:25) with lictors' rods took place; they are embarrassing events in a book dedicated to showing how compatible Christianity is with Roman hegemony. Obviously, Gallio did not order these last beatings. On the other hand, if the crowd beat Sosthenes, it is difficult to believe that Paul and Silas walked away unmolested. After all, they were the ones who caused the ruckus. In any case, Sosthenes' beating proved that Paul was a danger to his followers, not just his immediate colleagues and himself.

After however many beatings really took place, Silas's attitude toward Paul changed irrevocably. He never worked with Paul again. Silas had felt the lictor's rod in Philippi and witnessed resistance to Paul's message in Thessalonica and Berea. Now, in Corinth (having been led to believe that things were to be different), Silas found the old story was playing itself out again. This time, however, the violence had swirled beyond the messengers to Jews like Sosthenes and Crispus and God-fearers like Titius Justus who simply agreed with the message. Paul's position was a recipe for violence.

Silas had only one place to go. Acts doesn't want to admit what happened and never refers to Silas again after his arrival in Corinth. But his natural home was Jerusalem, and he returned to James with the news of Paul's extension of Jesus' message to pagans, and especially his insistence on calling all believers "Israel" whether or not they were Jews. And he told James what had happened in Corinth and elsewhere. That trip to Jerusalem explains what James did next, with catastrophic consequences for Paul.

Paul knew very well that Silas's departure was bad news, and he acted decisively, although what he did to defend himself took some time. He proceeded to the eastern port of Corinth, called Cenchreae, "shearing his head in Cenchreae because he kept a vow" (Acts 18:18). He observed the same Nazirite practice that James encouraged in the

Temple, because Paul was heading for Jerusalem. He intended to make good his promise to "remember the poor" from money he had managed to collect in Philippi, Thessalonica, Berea, Athens, and Corinth, offering help to the community in Jerusalem at the same time that he personally—as a pious Nazirite[15]—brought the sacrifice into the Temple.

Priscilla and Aquila supported Paul in this, although they did not go all the way to Jerusalem, but stopped at the port city of Ephesus on the way (Acts 18:18–19). Paul made his pilgrimage alone.

Keen though Acts is to link Paul closely and sympathetically to the circle of James in Jerusalem, the text is laconic about this pilgrimage to the Temple. "He greeted the church, and went down to Antioch" (Acts 18:22): nothing more. Not a word about how long Paul stayed in Jerusalem, what happened, or his contact with James. Not even a description of a warm reception in Antioch. This was not a happy trip; from the point of view of Acts, the less said about it the better.

Things had changed in Jerusalem, and they were changing even more drastically in Antioch. Between Paul's visit in 46 C.E. and his pilgrimage in 52 C.E., James' position had grown stronger and he became dubious of Paul's teaching. Prompted by Silas's news of what had happened in Macedonia and Achaia, James issued a decree, backed by Christian leaders in Jerusalem. This decree presented Paul with a cold shoulder in Jerusalem and produced a heated exchange with Peter in Antioch.

James simply disagreed with Paul: Gentiles baptized in Jesus' name without circumcision were no Israelites, in his view, but a people called by God to support and sustain Israel. To insist on this, James decided to send an encyclical to believing Gentiles commanding them "to abstain from the pollutions of the idols, and from fornication, and from what is strangled, and from blood" (15:20).[16] The Torah's specific requirements for Jews in particular could not be imposed on Gentiles, but accepting the God of Israel implied acknowledging that parts of the Torah spoke to humanity as a whole.

The rules set out by James tended naturally to separate believing

Gentiles from pagans. They had to refrain from feasts in honor of the gods and from foods sacrificed to idols in the course of being butchered and sold, although the devotion of animals in the market to one god or another was common practice in the Hellenistic world.[17] They had to observe stricter limits than usual on the type of sexual activity they might engage in, and with whom: marriage with close relatives was fashionable in the Hellenistic world, but forbidden in the Book of Leviticus (18:6–18). They had to avoid the flesh of animals that had been strangled instead of bled, because that method of slaughter left blood in the meat, and they were not to consume blood itself. These strictures are consistent with James' position at the time he decided Gentile believers did not have to be circumcised: God had co-opted a people from the Gentiles (Acts 15:14), and now he said they had to be similar to Israel and supportive of Israel.

James links his strictures to the fact that the Torah is well and widely known (Acts 15:21): "For Moses from ancient generations has had those preaching him city by city, being read in the synagogues every Sabbath." James and his supporters composed this encyclical without Paul's participation or knowledge, after Silas returned from Corinth. James told Paul what he had done only after the fact (as Acts 21:25 admits), and Paul never accepted all the requirements James imposed on believing Gentiles. It meant that all pagans had to become God-fearers in order to be baptized: they had to abide by the Torah.

What cut Paul worst was that Silas became James' envoy to bring that encyclical to Antioch (Acts 15:22, 27, 32–34). Silas had become Jerusalem's agent to stamp out Paul's teaching. Even Peter, in Antioch to promote the baptism of God-fearers, accepted the decree of James— as did Barnabas, the most prestigious Christian resident of the city. After all, James' decree only regularized what it meant to be a God-fearer; that endorsed Peter's vision, although it denied Paul's visionary redefinition of Israel. Paul, newly arrived in Antioch from Corinth by way of his frosty reception in Jerusalem, stood alone.

Acts does not report this confrontation at all. It was too embarrassing for that book's rosy perspective on primitive Christian unity. Paul, on the other hand, not only reported the dispute, but proudly related his own virulent part in it (Galatians 2:11–13): "But when Cephas came to Antioch, I stood up against him to his face, because he was condemned. Because before some came from James, he used to eat with the Gentiles. But when they came, he backed away and separated himself, fearing those of the circumcision. And the rest of the Jews were made hypocrites with him—so that even Barnabas was carried away with their hypocrisy."

Fired by his passion for his own opinion, Paul calls *any* appeal to ancestral Judaism "circumcision," as if not eating blood were the same thing. When Peter and Barnabas fall in with the policy of James in regard to purity, Paul calls that a hypocritical fear of the circumcision-backers (Galatians 2:11–13); when unnamed teachers actually urge circumcision on Gentiles, Paul tells them to operate on themselves (Galatians 5:1–12). Once Paul had eagerly desired James' authorization. Now, all who disagree with him are circumcisers in his mind, whether they really want circumcision or not.

Paul's virulence is a matter of principle as well as passion. He insisted that, because believers *were* Israel, in toto, they had to eat with one another, and to hell with James' new decree. That meant that God-fearing as well as Jewish believers were to join in mealtime celebrations with people who ate idol-meat (and may well have owned lamps and ceramics decorated with pagan gods). What Paul was asking for was completely consistent with his own position—and for that very reason untenable in Antioch as well as in Jerusalem.

As he said, he was opposed by Peter, Barnabas, the envoys of James (including Silas), and "the rest of the Jews." He was a minority of one among the leaders in Antioch. He describes himself as triumphant in a logical argument against Peter (Galatians 2:14–21). But this triumph was only in retrospect and largely in Paul's own mind. Paul left Antioch; Peter and Barnabas remained. The decree of James carried the day, and Paul was now effectively an excommunicant from his own movement.

part three

THE APOSTLE

OF CHRISTIANITY

· 8 ·

THE EPHESIAN CATAPULT

IOUS HISTORY MAKES Paul's exit from Antioch into a well-organized "missionary journey." But his leaving in 53 C.E. involved neither a hopeful mission nor even a strategic retreat. It was a rout.

Peter and Barnabas remained in Antioch, insisting that Gentile Christians had basic requirements of purity to attend to if they expected to mix with Jewish disciples. James' policy that all believers were required to refrain from idols, blood, and sexual impropriety had triumphed, would prevail for decades to come, and exercises an impact to this day in Christian attitudes about religious art, the preparation of food, and sex. The Puritans centuries later were called Puritans for a reason. Their overt obsession with purity reveals concerns that lie beneath the skin of most forms of Christianity. That attitude was in; Paul was out.

Effectively excommunicated from Antioch, he took off. True to its technique of using compact travelogues to gloss over painful confrontations, Acts makes Paul sound like a tourist as it boils months of searching for a new haven into a single clause (Acts 18:23): "He passed a certain time and left [Antioch], going through the Galatian region and Phrygia in order, shoring up all the disciples."

Not even Acts' rosy scenario can claim that Paul actually stayed in any of Galatia's towns. They closed themselves off to him. The leaders of the nascent Christian movement in Antioch had directed the people of Galatia to live in a way that contradicted Paul's claims. Later in the same year that he passed through Galatia, in 53 C.E., he wrote a letter to congregations there in which he admits that the Galatians had turned from him (Galatians 1:6–9):

> I am astounded that you defect so quickly from the One who called you in Christ's grace to another gospel! Not that there is another, although some disturb you and wish to pervert the gospel of Christ. But even if we or an angel from heaven announces other than what we announced to you, he will be damned! As we said before and I now say again: if anyone announces to you other than what you received, he will be damned!

As it goes on, this letter becomes even feistier, filled with argument, invective, polemic, and pleading. It reflects what Acts tries to conceal: the region where Paul had enjoyed his greatest breakthrough among Gentiles shunned him after he was pushed out of Antioch.

Somewhere, somehow, he needed a soft landing. That had to be in a city outside the sphere of influence of his apostolic opponents. Hard experience in Galatia had taught Paul how far and how deep that influence extended. While Paul had made his most recent trip to Jerusalem, Priscilla and Aquila had disembarked in Ephesus (Acts 18:18–21) on the western coast of Asia Minor. He barely knew this city, but at least it was off the map of Antioch's hegemony and even Jerusalem's. Once again Priscilla and Aquila offered him a haven, much as they had done in Corinth.

Paul journeyed west by caravan, covering five hundred miles of tough, dangerous terrain and encountering the perils and pains of travel over Asia Minor's highlands (Acts 19:1). Traveling without the backing of Antioch, he worked off his fare with his hands. The caravan probably crossed the plain of Cilicia, briefly entering Tarsus, then mounting through the Cilician Gates. Neither Paul nor Acts mentions if he sought any solace or help from his family, and his route lay north of his old itinerary with Barnabas.

He traveled quickly, with only indirect contact with the places he had visited with Barnabas in Galatia, the site of his stoning and eventual recovery. What he heard about the Galatian communities enraged him; he felt betrayed. The people to whom he had announced the message of Jesus had accepted the practices of his opponents in Antioch, whose bragging about circumcised flesh (Galatians 6:12–13) promoted the conventions of this world and betrayed the radically otherworldly power of Jesus.

But his opponents had won. Paul had left Antioch defeated. Damascus remained closed to him. The condition of any return he might make to Jerusalem involved cash contributions, and James' new teaching made him barely welcome there. Even the piddling villages and towns of Galatia joined the growing list of places where Paul was persona non grata.

Inauspicious though his flight to Ephesus was, this period, between 53 and 56 C.E., marks Paul's emergence as a major authority within the primitive Christian movement, an apostle for the faith of Gentiles in the Diaspora and therefore—after his death—what Christians from the second century on would call "the Apostle" of the whole Church. This was the most remarkable turnaround in his remarkable life.

· · ·

WITHOUT PRISCILLA AND AQUILA, none of this could have happened. They provided for Paul's soft landing in Ephesus and helped develop the most favorable setting he ever enjoyed as an apostle. They had arrived in Ephesus a good year before Paul did, stopping there as Paul traveled on to Jerusalem. It was natural for Priscilla and Aquila to stop at Ephesus, a beautiful Hellenistic haven of Greek culture on the western shore of Asia Minor. Unlike Paul, they had no Nazirite vow to complete in Jerusalem and no particular connection with James. They simply numbered among the dozens of freelance teachers telling about Jesus.

This commercially vibrant center with its synagogues, philosophical schools, and thriving port was a perfect fit for them, and what was good for them was good for Paul. Or it could be good: if he could be kept out of contention in synagogues over his pet theme. With Silas out of the way, who had insisted on Paul's connection to the institutions of Judaism, this should have been easier than it had been in Corinth—and in fact Ephesus made it possible. Not to take anything away from Paul, but it was Priscilla and Aquila who enabled him to convert his defeat at the hands of his colleagues in Antioch into a dramatic thrust for his own interpretation of Jesus' message. They took him in and provided him with a platform and a network of connections such as he had never known before and would never enjoy again.

Ephesus boasted several synagogues, lecture halls, and theaters, temples for Hellenistic deities, a famous brothel, splendid baths and mansions, and giant tenements. Traders transported goods both overland toward the east and by ship south into the Mediterranean through the Aegean Sea.[1] By early in the second century the city had a spectacular library, and collectors no doubt treasured their scrolls when Paul arrived in 53 C.E.

Ephesus was a jewel of Hellenistic culture, more Greek than the eastern cities of Asia Minor. It had escaped many of the polarizing controversies that plagued other cities. Jerusalem seesawed between Judaic piety and Roman occupation; Tarsus teetered on an identity crisis between its provincial roots and aspirations to grandeur; Damascus could never figure out whether it was more Nabatean or Roman, oriental or Western; Antioch on the Orontes bore a Persian name even as a major hub of a different empire. Ephesus wasn't beset by the underlying cultural struggles that had persistently ensnared Paul in those other cities.

What seemed promising territory to Paul was equally suitable to other Christian leaders. When Priscilla and Aquila arrived in Ephesus, they found a welcome for the message about Jesus, but that was because an Egyptian teacher named Apollos had gotten there before them (Acts 18:24–28). Apollos came from the Jewish quarter of Alexandria, a master of both philosophical rhetoric and Israel's Scriptures. He taught "accurately" about Jesus, Acts says (18:25), but his view of baptism differed from Priscilla's, Aquila's, and Paul's. He knew "only John's baptism."

Acts presents that peculiarity as if it were a detail to be corrected, and Priscilla and Aquila go on to put Apollos right about his little mistake. But the depth of the difference between Apollos and his tentmaking confreres shines through Acts' attempt to cover up a profound controversy.

Apollos preached a version of Jesus' message that Priscilla and Aquila could not accept. For Apollos, Christian immersion was the same repeatable rite practiced throughout Judaism, a ritual for purification by water in the manner of John the Baptist[2] and other Jewish immersers.

Priscilla and Aquila understood baptism very differently: it was the moment, dramatic and unrepeatable, when a believer received the same Spirit that had descended upon Jesus when he immersed in the manner of John, and which poured out of heaven when God raised Jesus from the dead. That was central to the teaching and vision of Peter and all who followed him, Paul included.

But Apollos's message fit in well among the synagogue practices of Ephesus. So well in fact that Apollos decided to prolong his lecture tour and proceed to other Greek-speaking cities. He carried with him letters of recommendation from various Christians in the synagogues of Ephesus (Acts 18:27–28). His perspective, a matter of extending loyalty to the Torah and the rituals of Judaism among Gentiles, represented a serious challenge to Priscilla and Aquila. Ignoring him was not an option.

For Apollos, Jesus realized exactly what the Torah was supposed to be: the will of God enacted. Jesus' baptism was a case in point. He followed the law of immersion and had been anointed by God for his obedience (Acts 18:28)—he was the "Christ," the "anointed" in Greek *(khristos)*, just what Messiah *(mashiach)* means in the Scriptures of Israel.[3] Apollos had mastered the art of rhetoric more than any other Christian teacher, including Paul; he seems to have presented the Torah as the culmination of prophecy and Christ as the culmination of the Torah.

Priscilla and Aquila were in no position to simply correct Apollos, as Acts would have us believe; they were tent-makers from Pontus—no match for the philosopher from Alexandria. To counteract Apollos's influence, they needed help. If Peter's vision about the outpouring of Spirit in baptism was going to make its way in Ephesus, they had to find an authoritative advocate of this teaching.

Paul could offer something Priscilla and Aquila could not. He came to Ephesus as an acknowledged apostle despite the controversy he had stirred up. The risen Jesus had appeared to him; the two greatest centers of Christianity, Jerusalem and Antioch, had delegated him to preach his gospel for the pagans. He knew Peter personally and put Peter's vision into practice. For all the depth and rancor of his disagreement with the older Galilean apostle, Paul never ceased to represent the Petrine message he had learned in Jerusalem in 35 C.E.

So, estranged from Peter in Antioch, Paul nonetheless arrived in Ephesus and contradicted Apollos's teaching with Peter's message about receiving God's Spirit. The diversity of the primitive Christian movement combined with the uncertainty of communication among its communities allowed for this kind of ambivalent stance. Agreeing with Peter about the Spirit while contradicting Peter when it came to pagans acknowledging the Torah—Paul crafted his trademark theology in Ephesus. It is the perspective that marks his letters and has characterized Pauline Christianity ever since.

When Paul came to Ephesus, he found a dozen men and their households who had been baptized by Apollos (Acts 19:1–7).[4] They knew only John's immersion: receiving the Spirit directly from the risen Jesus was a new idea to them. In fact, they said they hadn't even heard about the Holy Spirit (19:2). To get them to the point that they not only associated Jesus with the Spirit but also experienced the Spirit would take authority and talent. Priscilla and Aquila realized that Paul had both of those, in spades.

What separated Apollos from Paul was not Jesus' status as Christ, which Apollos was especially skilled at demonstrating from the Scriptures (Acts 18:28). The crux was rather the Spirit of God, which for Paul (following Peter) descended upon each believer at baptism, as it had on Jesus at his baptism. By calling out "*Abba*, father" as Jesus had, believers became God's children, adopted by God, and heirs of the same parentage that Jesus enjoyed as God's Son (Galatians 4:6, 7). Paul articulates exactly this conviction based upon the experience of baptism in the letter he wrote to Galatia soon after his arrival in Ephesus.

But Paul's declaration of the Spirit was not only a matter of invoking the teaching of Peter. What survived all his troubles in Jerusalem and Antioch was his incomparable capacity to bring people who listened to him to the point that they could feel Christ revealed within them. His letters were written to congregations that had already experienced his hypnotic power: that was the strength of his connection to them. For that reason these letters do not exactly repeat his words to them when he first awakened their faith in Christ. But he does use phrases that echo what he said to them initially, and they give us a pretty good glimpse of his method.

Paul was never afraid to refer to himself, especially if the reference emphasized his own human weakness. Paul's *ego,* his use of the word for "I," fueled his rhetoric. "I" means not only "I," but any "I" that stands before the reality of God (Galatians 2:19c–20): "I have been crucified with Christ. I live—yet no longer I—but Christ lives in me. And the life I now live in flesh, I live by the faith of God's Son, who loved me and gave himself for me." This is nothing other than Paul's experience on the road to Damascus, and on many hard roads after that, put into words and conveyed to others.

Part of the method was a dramatic presentation; Paul was proud that he could portray Jesus Christ crucified so vividly that his audience felt they were seeing the scene (Galatians 3:1). But the point was not just pathos. Knowing God's Son meant realizing that his dying and rising again awakened the resurrection principle within every believer. "The life I now live in flesh, I live by the faith of God's Son"— the way Jesus found to eternal life was open to anyone who accepted his Spirit.

This moment was so intimate a connection to Christ, Paul said (Galatians 4:9), it was more than just knowing God and more like being known by God. As he wrote in another letter he composed in Ephesus, God disclosed esoteric wisdom, the secret knowledge of his own nature, to every believer at baptism, "Because the Spirit searches everything, even the depths of God" (1 Corinthians 2:10). To "live by the faith of God's Son" involved being in a relationship with God that was so close, it meant more than understanding God or believing in God. By the force and suffusion of Spirit, the core of one's being became divine in a transformation whose meaning was infinite, beyond the capacity of the human mind to grasp.

Paul was so successful in Ephesus, he baptized these followers of Apollos again, laying hands on them as Ananias had laid hands on him.[5] Infused with the Spirit, they spoke in foreign tongues and prophesied (Acts 19:6). Acts and Paul agree that Spirit-possession in a communal setting could result in prophecy (Acts 2:1–41; 1 Corinthians 12:10). In expanded states of consciousness, believers spoke the tongues of other human cultures and of angels, declaring God's intentions for humanity in the manner of the great prophets of Israel.

Primitive Christianity, Paul's Christianity, was a religion of the Spirit and of Spirit's power in the community of believers. Scholars still sometimes deny or downplay this aspect of Paul's activity in an attempt to emphasize his work as a dogmatic theologian. But he knew where his authority came from (2 Corinthians 12:12): "The signs of the apostle were produced among you in all endurance—signs and wonders and powers."

Paul did not much like having to remind people of these accomplishments: to him that was bragging, and only fools bragged (2 Corinthians 12:11). After all, God's kingdom was not a matter of talk, but of power (1 Corinthians 4:20), the power of Spirit. Yet for all his reluctance to get into a bidding war over whose signs were bigger, Paul does state that signs attested his apostolic authority. They were the kinds of things he believed people shouldn't need reminding about.

Paul saw no dichotomy between the Spirit that acted in him

through Jesus and the force of the arguments he made. Together they effected a "demolition of strongholds" (2 Corinthians 10:4). That was his purpose, whether the fortress to be demolished was a harmful demon or a dumb argument. In Ephesus, Paul proved that Word and Spirit went together. He combined the authority of Peter's view of the Spirit with his own capacity to assist the birth of Christ in the heart of every believer.

· · ·

IT TOOK HIM THREE MONTHS to make Ephesus work for him fully; once he figured out a successful strategy, however, he parlayed it. The Book of Acts flags the vital difference Ephesus made to Paul in its peculiar, understated style (19:8–9): "Entering the synagogue for three months he spoke frankly, debating and persuading concerning the kingdom of God. But when some were hardened and opposed—insulting the way before the multitude—he removed from them to separate the disciples, debating every day in the school of Tyrannus." Never has a more fateful move been more blandly indicated.[6]

In Ephesus, Paul at last figured out that, if you really believed you were the Israel of God, then you did not need the approval of local synagogues. If they bother you, rent a hall—what we would call a storefront church. For the first time on record, Christians claimed public space, not as a subgroup from a synagogue but as people convening for their own worship.

Paul insisted on his own way of thinking more than anyone in the New Testament, but he was also its most flexible tactician. With a hall at his disposal, he could simply call a meeting. The Greek term *ekklesia* (church) refers to a meeting, including an assembly such as might be called in a town or a village. All he needed to make his new model work was some kind of local reputation to attract people. In that regard he had no problem at all.

Acts relates an episode that reveals Paul's growing fame in Ephesus (Acts 19:11–12). He had become known as an exorcist in Ephesus, as he had in Philippi. People began to take the cloths he used to wipe his

The Ephesian Nike (photo courtesy of the author). Idolatry could be beautifully done, posing a threat to both Judaism and Christianity. This rendering of "Victory" (Nike), located between a musical theater and the center of the city, was probably completed after Paul's time in Ephesus, but represents the kind of competition he was up against there.

hands and face and his work apron, and applied them to people afflicted with demons. The alien powers departed, and those who had been troubled became well.

This story offers an insight into how Paul's sense of the power of the gospel could be converted into local beliefs and practices. It doesn't need to be fully accurate in its particulars to give us a clear sense of how this process could work out.

Paul's prowess became so well known, some Jewish exorcists who claimed high priestly descent—called "the sons of Sceva"—took to conjuring the demons in what they took to be the Pauline manner. They intoned: "I adjure by the Jesus whom Paul preaches" (Acts 13–17). According to Acts, they learned to their cost that Paul's exorcisms were not mechanical techniques, but an assertion of Spirit. When they used their formula on a recalcitrant demon, it replied, "I know Jesus, and I am familiar with Paul, but who are you?" The evil spirit overpowered them, stripped them naked, and sent them beaten and bleeding from the scene.

Acts tells the whole story as a kind of joke, against high priests and Jewish exorcists generally, and the detail that there were seven sons of the high priest is an obvious flip-side comparison with the seven deacons of the primitive Church in Jerusalem. (Here again, a story in Acts spins shamelessly.) But this is just the kind of tale that built up Paul's reputation in Ephesus.

Spirit's power in Paul's mind and practice was worked out by means of exorcism: the inrushing force of the divine kingdom destroyed the demons' fortresses on the earth. This miraculous power played out in Paul's struggle with Satan (who could disguise himself as an angel of light; 2 Corinthians 11:14). His campaign was part of the underlying, spiritual warfare that was more fateful than any war the world could wage (2 Corinthians 10:4): "For the weapons of our warfare are not of flesh, but powerful in God for the demolition of strongholds." The struggle for humanity was an intellectual and emotional combat that centered on the conquest of evil in the human heart.

Paul's Stoic orientation comes out in his understanding of exorcism as it does in his teaching of the "body" of Christ.[7] Just as the believer was incorporated into the identity of Jesus by baptism, so the Spirit of God's Son transformed every believer into God's child with the personal awareness of God as Father. That chased out the unintegrated, demonic fragments of personality that can undermine a person's being. Paul was clearly aware of Jesus' words: "If I by the Spirit of God throw out demons, then God's kingdom has come upon you" (Matthew 12:28). But where Jesus' view of that transformation focused on the defeat of Satan in the physical world, the focus of Paul's combat was the rational soul of a Stoic, where the awakened consciousness that one was a child of God that emerged during baptism was the seal of Spirit's power.

Paul's claim of authority over Satan goes back to Jesus' vision: Jesus saw Satan fall (Luke 10:18) when his apostles commanded unclean spirits to depart. However confident this assertion, Jesus also finds himself tested by Satan (Matthew 4:1–11; Mark 1:12–13; Luke 4:1–13), and Paul openly admits (2 Corinthians 12:7–9) that he could never free himself of the "thorn in the flesh, an angel of Satan."

Neither Paul nor Jesus ever claimed an effortless victory over evil. They saw the struggle with evil itself, whether in the physical world or within one's soul, as a sign of the kingdom's arrival. For Paul, as for Jesus, divine Spirit, not personal power, overcame evil, and the rude force of the exorcist meant more than elaborate techniques of magic. So Jesus is depicted as entering into shouting matches with the unclean spirits, and Paul speaks of battling at the strongholds of Satan.

Fifteen centuries later, Martin Luther—a peerless interpreter of Paul—frequently spoke of Satan as a genuine force, and a force to be treated roughly:[8] "When the devil comes at night to worry me, this is what I say to him: 'Devil, I have to sleep now. That is God's commandment, for us to work by day and sleep at night.' If he keeps on nagging me and trots out my sins, then I answer: 'Sweet devil, I know the whole list. Also write on it that I have shit on my breeches. Then hang that around your neck and wipe your mouth on it.' "

The crudity of Wittenberg's most famous monk in this case carries on the abrupt, unmethodical confrontation with evil practiced by Jesus and Paul. It is a far cry from the resort to elaborate formulae, ancient and modern,[9] the stock and trade of professional exorcists.

· · ·

PAUL'S SUPREME CONFIDENCE in Spirit's capacity to work in him and through him defies complete explanation. Where he found the resources to persevere will always baffle us, but his successful method is literally an open book, because he wrote letters. These were not just conventional communications, but deliberate assertions of his spiritual power across Asia Minor and later into Greece and Rome. Every letter was a catapult, crafted to project his message, his authority, his exorcistic might into communities many miles from Ephesus. Paul exerted his impact within communities swept up in the first-century tumult of prophecy, conflicting loyalties, controversy, exorcism, and healing.

Acts' story of the sons of Sceva provides a window on the boisterous goings-on involved in Christian worship. Ephesus provided ample tenements, where collections of believers gathered. They shared meals in the presence of the risen Christ; they sang, spoke God's praises in their own and foreign tongues, in the mysterious language of angels. They heard Israel's Scriptures read and prophecies announced in the name of Jesus, then listened to teachings about what they had heard. They agreed to the baptism of new members and arranged for their immersion at night, in natural sources of living water, triumphing over the forces of evil.

These rambunctious goings-on and meetings in the "school of Tyrannus" (Acts 19:9) assured the notoriety of Paul's congregation. He was its undisputed leader, a distinguished visitor who had a long pedigree of accomplishment and the scars of persecution, boasting personal acquaintance with the most prominent apostles of his movement. He regularly instructed, cajoled, and corrected the whole gathering.

As Paul spoke, he laid his hands on some of his audience, young and old straining forward to receive the Spirit of Christ. This moment of physical contact was deeply affecting, and it cost him in emotional terms. He felt, he once remarked (Galatians 4:19), like a woman in labor, afflicted until Christ was formed in the midst of the congregation. Manifesting this Spirit was the purpose of Paul's suffering and work.

When he wrote from Ephesus, flushed with the triumph of correcting Apollos's views in meeting after meeting, he spoke with the authority of an exorcist. In fact, what he wrote from Ephesus was intended as an act of exorcism—at a distance. The result was a letter that changed the conventional understanding of what a letter could do, and created Paul as a literary persona.

IN EPHESUS, Paul took on the mantle of an apostle in his own right, writing to the Galatian congregations, the scene of his stoning, to insist that the mealtime apartheid between Jews and non-Jews that James, Peter, and Barnabas had imposed in Antioch contradicted the message of Christ. He wrote entirely on his own authority and with character-istic bluntness.

Luther called Paul's letter to the Galatians "My dearest little epistle, to which I plighted my troth." He loved it, of course, because it pro-vides the clearest statement there is of Paul's rejection of the Law of the Torah in favor of Christ's grace. Read through the lens of the sixteenth century's governing concern—the dichotomy between "faith" and "works"—this letter is the Magna Carta of Protestantism, excoriating a reliance on one's own efforts to achieve salvation and relying instead on the unmerited mercy of God.

But if Paul was so opposed to "law," why does he say toward the end of this same letter, "Bear one another's burdens, and thus fill up the Law of Christ" (Galatians 6:2)?[10] Part of the answer to that question is that he did not think in the same categories that thinkers since the Reformation have used. To him "faith" and "works" were part of a single, seamless action because he did not conceive of human beings as isolated units, with intentions inside their hearts and activities outside their bodies. The membrane between the spiritual and material worlds was permeable. People lived in both spheres at once. In fact, to the heart awakened to Spirit, there was no difference between the two.

This letter blazes with an intensity as great as Luther's, but with a dif-ferent focus. Paul is openly disgusted with the behavior of old sup-porters back in Galatia and filled with newfound pride. His victories in Ephesus—converting congregations away from Apollos's view of bap-tism to Peter's, establishing the first independent Christian church in a public space—confirmed him as an apostle in the estimation of a great city, not merely by his own assertion or in the grudging acknowledg-ment of his predecessors in Jerusalem and Antioch. Let the Galatians try to dismiss him now! How could these bumpkins spurn him when a real city was embracing his message and his status?

He enjoyed so many resources from his success at Ephesus, he could arrange for a secretary[11] to help him compose a letter to the Galatians.

Completely his responsibility, this missive so bristles with Paul's temperament that at one point he snatched the papyrus reed from his assistant and wrote: "Look at the big letters I write to you in my own hand!" (Galatians 6:11). He was no professional scribe and needed help to get his thoughts down.

The editorial help did not dilute his character. This letter opens with a slap in the face—Paul pretending to astonishment (as we have seen) "that you defect so quickly from the One[12] who called you in Christ's grace to another gospel!" (Galatians 1:6) Letters in antiquity normally began with an extended greeting and effusive compliments. After all, the reading of any communication involved at least a small audience—including the emissary who brought and often read the scroll, a scribe and serving staff who might be called on to devise an answer, as well as the recipient himself (or herself) with any friends or family who were involved. Under those circumstances, buttering up the recipient to accept the point of the message was such an obviously good idea that it became a convention, which, in most of his letters, Paul sensibly followed.[13] But Paul didn't feel the least bit complimentary toward the yokels of Galatia. They are, in his own words, "you stupid Galatians" (3:1). He uses every bit of bias against the Celts of Galatia, every trick of sarcasm, every appeal to sentiment, every logical argument he can muster to shame them into agreeing with him.

Paul is so tough, clear, and wound up that he reveals more about his background in this letter than he does anywhere else. But the letter's force resides in its ferocious attempt to exorcise the Galatians of the false messengers that in Paul's mind would destroy the message of Christ. The issue is not merely that they are listening to other teachers. Paul might have been vain, but his motivation was not mere vanity. He was incensed because the non-Jewish believers whom he had initiated into the Spirit of Christ were now willing to accept circumcision, keep the calendar of Judaism, and accept the strictures of James about what they could eat, how, and with whom. The success of those who insisted on these teachings is measured by the fact that they were active in Galatia while Paul was not. To him they were anathema.

His crude language betrays the virulence of his feelings. People who want to circumcise Gentiles for the sake of Christ should just "cut off" their members (Galatians 5:12); keeping the festivals and Sabbaths of Judaism is as bad as serving idols (Galatians 4:8–11); observing purity at meals is hypocrisy (Galatians 2:13). By the time he wrote this letter, Paul had traveled very far from the original extension of Peter's gospel to God-fearers. He went way beyond even the permissive mixing of Jewish and Gentile believers that he had encouraged in Antioch. Now he was on the attack: he blasted any gesture by Gentile Christians toward an acceptance of Judaism.

Paul's thought had changed, and he said that the Torah itself had become an obstacle to the message of Christ. Now he saw any messenger opposed to him—human or heavenly—as damned. Any agent that drew the Galatians from his message was a sorcerer, who bewitched them (Galatians 3:1–5) to betray the crucified Christ and the Spirit that moved within them. The Paul of this letter is an exorcist, and he exorcises his audience of any force—Pharisaic, Jewish, Christian, apostolic, or local—that might divert them from his perspective.

. . .

PAUL'S FEROCIOUS LANGUAGE reflects the drama he believed he had to play out: the world as everyone knew it was truly about to come apart. You could be saved from that complete dissolution by one, single power: God's. There was no other feasible resort. The absolute imperative for the Galatians was to maintain their loyalty to Christ, "who gave himself for our sins, so that he might rescue us from the present evil age" (Galatians 1:4). From that source and that source alone, "grace" (kharis)[14] was offered (Galatians 1:3); God's favor in allowing people to survive the imminent cataclysm and live in the power of the eschatological kingdom.

For Paul, as for primitive Christians generally, the message of Jesus was an announcement of victory, an euanggelion ("gospel" in Old English). The meaning of this term in Greek as well as in Aramaic (besora) makes it clear that Paul and his peers were referring to real triumph—in the ultimate field of battle. (That is why the modern translation "good news" strikes me as flaccid.) Paul insisted tirelessly that this victory was won for us apart from our own doing. God dispensed his compassionate power as "grace," an undeserved favor for which thanks is due.

Everything depended on remaining loyal to this saving power. Defecting to "another" triumphal message (as if there were such!) was fatal. Paul is trying to save the eternal lives of those who read his letter in Galatia. That's why he takes no hostages in his argument, allows no concessions, and uses such violent rhetoric and invective.

That is why, in asserting his own apostolic authority, he calls Peter and Barnabas hypocrites (Galatians 2:11–13) and flaunts his contradiction of Peter and other apostles when they try to apply laws of purity to Gentile believers. He then proceeds to the heart of his argument (3:1–3): "You stupid Galatians! Who bewitched you, not to obey the truth, before whose eyes Jesus Christ was portrayed crucified? I only want to learn this from you: Did you receive the Spirit from works of law, or from hearing with faith? Are you so stupid!? Having started with Spirit, do you now finish with flesh?"

The antithesis between Spirit and flesh, between gospel and custom, between divine grace and human intention, was basic to Paul's position because, on the road to Damascus, Christ appeared to him as the triumph of Spirit over every convention, even the Torah. That experience explains Paul's famous teaching of justification by faith—the pivot on which the Reformation turned. He articulates what he means by this in Galatians, spelling out how he sees the uncovering of God's Son within the believer as superseding the place of the Torah (2:19–21): "For I through the Law am dead to the Law, that I might live in God. I have been crucified with Christ. I live—yet no longer I—but Christ lives in me. And the life I now live in flesh, I live by the faith of God's Son, who loved me and gave himself for me. I do not refuse the grace of God; for if righteousness were through law, then Christ died for nothing."

Here is the heart of what Albert Schweitzer called Paul's mysticism:[15]

the conviction that identifying oneself with the crucified Christ by baptism enables one to participate in the power of his Resurrection. Paul's spirituality derives from Peter's teaching: baptism is precisely when one is identified with Christ and made a recipient of Spirit. That becomes the sole principle of Pauline ethics, what Paul called "the Law of Christ," taking the place of the Torah of Moses.

When Paul calls his readers stupid, he is pursuing the same thought in a ferocious key. However critical he is of them, he still refers to the portrayal of Jesus' crucifixion as the occasion of their receiving Spirit (Galatians 3:1–3). But he insisted ruthlessly on his radical and unique claim that baptism totally changes a basic axiom of what the Scriptures of Israel mean. The Spirit defines "Israel"—the people of God—in a completely new way (Galatians 6:15–16):[16] "For neither circumcision is anything, nor foreskin, but a new creation. And as many as hold to this standard, peace upon them and mercy—even upon the Israel of God."

Right here, Paul does what Peter didn't do, what Barnabas never did, what James could not conceive of: he redefines what "Israel" means in terms of the Spirit. Spirit, received in baptism, takes the place of circumcision as the measure of who the people of God are.

That is why Paul demands that even Jewish followers of Jesus, once baptized, should ignore their own rules of purity at meals for the sake of fellowship with Gentile disciples (Galatians 2:11–21). While James and Peter and Barnabas accepted that Jewish followers of Jesus and non-Jewish followers of Jesus could pursue their own customs, Paul insisted that Christ supplanted the force of all such conventions. Christians not only could eat together, they *had* to eat together, in spite of the Torah!

To his mind this was not a big demand: after all, God had just declared, by the fiat of raising his Son from the dead and shedding his Spirit on all who were baptized in his name, that by grace Greeks were no longer Greeks, Jews no longer Jews, slaves no longer slaves, free people no longer free, women no longer women, men no longer men (Galatians 3:26–29), because there was just a single Israel, gathered by Spirit, according to God's primordial intention.

. . .

YEARS BEFORE, his own experience on Sinai had convinced Paul that the law that came from Arabia was not the true mother of faith (Galatians 4:22–31). Rather, faith's mother, the true covenant to which the Torah is only a prologue, is the Spirit that comes from belief in Christ. So thoroughly did he see the meaning of the covenant in Christ, he had come to compare every believer at baptism to Abraham, the father of the covenant people (Galatians 3:6–7). For Paul the faith one has in Christ is identical to the faith in God that Abraham showed: that is why, at the close of the letter to the Galatians (6:15–16), he will claim that faith makes "Israel" as a "new creation." Faith is not just a matter of belief; it is how the individual and the community join themselves to the one reality that will survive and supersede the present pattern of the world.

The obvious alternative to Paul's claim is that Abraham's example is better followed by pursuing the Law than by ignoring it. In considering that alternative, Paul makes his great contribution to the Christian interpretation of Scripture.

Paul uses Scripture *against* itself to prove that it is not a single, literal authority. He does that by quoting Scriptures[17] that are on opposite sides of the fence (Galatians 3:10–11): "As many as are from works of law are under a curse, because it is written, 'Cursed be everyone who does not remain in all the things written in the book of the law, to do them' [Deuteronomy 27:26]. But it is clear that no one is justified before God by the law, because 'The righteous one shall live from faith' [Habakkuk 2:4]." These two principles are in conflict: one says you have to put all the law into practice, and the other says you need only faith.

Christ resolves this conflict, according to Paul. Christ himself became a curse, because he was hung on a tree as an executed criminal, an accursed person according to the book of Deuteronomy (Galatians 3:13–14): "Christ redeemed us from the curse of the law, becoming a curse on our behalf; because it is written, 'Cursed is everyone who hangs upon a tree' [Deuteronomy 21:23]. So the blessing of Abraham extends to the Gentiles in Jesus Christ, and we receive the promise of the Spirit through faith."

So there was indeed a curse at the heart of the Law, but Jesus broke the curse by dying. His death brought Resurrection and an outpouring of God's Spirit, in which even non-Jews can share. God had promised Abraham, "In you shall all the Gentiles be blessed"; now, faith in Christ made that happen (Galatians 3:8, citing Genesis 12:3). Paul's logic is as tight as his passion is insistent, but it is only convincing if you accept his axiom that the Torah and the Spirit are at odds—and can follow his juggling with texts.

For Paul and Christianity after Paul, the cross of Christ is the intersection where the Torah stops and the Spirit begins for all humanity. It is more than an event in history, because the meaning of the Scriptures and of all human history revolves around its truth. The cross becomes the pattern of human suffering transmuted into fulfillment.

Two elements stand out clearly in Paul's interpretation of Scripture. First, the use of Scripture against itself, in order to map a conflict within the text, turns out to be a governing concern. In that way, Christ is invoked as the principle and the power that resolves the conflict, so that promise and faith triumph over the Law. Following this dialectical principle, there is a corollary: Law has only a provisional function within human experience. Promise (as in God's promise to Abraham) is the vocation of humanity. The fulfillment of promise— realized by identification with Christ—is the destiny of belief. The meaning of human existence is not static, but *progressive*, and that progress takes people beyond the Law.

Both elements of interpretation, the dialectical and the progressive, are rooted in the experience that Paul ceaselessly replayed in his own mind and conveyed to others: baptism into Christ releasing the Spirit of God within the believer. Once you see that as the point of Israel's Bible, you have no problem when those Scriptures contradict one another. Paul's policy is the reverse of claiming that Scripture always says the same thing in the same way. Instead, he argues that Scripture is at odds with itself, until the faith of Jesus Christ is understood to be the purpose that the various texts anticipate. That dialectical perspective leads on naturally to the progressive perspective, in which human experience reveals that the promise of faith makes every other standard, including the Law, of only provisional value.

. . .

"NO WAY I CAN BOAST except in the cross of our Lord Christ Jesus, through whom the world has been crucified to me and I to the world" (Galatians 6:14). Just as the cross of Christ means that the Torah uses up its capacity to regulate behavior, because Christ became a curse to the Law (Galatians 3:13), so the world loses its capacity to constrain Paul himself. Its capacity to mold Paul's behavior is lost. That is why he found the resources in Ephesus to break free of Jerusalem and Antioch.

Ephesus gave him something he had never dreamed of: a base of power. That came from his work as an exorcist and from the economic and political resources that Priscilla and Aquila put at his disposal. Paul acknowledged his debt to them in another letter he wrote from Ephesus (1 Corinthians 16:19), where he conveys the greetings of "Aquila and Priscilla . . . with the church that is in their house." This is the earliest reference to what scholars have called "the house church," a unit of Christian worship and instruction based not in public halls, outdoor meetings, or cramped tenements, but in homes of wealthy converts.

"In my father's house are many mansions," Jesus says in John's Gospel (14:2). The King James Version translates that saying accurately, although more "modern" versions have changed "mansions" to "rooms" in the interest of plausibility. But recent excavations in Ephesus (where John's Gospel, like several of Paul's letters, was composed) have recently uncovered a huge complex of stately abodes inside a common building. Just as Ephesus had the allure of the Hamptons in the ancient world, so some of its housing included condominiums for the newly rich, upwardly mobile elite. In their ownership of a house that could serve as a congregational meeting place, Aquila and Priscilla clearly belonged to that elite. The mansions of Ephesus boasted atriums with fountains, baths, and philosophical salons, some with busts of ancient sages adorning the walls. In such a room Paul held court, arguing, debating, interpreting Scripture, exhorting his hearers to realize their gift of the Spirit in baptism.

Indeed, part of Paul's appeal in Ephesus, as he proceeded to correct the teaching of Apollos in congregation after congregation, was that he represented not only apostolic authority but also the prestige of wealth. Priscilla and Aquila were in the vanguard of Christianity's upper-class sympathizers (although later legends that make Priscilla an aristocratic Roman matron push the couple's status too far). The pagans among them could not let their sympathy blossom in public because that would involve denying the gods of Greece and Rome. But Priscilla and her husband were Jews; they were not expected to go along with Hellenistic pantheism and could be open in their agreement and friendship with Jesus' followers. Their strict monotheism together with keeping circumcision, the Sabbath, and rules of kashrut and sacrifice were already permitted under Roman law. They could and did open their house to Christians.

The house church became a vital center for Christianity owing to the wealth and influence of its owners. The tenement church, the guild church, the clandestine meeting by a river or stream by no means disappeared, because house churches were not egalitarian and did not welcome all Christians in the community. But they did provide for privacy in speaking of Paul's most controversial ideas, an insulation from public scandal and violent dispute.

During most of his time in Ephesus, Paul could freely move about town, visiting tenements, guilds, houses, and pickup meetings with the assurance of material support from Priscilla and Aquila and other wealthy patrons. But in their house he could most openly speak his mind, and a willing secretary sometimes took down his words and helped frame them into a decent composition.

Paul's letters often display intellectual hyperactivity. He says more than needs to be said; he stretches arguments to their breaking point.

That is to some extent a matter of his temperament, but we need to keep in mind that when Paul wrote, he was playing to his local audience as well as addressing people far away. Grabbing his own secretary's reed to impale the foolish Galatians with yet another argument, telling his enemies to mutilate themselves—all this was theatrical stuff, designed more to entertain the Ephesians than convince the Galatians. His letter to these Celts must have sounded in Ephesus like an extended Irish joke.

It did not play in Galatia. There is no indication that Paul ever returned to that region, although communities in Asia Minor nearer to Ephesus did feel his influence. Telling the Galatians that they needed to have arguments spelled out in big letters, calling them stupid, referring to their ancient ancestral religion as silly idolatry, accusing them of mindless treachery: that is not the stuff of convincing argument. The letter to Galatia established his position in Ephesus, but it failed to move its intended recipients. More than a century after Paul there is excellent evidence that the Galatians were in fact keeping the calendar of Judaism, celebrating Easter in a tight correspondence with Passover, and observing regulations of food purity.

Paul no more drew them from their attachment to traditional Judaism than he convinced them that anyone who believed in Christ—Jew or Gentile—belonged to the Israel of God. The salons of Ephesus ate that argument up, not the Celts of Asia Minor's highlands.

In Ephesus, surrounded by sophisticated listeners in a salon, he could get away with saying that to be "Israel" you needed no law, no circumcision, no festal calendar, only faith in Christ. According to Paul's splendid revisionism, God had changed the whole definition of what it means to be his chosen. The audience relished his attacks on the backwoods Galatians and the literal-minded Judaizers.

Paul opened up radically new ways to think and feel about how God was changing the world. Although there is no reason to suppose that social barriers were instantly forgotten, it is plain from many, many texts that Christians put a premium on rejecting the social status of this world in favor of the grace of the world to come. If you could go that far, why not take the next step? Why not say that there was no longer Jew or Greek in the new kingdom that God had introduced with the Resurrection of his Son? The world was being made new. It demanded a new Israel. Paul had become its Moses, nestling on the luxurious couches of some of Ephesus's wealthy and open-minded citizens.

· 9 ·

GREEK FIRE

I N EPHESUS, Paul had emerged as an effective exorcist, a creative
exponent of Peter's teaching, and a powerful writer. Even Apollos's followers embraced his message about Spirit. At this
time Paul referred cordially to Apollos (1 Corinthians 16:12)[1] along
with many other colleagues and friends. He dispatched letters to distant congregations and his unforgettable rhetoric, which made the
rounds by word of mouth as well as on papyrus scrolls, brought him
fame.

Success bred ambition in Paul, as it does in most intellectuals.
Ephesus awakened the aspiration in his heart to bring his message about
Jesus to the Greco-Roman world as the one true gospel. His distinctive theology, as we have seen, embraced Peter's teaching about Spirit,
although he rejected Peter's and James' demand that Gentiles had to acknowledge the Torah as God-fearers did. Both in what he offered and
in what he did not demand, Paul knew he had crafted a vision that
could penetrate any culture.

In his mind, Ephesus was his spiritual beachhead for an invasion of
Greece. Armed with his new literary powers, he would reverse his earlier setbacks in Corinth. Antioch and Galatia to the east could take care

of themselves. They might excommunicate him, but his success in Ephesus proved that he didn't need their authority. He would press to the west, as he had agreed to do almost a decade earlier in Jerusalem. His confidence had never been greater.

His tactical flexibility was also at its height. Between what he wrote to the Galatian churches and what he wrote to their Corinthian counterparts (55–56 C.E.), there is a shift in tone and tactics. He had learned that expressions of open contempt were counterproductive. He doesn't say, "You stupid Corinthians!"[2] He had discovered more powerful means to project his authority from one city to another.

· · ·

PAUL BELIEVED HIS POWER resided in the Spirit that he aroused in his audience. That was so in Ephesus, and he thought he could make it happen in Corinth, where, just three years earlier, he had run into his old trouble with synagogues. His Ephesian experience suggested that the variety and pluralism of Hellenistic cities like Corinth might make them fertile ground for the salon Christianity that Priscilla and Aquila enabled him to develop. By writing a series of letters to Corinth, he wanted to remake his reputation there and fashion at least some Corinthian congregations into the salon model he had pioneered in Ephesus.

What English Bibles call "The First Letter of Paul to the Corinthians" is really just the first letter we happen to have from Paul to communities in Corinth, not the first letter he ever wrote them. He indicates that letters had been passing back and forth for some time and that the Jesus-salons Paul wanted to see started had prospered in the city. His principal informants were people from the congregation who met in the house of a woman named Chloe. By letter and personal contacts through trade, they kept Paul abreast of developments.

Paul wrote 1 Corinthians to deal with just the kinds of divisions you would expect in a salon culture (1 Corinthians 1:11–12): "Because it has been made clear to me about you, my brothers, by Chloe's people, that there are contentions among you. I mean this, that each of you says, 'I belong to Paul,' 'I belong to Apollos,' 'I belong to Cephas,' 'I belong to Christ.' "

Each salon claimed to be smarter than the next. Its members identified themselves by their favorite hero—Paul or Apollos or Peter. Salons are talking shops. Their intellectual ferment makes them appealing to educated people. They are often competitive and love their reputations as much as they love ideas; for them being in intellectual fashion is life's greatest pleasure while being out of fashion is more painful than sin itself. They try to trump each other. In the case of Corinth, some upwardly mobile warriors in the art of rhetoric got to saying—our hero is Christ.

Christian one-upmanship and disunity is not a recent invention. Once the congregation is a salon, defined not by connection with a synagogue but by the teacher who founded it, you can wind up with as many different kinds of churches as there are teachers. In the first century as in the twenty-first, the tendency toward factionalism came with the territory of extending Jesus' message to Gentiles.

Divisions among salons in Corinth threatened to undermine Paul's teaching that all believers receive a single Spirit. So he let his temper show (1 Corinthians 1:13): "Is Christ divided? Was Paul crucified for you, or were you baptized in Paul's name?" He got so worked up over his theme that he says he is happy he baptized only Crispus and Gaius, declaring categorically, "Christ did not delegate me to baptize, but to announce the Gospel" (1 Corinthians 1:14, 17). Yet he had to admit, "I did also baptize Stephanus's household—anyway, I don't know whether I baptized anyone else" (1 Corinthians 1:16)—a rhetorical shrug of the shoulders.

The self-assurance of this opening gambit is as striking as his cool assertion of authority. Look, he says, "I planted, Apollos watered, but God made for growth" (1 Corinthians 3:6). Unlike the case in Galatians, he doesn't go into a long explanation about his relationship with the apostles in Jerusalem. He presents no extended arguments on the basis of Scripture, and he refuses to beg or plead. He is confident enough that he makes a little joke about Apollos "watering" people—

a sly allusion to repeated immersions without reference to Spirit, which Apollos had practiced before Paul won him over to the teaching of Peter.

Paul stakes his claim to authority on the basis of the disclosure of Christ that brings the Spirit. Spirit in his mind was the one substance that could endure the conflagration that was to come (1 Corinthians 3:10–17). Whether you thought of the final dissolution of the world as the Stoic *ekpurosis* or the Jewish *Gehenna*, Paul insisted, Spirit alone could withstand that fire. Spirit was the greater fire, the eternal burning that Isaiah saw (Isaiah 33:14). Whatever was not of Spirit would perish.

Better than any other teacher in the New Testament, Jesus included, he drew others into this vision of the Spirit's fire. He won them over with compelling rhetoric, making them realize that the purpose of meeting in Christ's Spirit differed from the symposial entertainments that were a staple in their culture.

A salon could effectively realize Spirit because it did not bring with it the baggage of the synagogue, where arguments about circumcision and food laws were bound to prevail. Although they had the potential to spell triumph for Paul, salons could at any time degenerate into chatting shops for theological ideas. That was a far cry from their true status as "the Israel of God," his name for congregations filled with Spirit.

The very pluralism that gave him an entrée into salons had to be tamed for his own view of salvation to be maintained. He could only conceive of such a vast, creative project at the top of his form. That was just where he was, about to turn fifty, in full control of his argumentative range. 1 Corinthians is, in literary terms, his greatest achievement, perhaps the finest single piece of writing in the New Testament. It is rich in insight, theology, and emotion, beautifully coordinated to the specific circumstances addressed, and filled with prose so vivid—especially as rendered in the King James Version—it can take its stand alongside the poetry of any culture.

Where is Paul's famous hymn on the eternity of love?—1 Corinthians 13 (v. 1): "Though I speak with the tongues of men and of angels, and have not charity, I am become as sounding brass, or a tinkling cymbal." Where does he explain how the whole Church belongs to the organic whole of Christ's body?—1 Corinthians 12 (vv. 12–13): "For as the body is one, and hath many members, and all the members of that one body, being many, are one body: so also is Christ. For by one Spirit are we all baptized into one body, whether we be Jews or Gentiles, whether we be bond or free; and have been all made to drink into one Spirit."

Where does he set out the importance and hierarchy of spiritual gifts?—1 Corinthians 14 (v. 5): "I would that ye all spake with tongues, but rather that ye prophesied: for greater is he that prophesieth than he that speaketh with tongues, except he interpret, that the church may receive edifying." Where is his account of Jesus' last meal with his disciples, the earliest Eucharistic text in the New Testament?—1 Corinthians 11 (v. 26): "For as often as ye eat this bread, and drink this cup, ye do shew the Lord's death till he come." Where does he spell out how Jesus was raised from the dead and how believers will be raised?—1 Corinthians 15 (vv. 50–52): "Now this I say, brethren, that flesh and blood cannot inherit the kingdom of God; neither doth corruption inherit incorruption. Behold, I shew you a mystery; We shall not all sleep, but we shall all be changed. In a moment, in the twinkling of an eye, at the last trump: for the trumpet shall sound, and the dead shall be raised incorruptible, and we shall be changed." These words have resonated for nearly two millennia since they were written; the chapters in which they appear are so masterful that, line for line, they have influenced Christian thought and practice more than any other Scriptures.

Paul wrote this letter knowing how good he was, and how high he stood in the estimation of his followers. In addition to his perennial ability, he had clout for the first time in his life and was very secure about using it. Having chided the salons for their factionalism, he asked them with studied majesty: "What do you want? Shall I come to you with a rod, or in love, in a spirit of gentleness?" (1 Corinthians 4:21)

That "rod" was a matter of the force he could exert when he was present personally, the kind of exorcistic power he was celebrated for in Ephesus. His letters deliberately try to invoke that power, and I Corinthians shows precisely how Paul thought his authority could be brought to bear in his absence. That was his step beyond the catapult he had unleashed in writing to the Galatians.

. . .

"Shall I come to you with a rod, or in love?" Paul struck so fiercely and accurately that commentators still struggle to get their minds around what he was doing at this point. It is hard to believe that Paul said what he said—harder still to accept that he meant what his words say. True, he was genuinely angry about some goings-on in Corinth. A man there was bedding a woman who had been his father's wife (I Corinthians 5:1). This was off the chart of permissible behavior even "among the Gentiles" and violated Paul's principle that everyone should "keep one's own vessel in sanctification and honor, and not in the passion of lust just like the Gentiles who do not know God" (I Thessalonians 4:4–5).

But what he then tells the salons goes beyond anger. He judges the Corinthians in absentia (I Corinthians 5:3–5): "For absent in body but present in the Spirit, I have already judged—as being present—the man who has behaved this way. In the name of our Lord Jesus, when you have gathered and my spirit is with the power of our Lord Jesus—turn over such a man to Satan for destruction of the flesh, so that the spirit might be saved in the day of the Lord."

Paul projects his own spirit into the worship of the Corinthian salons: "when you have gathered and my spirit is with the power of our Lord Jesus." He is there with the risen Jesus, judging an egregious case of impurity.

This kind of commanding confidence has prompted many of Paul's readers, ancient and modern, to accuse him of arrogance. His plan for the salons is clear and audacious. They are to meet as a séance. If the word "séance" seems strong to you, consider that the salons were already baptizing people who had died. They invoked the dead in prayer so that they could be retroactively immersed in Jesus' name (15:29).[3] Christ was an eternal reality, reaching backward as well as forward in time, not only across every physical boundary. These communities believed in life after death and invoked the presence of the departed in their worship. Among those invoked, Paul said that the risen Jesus and he, the absent Paul, would condemn the man who profaned his own body and the body of his stepmother.

In Paul's own mind he was a spiritual force alongside Jesus. Together they directed the course of worship, exorcised impurity, and focused the punitive power of the community of the chosen people.

"Absent in body but present in the Spirit"—this phrase is now a cliché. But in the way of clichés, it betrays the power that produced its wording in the first place. Paul's presence in the Spirit was no warm reassurance of his general goodwill, but a searing judgment, spurning the nameless man, casting him out into the world of the flesh, where destruction awaited him. Baptism made the body a temple by the indwelling of Spirit, and impure acts defiled that temple (1 Corinthians 3:16; 6:19; 2 Corinthians 6:16). Paul allowed for the possibility that such a person might finally be restored in spirit at the moment of apocalyptic destruction, but the fornicator had no part whatever in the transformed community of the faithful who enjoyed the presence and power of divine Spirit. Paul plainly says that it is *he* who decides who belongs to the body of Christ and who does not, and that he does that at a distance, "in the Spirit."

. . .

WAS PAUL SOME KIND OF shaman, whose powers included astral projection? He prided himself in the many "signs of the apostle" he performed (2 Corinthians 12:12), including exorcisms and healings. Visions sometimes disoriented him so much he couldn't say exactly where they occurred, "whether in body, I do not know, or outside the body, I do not know" (2 Corinthians 12:2). The Corinthian case of impurity brought him to the point where he claimed he catapulted his spirit into the city to exercise judgment with Jesus (1 Corinthians 5:3–5). How can his shamanic side be denied?[4]

After all, Jesus clearly exercises shamanic powers in the Gospels— when he stills the storm, appears to his disciples walking on water, and joins Moses and Elijah in the glory that surrounds God's chariot-throne, for example.[5] Paul associated himself with Jesus as an apostle of commanding spirit. But he went out of his way to stress his dependence on Jesus. Paul exorcised, healed, and experienced visions but fell short of the highest prophetic attainment of the Hebrew shamans: Elijah, Elisha, the Galilean mystics who joined the heavenly ascent of Enoch, and Jesus himself. They were so skilled in the vision of God's presence in his chariot that their disciples saw each of them associated with that chariot. The shamanic prophets not only had visions; they themselves *became* visions for their disciples.

Not every mystic is an adept of the chariot-throne, a Merkabah mystic. Paul's conversion shows that. In the same way, not everyone who speaks of projecting his spirit beyond his body to another location is a shaman. The Corinthians' worship did not center on the practices of Merkabah mysticism, a practice limited for the most part to territorial Israel, but the evidence for a different set of *Hellenistic* mystical practices in Corinth and elsewhere in the Diaspora is rich and deep.

During their worship, Paul says the Corinthians became "wild about spirits" (1 Corinthians 14:12). He provides the earliest description there is of the spiritual rapture that has inspired Christians, ancient and modern, to esoteric accomplishments that range from snake-handling to apocalyptic trance. These meetings peaked in communal ecstasy (1 Corinthians 14:26–33), crescendos of psalms, teachings, revelations, speech in strange languages, apocalypses, interpretations, and prophecies.

Paul encouraged that activity and more. The one Spirit of God produced all these blessings, and within the single body of Christ, God bestowed many different charismata (1 Corinthians 12:4–12): wisdom, knowledge, faith, healings, wonders, prophecy, discernments of spirits, strange new languages, and their interpretation.

These gifts in Paul's view amounted to guiding principles of the Church: apostles, prophets, teachers, wonders, gifts of healings, the willingness to support and to lead, varieties of tongues (1 Corinthians 12:27–31), culminating in faith, hope, and love (1 Corinthians 13). The mysticism of the Corinthian communities focused on the Spirit of God rather than the divine chariot-throne. These groups were no less committed than their Galilean counterparts, but the idiom of their spiritual practice was different.

Paul's description also makes it plain that worship in Corinthian salons could decay into chaos; he uses his own authority to wrestle unity out of their spontaneous outbursts. He wonders aloud whether a curious visitor to a salon church might not come to the conclusion that the participants were simply crazy (1 Corinthians 14:23). Spirit-possession and prophecy were regular features of magical and religious practice in the Greco-Roman world, but by any standard Corinthian spirituality could become strange.

Paul had to face that head-on (1 Corinthians 12:1–3): "Concerning spiritual matters, brothers, I do not want you ignorant. Because you know that when you were Gentiles you were led astray toward dumb idols: therefore I make known to you that no one speaking by God's Spirit says, Jesus be damned! And no one is able to say, Jesus is Lord, except by Holy Spirit!" There is only one reason Paul would have said this: some members of the Corinthian salons had declared their spiritual liberation from Jesus! They anticipated the Gnostic Christians of the second century who separated the man Jesus from the divine principle of Christ. Paul associates this separation with the idolatrous drift from god to god that typified Gentiles in his mind.

Magic had been part of the Corinthians' lives, and continued to exert its influence. Paul's task was to identify those magical elements that expressed Spirit (such as the invocation of Jesus' power and his own apostolic presence), exorcise those that did not (such as cursing Jesus), and to do that from the distance of Ephesus. Like a sorcerer, Paul could invoke his presence apart from his physical body.

The rich literature of magic from this period shows that the persona of the magus was prominent within the Greco-Roman world. Philo compares Moses to a magician and philosopher engaged in esoteric thought and practice (*On the Life of Moses* 1.1–95). In particular, because the Stoics conceived of the human soul as correlating to the divine *logos* that governed the universe, they could attribute the capacity to travel through time and space to the accomplished sage. Paul spoke as both a magician and a philosopher—in short, as an occult intellectual of both Judaism and Stoicism—when he called on the Corinthians to invoke his spirit in their worship.

Throughout 1 Corinthians, Paul, the exorcist, inveighs against idolatry. The issue for him is not an abstract challenge to monotheism, but reflects his awareness that the séances of Corinth were multiplying the "spirits" that were available; Christ indeed looked "divided." The case of the man "having" his father's wife (1 Corinthians 5:1) exemplified what Paul detested most: pagan indulgence and loose sex, trademarks of Corinth.[6] He shared the prejudice of millions of his coreligionists in believing that non-Jews, left to their own devices, would spend the whole of their time finding new gods to worship and inventing new permutations of sexual coupling.

. . .

DURING THIS PERIOD, Paul's confidence was at its height; the synergy between his standing in Ephesus and his impact on Corinth galvanized his thinking, and 1 Corinthians is the apogee of his rhetorical and intellectual achievement. His touch for the situation in Corinth was way ahead of his clumsy fulminations against the Galatians. He had Chloe, rich and influential, on the spot, and an even wealthier patron, named Stephanus.

Stephanus's contacts were as far-ranging as Priscilla's and Aquila's and, with his friends Fortunatus and Achaicus, he gave Paul a financial platform such as no other Christian teacher of the time enjoyed (1 Corinthians 16:15–18). With that kind of backing, Paul no longer needed to work with his hands or get financial support from Antioch or depend on friendly synagogues.

Not that he wanted any divorce from Israel: he boasted at least two colleagues who maintained their contacts with synagogues in Corinth. Sosthenes had taken the heat for Paul back in 52 C.E. and proudly coauthored the letter of 55–56 C.E. as Paul's junior partner (1 Corinthians 1:1).[7] Timothy, always an important contact man for Paul in Greece and the Hellenistic eastern area of Asia Minor, became Paul's personal agent in Corinth, his own "beloved and faithful child" (1 Corinthians 4:17). Timothy went from Ephesus to Corinth and back again both to represent Paul's teaching and to report on how this teaching was faring. By his mixed background, with his Jewish mother and Greek father, Timothy embodied the cosmic thrust of Paul's message, its uncompromising insistence that Christ transformed the whole of humanity.

No Christian thinker before or since has thought on so cosmic a scale, linking God's Spirit to humanity's and both to the transformation of the world. The picture he conveyed of what it meant for even small groups of believers to meet together involved them in a literal reshaping of the universe. The same Spirit that made the world, hovering over the face of the primeval waters and descending upon each believer at baptism, infused the meetings of every congregation, joining Paul's spirit and Jesus' power in the judgment that would free the world of its old shape and give it new form. That transformation was doubly powerful because at the same time it occurred at the intimate level of each believer's own body.

The transformation of body and self and world were all happening at once, "in Christ,"[8] as Paul repeatedly said. He articulated his prophetic philosophy of transformation with the certainty of a zealot and the precision of a scientist. When Paul described this bodily transformation, he reached back to his personal experience on the road to Damascus.

He crafted a metaphysical language of resurrection to refer to a reality beyond this world that nonetheless unmakes and remakes this world (1 Corinthians 15:35–44):

But someone will say, "How are the dead raised, and with what sort of body do they come?" Fool, what you yourself sow does not become alive unless it dies! And what do you sow? You do not sow the body that shall be, but a bare germ, perhaps of wheat or of another grain. But God gives to it a body exactly as he wants, and to each of the seeds its own body. Not all flesh is the same flesh, but one of humans, another flesh of animals, another flesh of birds, another of fish. And there are heavenly bodies and earthly bodies, but one is the glory of the heavenly and another of the earthly. Sun's glory is one and moon's glory another, and another stars' glory, because star differs from star in glory. So also is the resurrection of the dead. Sown in decay, it is raised in incorruption; sown in dishonor, it is raised in glory; sown in weakness, it is raised in power; sown a physic body, it is raised a spiritual body.

There is not a more exact statement of the process of resurrection in the whole of Christian literature, and Paul's words have had a firm place in Christian liturgies of burial. Their particular genius is the insight that resurrection involves a new creative act by God, what Paul calls a "new creation" (2 Corinthians 5:17; Galatians 6:15). Morally and existentially, the hope of the resurrection involves a fresh, fulfilled humanity.

When Paul thought of a person, he conceived of a body as composed of flesh, a physical substance that varies from one created thing to another (people, animals, birds, fish). But in addition to being physical bodies, people are also what Paul called "psychic bodies," by which he meant bodies with souls. Unfortunately, most modern versions of the Bible mistranslate this phrase. They distort Paul's language by having him speak of a "natural" or "physical body"; his own word at this point (1 Corinthians 15:44) is *psukhikon*, an adjective derived directly from the noun for "soul" *(psukhe)*. Bodies for Paul are not just lumps of flesh: they are self-aware or self-conscious. That self-awareness is precisely what makes them "psychic."

In addition to being physical body and psychic body, Paul says we are—or can become—"spiritual body." The first human being became "a living soul"; Jesus is the last Adam or final person, becoming "life-giving Spirit" (1 Corinthians 15:45). He is a new template for humanity. People can pass beyond being material and beyond their awareness of their own limited lives. They can become spiritual bodies: infused with Spirit, God-conscious, framed in Christ's image instead of Adam's (1 Corinthians 15:47–49): "The first person was from earth, dust; the second person from heaven. Such as the dust person is, so are those of dust; such as the heavenly person is, such are those of heaven. And just as we have born the image of the dust person, we shall bear also the image of the heavenly person."

That was why "We shall all be changed" (1 Corinthians 15:51): everyone, everywhere, without exception. God played for keeps, and his Spirit began its work in the little salons of Christians that dotted the Mediterranean world.

. . .

EVEN THOSE IN CORINTH who thought Paul was ugly and an ineffective speaker had to admit his achievement in this letter (2 Corinthians 10:10): "His letters, they declare, are weighty and strong, but his bodily presence weak and the discourse contemptible!"

Paul is proof that you don't have to be a genius all your life to break through and discover an idea of genius. His teaching in regard to resurrection, expressed in 1 Corinthians, gave Christianity the engine that powers its hope. Interpreting these words has naturally been a topic of controversy, but no believer can deny that this is a topic that demands controversy, because how one believes in resurrection defines the kind of Christian a person is.

Paul savored the genius of his idea. He insisted on it, along with Peter's teaching about Spirit, and on his own authority to catapult himself into Corinth. In his insistence, he ran up against the very nature of the salons that had been his making. Salons by definition can explore any idea and engage in any activity that polite company will tolerate. They are freewheeling, irreverent, and fully capable of replacing one intellectual icon with another. They trade in opinion and move freely from idea to idea.

The salon's leader, if he or she wants the group to focus on a single, radical idea, needs to harness the salon's discursive tendencies. Paul illustrates this process as he writes to the Corinthians. He goes to the heart of the salon's ethos and insists that, in its dedication to Christ, its very identity needs to change (1 Corinthians 1:20–24):

> Where is the sage, where the scribe, where the debater of this epoch? Didn't God render the wisdom of the world foolish? Because since— in God's wisdom—the world did not know God through wisdom, God took pleasure in saving those who believe through the foolishness of the proclamation. Since Jews demand signs and Greeks search for wisdom, we proclaim Christ crucified, an obstacle to Jews, foolishness to Gentiles, but to those who are called, both Jews and Greeks, Christ is God's power and God's wisdom.

Paul is saying that wisdom is not merely a matter of swapping opinions. Rather, it flows from Spirit, the informing power of the universe. So when he asks his rhetorical question—"Where is the sage, where the scribe, where the debater of this epoch?"—he has in mind only one answer. This present time, which was passing away, offered no wisdom and no agent of wisdom. Only the likes of Paul, delegated by revelation from the world to come, God's kingdom, could offer the truth that endures.

Paul admitted to being the "least of the apostles who is not worthy to be called apostle, because I persecuted the church of God" (1 Corinthians 15:9). But that did not make him feel inferior: "I don't think I come up short of the most eminent apostles. Even if I am an incompetent in discourse—that is not knowledge" (2 Corinthians 11:5–6). And he had no doubt about what he knew. He had explained to the civilized world how it was going to hell in a handbasket, and how the cross of Christ alone gave proof of life beyond the dust and ashes of final judgment.

HE AND JESUS, Paul insisted, mediated the world's final transformation. They understood the promptings of the Spirit; together they conveyed power and wisdom to congregation after congregation. 1 Corinthians is indeed weighty—and brilliant to the point of genius. But alongside that undoubted achievement, Paul also managed to estrange himself from the very communities he tried to discipline. What he said could seem blatantly self-serving. He had the knack of going a good step or two too far when things went his way, and his attempts to legislate on behalf of the Spirit of God struck many as shameless, insufferable, and arrogant.

He took the occasion of condemning the incest of the man with his father's wife to legislate about marriage. Or rather, to legislate against it (1 Corinthians 7:1–2): "Concerning the matters of which you wrote, it is good for a man not to touch a woman; but because of fornication, each man can have his own wife and each woman her own husband." He had never been married. The only recommendation he can come up with for marriage is that it is, as he says later—"better to marry than to burn" (1 Corinthians 7:9). Despite his inexperience and disinclination, he appoints himself the Ephesian Dr. Ruth.

All this, remember, centuries before the vow of celibacy became widespread in Christian practice. In fact, he admits his view is unusual, asking rhetorically (1 Corinthians 9:5): "Don't we have authority to travel with a sister as wife, like the rest of the apostles and the brothers of the Lord—even Cephas?" He knew he was out of step with his colleagues and recognized that it would have helped the perception of his status if he had married. His personal choice meant more to him than his status.

The promptings of the Spirit and his own preferences got mixed up in his mind within his role as an apostolic teacher. He openly says (1 Corinthians 7:7): "I want all people to be as I am myself, although each person has one's own gift from God, one person this way, and another that way." So which is it?: is everybody to be like him, or are all to be different?

Paul virtually admits to the tangle he is in by referring to Jesus' teaching about marriage: once two people married and became "one flesh," God demanded faithfulness and intimacy from the couple

(1 Corinthians 7:1–16).[9] Still, to Paul, marriage was an institution of this world, a world that was passing away (1 Corinthians 7:17–31). As far as he was concerned, he was an emissary from another, eternal world, a world that had no room for touching women. In heaven, flesh was irrelevant; copulating, like eating and drinking, had no place. In view of Jesus' teaching, Paul can't actually forbid marriage. But he can give his opinion (1 Corinthians 7:40), adding, "and I think I also have God's Spirit."

By this stage he had no doubt lost many of his Corinthian readers. Compared to James and Peter, he was making an extraordinary demand: to give up sex as a vanishing artifact of this world. Compared to Paul's teaching, even the requirement of circumcision by Christian Pharisees seemed moderate.

To this day churches try to save Paul from himself. They restrict his requirement to bishops (in the Orthodox Church) or priests (in the Roman Catholic Church) or friars (in the Anglican Church), or to those who wish to take on Paul's lifestyle as a personal vow (as in many churches, Protestant and otherwise). But they are defeated by Paul's words. For Paul, the end of the world was so near that intelligent, responsible believers should dispense with any encumbrance, marriage included.

Paul not only made peculiar demands about sexuality, he told the Corinthians what food to put in their mouths—and insisted upon the superiority of his own position. Never mind that it was changing all the time. No wonder that to many of his contemporaries he seemed not only shameless but insufferable.

The church in Corinth was grappling with the question of what to do about food sacrificed to idols (1 Corinthians 8:1). Many believers in Corinth had been dedicated idolaters prior to their baptism; that was one reason that Paul explicitly wanted his readers to separate themselves from the trappings of idolatry, which could include reveling and all kinds of prostitution (1 Corinthians 6:9b–10, see also 5:9–13): "Don't be deceived, neither fornicators nor idolaters[10] nor adulterers nor soft boys nor guy-lovers nor thieves nor enviers nor drunks nor revilers nor frauds shall inherit God's kingdom." Once

drunks nor revilers nor frauds shall inherit God's kingdom." Once
again he is crude, to the point, and makes life almost impossible for his
pious interpreters.

But why did that trenchant rejection of idolatrous custom not extend to the old practice of eating idol-meat? Paul insisted that what he
said in the dispute with Peter in Antioch still stood. Pagan believers
could not be compelled to observe rules of food purity, and that included James' stricture against eating idol meat. He even added a new
justification for his view (1 Corinthians 8:4): "We know that there is
no idol in the world, and that there is no God but one." Idols don't
really exist, Paul said, so you eat what you like.

But what if a host made a big fuss, offering a luscious roast in honor
of Artemis or Zeus or some other god? After all, the Corinthians came
from just this kind of background. Should a Christian just wolf down
the idolatry with the meat?

Paul responded by crafting his own version of James' stricture. If
you are at a meal and another guest is present who might actually believe in idols if you gave the example of eating idol-meat, then don't
eat the meat. Here (1 Corinthians 8:9–13) he invokes a fresh principle
to revamp his old position about idols: "Therefore if food trips up my
brother, I will not ever eat meat."

It is as if he were in a competition with James. James favored
Israelite circumcision while accepting Gentile converts; Paul priori-
tized celibacy and accepted marriage only as a necessity. James insisted
that idol-meat was not to be eaten; Paul was willing, in theory, to become a vegetarian if that was what it took to avoid giving offense by
eating meat. What were the Corinthians, living in the midst of idolatry, to make of Paul's teaching? When should they invoke the principle that idols were nothing, and when should they help others
not to engage in destructive worship? Paul was asking a lot, and he
knew it.

When pressed for his reasons, he demanded even more obedience
(1 Corinthians 9:1–2): "Am I not free? Am I not an apostle? Have I not
seen our Lord Jesus? Are you not my work in the Lord? If I am not an

apostle to others, yet I am to you, because you are my seal of apostolate in the Lord!" This assertion is so raw and vulnerable, many commentators have surmised that a different letter has been spliced in at this point. But the flow of thought is natural once you have allowed for Paul's temper and temperament, and for the simple fact that he knew his beliefs about idol-meat didn't square with his views on sexuality. In the one case he dismissed considerations of purity, and in the other he tightened them up.

He voices his awareness of this inconsistency with fearless clarity in an attempt to make it into a virtue (1 Corinthians 9:19–22): "Free from all people, I have enslaved myself to all, so that I might gain more. And I became to Jews as a Jew, so that I might gain Jews, to those under law as under law—not as being myself under law—so that I might gain those under law, to the lawless as lawless—not as being lawless for God, but within law for Christ—so that I might gain the lawless. For the weak I became weak, so that I might gain the weak. I became everything to all, so that I might by all means save some."

The heroic meter of this boast cannot conceal its insufferable incongruity. He observes food laws with Jews and ignores them with Gentiles; he refuses idol-meat when occasion demands but eats away at other times. Here he is telling the Corinthians exactly how he conducts himself in Ephesus; the Ephesians needed no reminder of his behavior. Writing to salon after salon, Paul composed a song for himself even as he addressed the concerns of fledgling communities of Christians in Corinth.

So Paul did seem arrogant. He even thought that his cultural preferences should outweigh local customs: in some ways everybody was supposed to behave as if they came from Tarsus. His peremptory command about women still takes people's breath away (1 Corinthians 11:5–6): "But every woman praying or prophesying with uncovered head shames her head, because it is one and the same to being shaven! For if a woman doesn't cover herself, she shall be shorn, and if it is disgraceful for a woman to be shorn or shaved—she will be covered!"

The *burka* we associate with Islam is no Muslim invention, but had been well established during Paul's time in Tarsus. He knew the Corinthians too well to know that he could not stop Greek and Roman ladies in their households flaunting flimsy linen, their curves, and the odd flash of pale skin. But he felt full enough of Spirit to insist that they cover up in meetings for worship. People who made their living from sexual license simply could not inherit the kingdom of God, and any display of female skin or hair ran a similar risk as far as Paul was concerned.

He tried to mount an argument for his aversion to female flesh, but this attempt was a ruin. First he says, thinking of the book of Genesis (2:22, leaving aside 1:27), "man is not made from woman, but woman from man," but then he turns around and remembers his own principle that "neither is woman apart from man nor man apart from woman," because both are equally from God (1 Corinthians 11:8–12). All he really manages to show is that he has no argument, and that he has let his own preferences run rampant.

He also insisted that women had no rightful part in community debate. Commentators have scoured ways to take the sting out of Paul's words on the subject, and when that fails, to attribute them to some later copyist. But this special pleading doesn't work. The phrasing is Paul's, the sentiment typically Pauline, the arrogance unmistakable (1 Corinthians 14:33b–35): "As in all the churches of the holy ones, the women in the churches will keep silent, because it is not appropriate for them to speak, but they shall be subordinated, just as the Law says. And if they want to learn something, they will inquire of their own husbands at home, because it is disgraceful for a woman to speak in church."

So much for Chloe, for Priscilla, for Lydia—however valuable they were to Paul, however equal to him in Christ. In this world, passing away though it was, he feared the turn-on of women's voices as much as the sight of their hair and skin. Those enticements could ruin a congregation; at one point he even suggests that the sight of female hair might distract any angels in church attendance (1 Corinthians 11:10).

Women were neither to be seen nor heard when men were around—apart from their husbands, that is, because marriage had cured them of flaming passion.

In his overwhelming concentration on Spirit, Paul had a real problem with flesh: the "one flesh" of a married couple, the flesh you eat, and female flesh. He fumbled with all those topics, experimenting with approaches as occasion demanded, never achieving consistency, convincing relatively few of his readers in his time or ours.

. . .

WITH PAUL at the safe distance of Ephesus, the Corinthians could keep up their lively correspondence with him and filter out his outbursts of temperament as they read, interpreted, qualified, or disregarded what he said. The Ephesians didn't have that luxury. They had Paul in their midst, well funded and as full of himself as he was of God's Spirit. Something had to go wrong, and it did.

The pluralism of Ephesus had enabled Paul to establish his base of influence. That pluralism was grounded in what scholars of religion call the syncretism of Greco-Roman culture, the "joining together" (as the term *sunkretismos* means in Greek) of the multiple cults and philosophies that streamed into the city, forming new hybrids and combinations. Paul represented a fascinating hybrid of Judaism and Stoicism: a philosopher-rabbi with a skillful and potent mix of beliefs, practices, and esoteric techniques he had learned in Tarsus and Jerusalem.

Yet the syncretistic culture of Ephesus drew his fire. In this case, literal fire went along with the fire of Paul's spirit. A single verse in Acts, describing what some of Paul's followers in Ephesus did, provides everything we need to know to understand why—despite all his success—he had to depart from that city, and why he never returned (Acts 19:19): "A large number of those who had practiced charms brought together the books and burned them in front of all, and they estimated their prices and hit upon fifty thousand silver drachmas."

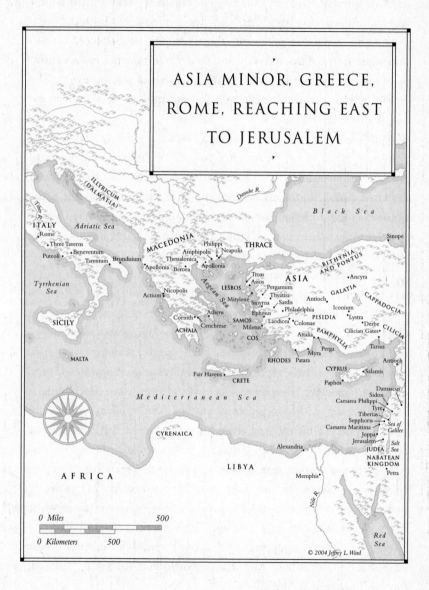

ASIA MINOR, GREECE, ROME, REACHING EAST TO JERUSALEM

Black Sea

ITALY
Adriatic Sea
Rome
Three Taverns
Puteoli
Beneventum
Tarentum
Brundisium

ILLYRICUM
(DALMATIA)

Danube R.

Sinope

MACEDONIA
Philippi
Amphipolis
Neapolis
Thessalonica
Apollonia
Apollonia
Beroea

THRACE

BITHYNIA
AND PONTUS

Tyrrhenian Sea

Nicopolis
Actium

Troas
Assos
ASIA
Ancyra

Aegean Sea
LESBOS
Pergamum
Mitylene
Thyatira
Smyrna
Sardis
Ephesus
Philadelphia

Antioch
GALATIA
CAPPADOCIA

Iconium

SICILY

Athens
Corinth
Cenchreae
ACHAIA
SAMOS
Miletus
Laodicea
Colossae
PISIDIA
Lystra
Derbe
CILICIA
Cilician Gates

COS

Attalia
PAMPHYLIA
Perga
Myra
Tarsus

MALTA

RHODES
Patara

Antioch

Fair Havens
CRETE

CYPRUS
Salamis
Paphos

Mediterranean Sea

Damascus
Sidon
Caesarea Philippi
Tyre
Tiberias
Sepphoris
Sea of Galilee
Caesarea Maritima
Joppa
Jerusalem
JUDEA
Salt Sea
NABATEAN KINGDOM
Petra

CYRENAICA

Alexandria

LIBYA

AFRICA

Memphis

Nile R.

0 Miles   500

0 Kilometers   500

Red Sea

© 2004 Jeffrey L. Ward

In his conviction that there is no true idol in the world, as he told the Corinthians, Paul got his Ephesian disciples—or at least the most zealous of them—to burn their own idolatrous scrolls in public—the expense be damned together with those who served such idols! He had catapulted spiritual fire into Corinth to deal with fornication and now, in 56 C.E., he had his followers set the trappings of idolatry alight. The same zeal that had once made him a persecutor of Jesus' movement found a new target.

Paul knew the danger he was in: he had publicly insulted the Ephesian ethos of toleration. Acts speaks of his planning to leave Ephesus for Jerusalem right after the book-burning (Acts 19:21), and at the close of 1 Corinthians he confirms that intention. Realizing that Ephesus could no longer serve him as a safe haven, he hatched a new and desperate scheme. With support in Ephesus crumbling and Antioch off limits, he decided to return to Jerusalem.

Despite his frosty reception there by James in 52 C.E., Paul's previous agreement with James and his colleagues in 46 C.E. to collect resources for the "poor" of Jerusalem (Galatians 2:10) still stood. He plotted a triumphant return to the holy city, bringing with him another collection for the Nazirites of James' circle, greater than his earlier gifts, together with his new reputation as a zealous activist against idolatry. His plan included a journey to Corinth and north into Macedonia as well as contact with congregations in Asia Minor, all in an effort to swell the size of his offering. Paul leaves no doubt that this time he hopes to raise a lot of money quickly (1 Corinthians 16:1–4): "Concerning the collection that is for the holy ones, just as I ordered the churches in Galatia, so you do, as well. Every first day of the week, each of you will set aside from his own, storing whatever he prospers in, so that when I come collections don't happen. When I have arrived, whomever you approve, these I will send with letters, to bear your grace to Jerusalem. And if it is worthwhile for me to proceed, they will proceed with me."

Real money, together with his success in Ephesus, would bring him the support of Jerusalem. That was his gamble, and he states explicitly that he won't even try it unless his efforts prove "worthwhile." With support from wealthy congregations like those in Corinth, he would no longer need to use Ephesus as a base. He offered to bring donors in his entourage for the Jerusalem pilgrimage, but it was a matter of pay before you go.

Although he expressed urgency to get on with his projected journey, he also acknowledged that he had to remain in Ephesus until Pentecost (1 Corinthians 16:5–8). His succinct description of the situation is characteristic (v. 9): "Because a great and effective gate has been opened to me, and opponents are many." Nothing like lots of enemies to make his apostolic day.

In fact, what Paul considered a wonderful opportunity was a riot that nearly got him killed. The events are reported in Acts (19:23–41). They turn on the attitude toward Paul, not in any churches or synagogues in Ephesus, but in the city at large. His public profile in the school of Tyrannus, capped by burning scrolls in a public square, had brought him head-to-head with hard realities, economic as well as religious.

No visitor to Ephesus can fail to be impressed with the magnificent sculptures of the gods and goddesses of the local pantheon. To this day a beautiful statue of the goddess Nike (Victory) lies just to the north of the odeon, looking for all the world like a renaissance angel. The care of the workmanship is stunning; so was the expense involved. Along with work in stone, Ephesian craftsmen made household idols in silver and gold. These little gods were more affordable than larger sculptures.

Paul's preaching was more aggressive than the usual Jewish objection to idols. He didn't even accord them the respect of treating them as dangerous. He said they were useless, and if his followers treated scrolls like firewood, what would they do to the silver images of Artemis? She was the great protector of the Ephesians, named after the Greek goddess of the hunt, but boasting the form of Kuballe, the flesh-eating matriarch of Asia Minor's pantheon. Her temple outside the city was one of the seven wonders of the world.

A local silversmith named Demetrios came to Artemis's defense. He whipped up Ephesian pride against Paul, citing his threat to the trade in idols and his affront to religious piety (Acts 19:24–27). Demetrios's mob stormed through Ephesus, shouting out "Great is Artemis of the Ephesians!"; they beat Paul's followers and tracked down the apostle himself. Public order threatened to dissolve completely. Two of Paul's disciples, Gaius and Aristarchus, were dragged into the enormous theater, a place for spectacle, pageant, gladiatorial combat, and the execution of prisoners using wild animals. Thousands of people filled the stone benches, joining in Demetrios's chant, "Great is the Artemis of the Ephesians!" (Acts 19:28–34) In the contest between the new religion Paul preached and civic pride, civic pride won hands down.

Paul himself was imprisoned. This was probably the third time his back encountered the lictor's rod. According to Acts, officials did not permit him to go to the theater to defend himself before the crowd. Yet he said to the Corinthians, "If by human standards I fought with beasts in Ephesus, what benefit is that to me?" (1 Corinthians 15:32) Was he dragged out into the theater after all and threatened with animals? Probably not—the officials clearly appreciated that putting Paul in the middle of a violent dispute was a bad idea. That qualifying phrase Paul uses, "by human standards" *(kata anthropon)*, suggests that he had to argue with officials while Gaius and Aristarchus were actually in the arena. By keeping Paul out of the way, the officials calmed the rioting audience with their own arguments.

For all his achievements, his mastery of the language and practice of the Spirit, Paul had ruptured the peace of Ephesus. During the riot even the Jews of the city had been shouted down when they tried to intervene on Paul's behalf (Acts 19:33–34). By acting as he did, aggressively attacking the ancestral religion of his host city, he had made himself, many members of his movement, and those Jews who defended him contemptible in Ephesus.

He never did return, and it is hard to believe that caused widespread lamentation. To the civic authorities the book-burning apostle rivaled the rioting silversmith in nuisance value—and provided no economic benefit. Paul himself, for all his brave words about the "great and effective gate" Ephesus had opened to him, knew that the riot had closed the door to any hope of his remaining there. Jerusalem—and therefore the success of his collection for the Nazirites in that city—held out the last chance for Paul to have his apostolic work endorsed.

· 10 ·

SACRIFICE IN THE TEMPLE

P AUL'S EPHESIAN BASE had crumbled; Demetrios's riot
trampled more than three years of constructive work. Paul's
congregations could no longer harbor their iconoclastic apostle—he put them at risk of mob violence. Ferocious pride and absolute confidence in his apostolic calling pushed him to attempt his most
audacious maneuver ever. Now, as before, defeat ratcheted up Paul's
ambition: resistance only proved to him that the apocalyptic crisis
was imminent. He decided to move himself and his closest colleagues
to—of all cities—Rome. Paul wanted to make the Ephesian fracas
into an opportunity for the great, westward sweep of the gospel that
Isaiah had predicted, and that had impelled his vision since his time
with Silas.

He spelled out his planned itinerary and acknowledged the impossi-
bility of staying around Ephesus in his letter to the Romans (15:23–25):
"But now I no longer have a place in these regions, but I've had a longing to come to you for many years, whenever I proceed into Spain.
Because as I proceed through I hope to see you, and to be provisioned
by you there, if I may first enjoy you a little. But now I proceed to
Jerusalem, ministering to the holy ones."

First offer the collection in Jerusalem; then travel to Rome and on to the west. That was the plan, plainly specified, a single plan, not two unrelated projects for travel. For Paul the road to Rome led through Jerusalem. Only by traveling from there could he arrive in Rome as an apostle delegated by the top leaders of his movement. At the time he wrote to the Romans, he was by his own admission an apostolic refugee without a "place" to call his own, because he had worn out his welcome in Ephesus. He could do with a more impressive introduction than that. Moreover, his pilgrimage to Jerusalem focused efforts throughout the churches he contacted to support the "holy ones" there and at the same time give Paul himself material support. His reference to being "provisioned" by the Romans was not an incidental concern. The sacrifice in the Temple and the extension of the gospel as far west as the mind could conceive were for Paul two movements in a single, divine symphony.

The particular situation of the Roman churches made Jerusalem's endorsement all the more important for Paul. Priscilla and Aquila were in a position to warn him of the damage caused by Claudius's edict in 49 C.E., which expelled many Jews from the city. True, this meant that Gentile Christians now outnumbered Jews who believed in Christ, but it also made relations difficult between the two groups; fresh outbreaks of violence threatened. Anyone who increased the risk of turmoil among Christians in Rome also increased the odds of yet another disastrous imperial edict.

To do any good, Paul had to arrive in Rome as a reconciler of Christian Jews and pagan Christians. By his agreement with James and Peter and John in 46 C.E., he was the apostle of the Gentiles (Galatians 2:7–10), so his ambition to go to Rome was natural. But his track record as a reconciler was dismal. He had to show that he was acceptable among Jews by personally offering his collection for the Nazirites and taking part in Temple sacrifice. Cold-shouldered by James in 52 C.E., by the time he wrote to the Romans five years later he had decided to bet everything on his latest and largest offering in Jerusalem.

That would open up the opportunities in Roman congregations he would need in order to succeed. His gift for believers in Jerusalem would be so successful, so public, that James and the senior leadership there would help establish him in a new city, the center of the Roman Empire.

Paul put the same energy into his collection that he devoted to explaining the revelation of God's Son within each believer: for him, both were works of the Spirit. With hindsight, his effort to overcome all the opposition to him by means of his giant gift may seem hopelessly optimistic, but there is no hint of despair on his part. The ferocious passion that threw him into combating idolatry in Ephesus showed itself again.

He found refuge from the danger in Ephesus in the same port from which he had staged his mission to Macedonia a decade before, Troas.[1] Now he would return to those Greek cities to build up funds for the offering in Jerusalem. Timothy and Titus were his assistants. One approached the circumcised; the other, Gentiles. Through these disciples, Paul vicariously became all things to all men.

Paul initially targeted the northern part of Greece for fund-raising. Communities such as Philippi (see Acts 20:6), Berea, and Thessalonica were ready to support Jerusalem's poor. Solidarity with those who worshiped with James in the Temple was an undisputed part of Christian identity for the Macedonians. Silas and Paul together had taught them that sending funds to Jerusalem was the way all believers—both Jews in the Diaspora and Gentiles—could join with the sacrifice of Israel. The Nazirite vow that James practiced himself, and encouraged others to undertake, made Jerusalem the natural focus for every follower of Jesus who took the Israelite character of the movement seriously.

The Macedonians gave generously, and that encouraged Paul as he turned to the more ticklish Corinthians in Achaia, the southern part of Greece. He knew from the beginning that he was going to have problems. He mentions Timothy in 1 Corinthians (16:10–11) and hopes that no one in Corinth will "despise" the young man. That is a rare indication of Pauline uncertainty. He thought there might be trouble, and there was. The Corinthians refused Timothy and insulted Paul when he was at his most vulnerable as an apostle.

Paul tells the sorry tale from his side—as well as Timothy's, since the two men wrote some of this correspondence together—in 2 Corinthians. This "epistle" assembles parts of various letters: fragmented expressions of anger, remorse, ambitious schemes, disappointment, and desperate hope.[2] But the emotional story behind all this is pretty straightforward, and we can infer the Corinthians' response from what Paul says.

In his ploy to raise funds, Paul boasts to the Achaeans how generous the Macedonians were (2 Corinthians 8:1–6):

> We want you to know, brothers, the grace of God that is given among the churches of Macedonia, because in a great ordeal of tribulation the abundance of their joy and their deep poverty abounded into the wealth of their generosity. For according to their capacity—I attest, beyond their capacity—they voluntarily besought this grace from us with a great appeal: partnership in the ministry that is for the holy ones. Not merely as we had hoped, they gave themselves first to the Lord and then to us through God's will, so that we summoned Titus so he would complete in you this grace that he had initiated.

Paul follows up this portrayal of generosity with the not-so-gentle reminder that the Corinthians are richer than the Macedonians (2 Corinthians 8:7). In any case, he says—always taking the stance that he is giving "an opinion," not bossing anyone around (8:10–12)—the Corinthians really ought to do what they said they were going to do. Compared to his brilliant analysis of Spirit in 1 Corinthians, the rhetoric here is loosely wound. The supreme confidence of his earlier letters does not always come through in 2 Corinthians. The attempt to manipulate the Achaeans with the example of the Macedonians is transparent, and the thunderous majesty of his best arguments is absent.

As if sensing the low voltage of his appeal, Paul adds a tangential argument. The Corinthians should help those in Jerusalem against the day when Corinth might be in want. This plea is also designed to defang the argument that Paul is burdening the Corinthians for his own benefit (2 Corinthians 8:13–15). Paul sends Titus as his personal representative for the collection, along with two other unnamed "brothers" (probably Timothy and Sosthenes; 8:16–24). Titus takes the lead as an uncircumcised believer among the mostly uncircumcised Corinthians. But all three of them had to take the brunt of a rough reception for Paul's project.

The next chapter of 2 Corinthians, representing part of a separate letter, shows that relations broke down; Paul's changed tone breathes desperation. The project has clearly run into problems in Corinth. In the face of complaints, he finds it necessary to explain why he had sent "the brothers" (Titus and company) without coming personally. He makes the lame excuse that he had been bragging in Macedonia about the generosity of the Achaeans and wanted tangible support for his boasting (2 Corinthians 9:2–5). This is quite a confession: evidently he had been telling the Macedonians the kinds of things about the Achaeans that he had been telling the Achaeans about the Macedonians. The foolishness of trying such a gambit pales in comparison to the foolishness of owning up to it.

Why this sudden, self-debilitating rush of honesty, the admission of his elementary shell game? The truth came out only because Paul was acutely embarrassed and he panicked. Despite what he had told the Macedonians about the Corinthians' wealth and enthusiasm, Titus and the brothers must have returned virtually empty-handed from Corinth for Paul to have admitted to his own desperation.

Paul pleads with the Corinthians, reminding them that the collection is a collective sacrifice by all believers, directly offered by Israelites, but on behalf of Gentiles as well (2 Corinthians 9:12–14): "The ministry of this service not only replenishes the needs of the holy ones, but also abounds through many thanksgivings to God. Through the ordeal of this ministry, they glorify God for your subjection by professing the gospel of Christ and the sincere partnership with them and with all, and by prayer for you they yearn for you because of the surpassing grace of God in you."

The cornerstone of his agreement with James and Peter endured, solid as ever for all the difficulties involved: Paul's work among the Gentiles was to support the community of believers who sacrificed in Jerusalem and prayed on behalf of all.

This pact enabled the Corinthians to be included in the worship of Israel. Their offering would penetrate into the sanctuary that they as Gentiles could not physically enter, the sacred place where Jesus and the prophets had predicted the whole world would be transformed. This was not an opportunity to mess up. Tightfistedness will be met with divine stinginess: sow little, reap little (2 Corinthians 9:6), Paul said. Just as he demanded the benefit of the Temple for all believers, the Israel of God as he called them, so he required them to participate in the offering to the God of Israel in Jerusalem.

An appeal for funds against a background of disagreement is a recipe for pastoral strife, and the reaction of some Corinthians was scathing. They said Paul was as weak and anemic in person as he tried to be commanding in his letters. He quotes their criticism (2 Corinthians 10:1, 10), so deeply did it sting. In a cooler moment he said of this whole section of 2 Corinthians (2:4, speaking of chapters 10–13), "from much tribulation and anguish of heart I wrote to you through many tears."

Titus and his colleagues returned empty-handed, and Paul had personally stormed into Corinth (2 Corinthians 12:14–13:2). At last face-to-face with the salons, reality set in: there was no collection readied, no willingness to make arrangements for it, no recognition of Paul's preeminence. This bitter personal experience unleashed his fury. That is why he launched into his fierce defense of his apostolate, writing "through many tears," speaking of himself more baldly than in any other place. This section of 2 Corinthians is as raw and scrappy as 1 Corinthians is well crafted and controlled.

Usually you have to dig to find Paul's affect; in this case it is a matter of weeding through a host of full-throated, nervy feelings to get at those that lie closest to his heart. Yet right through this tough missive, Paul's rage turns on the issue of his authority. His pride and his vulnerability come tumbling out all at once as he speaks of "weapons" that he acknowledges he cannot wield until the salons accept him again as their apostle (2 Corinthians 10:3–6): "Walking in flesh, we do not make war as flesh does. Because the weapons of our warfare aren't of flesh, but empowered by God for the demolition of strongholds. We demolish reasonings and every superior notion lifted up against the knowledge of God, taking every thought captive for the obedience of Christ, ready to avenge each transgression, when your obedience is fulfilled."

His claims may seem outlandish and abusive, but they come without a shred of circumspection. In that lack of restraint Paul reveals his inner energy: the force of Spirit, changing this world, was so vital in his mind that the opposition of the futile world of flesh was a badge of honor. Never has a writer stood more naked in his sincerity.

How people measured him, by this world's standards, finally did not matter. His measure, says Paul, is how God gauges him (2 Corinthians 10:12–18).[3] Those who resist him, including those boasting apostolic authority, are false apostles (11:13), announcing "another Jesus," "another spirit," "another gospel" (11:4). They claim to be superior apostles (11:5); they boast of being Israelites of Abrahamic descent in command of the Holy Scriptures as well as Christ's ministers (11:22–23), but they are deceivers (11:14)—as deceptive as Satan himself!

The eloquent appeals for unity in 1 Corinthians go out the window here when he compares his apostolic colleagues to Satan, "who disguised himself as an angel of light" (2 Corinthians 11:14). He dismissed his competitors as servants of the god of this world of passing flesh. Paul insisted that only he was right and that the authority of any other apostles was to be exorcised from Corinth. He knew the politics of the situation were against him. That's why he speaks here—and only here—of his prophetic "signs" (12:12) and of his spiritual ascent to heaven (12:2–4). Humiliated during his personal fund-raising visit to Corinth, he was prepared to come for "a third occasion" (12:14). That is a threat grounded solely in his eschatological authority to speak on behalf of the spiritual world that was coming to replace the world of flesh.

He fulminates that any greed should have been attributed to him over the collection: he had relied on the Macedonians for support during his visits in Corinth (11:7–11). No profit was involved; the collection went beyond a practical matter, into the heart of the gospel. If they failed to heed him this third time (13:1–2) he would not spare them.

The bitter finale of 2 Corinthians burns with the logic and the passion of Paul's whole view of his apostolic authority (13:10): "For this reason I write this when absent: that when present I do not have to use the authority relentlessly that the Lord gave me for building up, not for demolition."

The one thing that mattered, the new creation of Spirit that was to replace all flesh, so obsessed Paul, so absorbed his sense of what was real, that he was prepared to use that reality to condemn to nonexistence whatever resisted it. This spiritual warfare was the dark side of his exalted, poetic teaching concerning the resurrection of the dead in spiritual bodies, because if anyone fell short of the requirements of Spirit, that meant consignment to hell, the destruction of flesh.

Paul never did go to Corinth for this final, personal confrontation. His last, conciliatory communication to the Corinthians (2 Corinthians chapters 1–7) is directed not only to the city but to Achaia generally (1:1). That was the best leave-taking he could manage, an attempt to reduce the importance of the Corinthian rebellion by speaking warmly of the region as a whole.

Paul looks back on what he had written so hurtfully "through many tears," trying for a valedictory mood, but with his prose still sputtering (2 Corinthians 7:8–9): "For even if I grieved you in the letter, I do not regret that—even if I used to regret—I see that this letter, even if it grieved you an hour—now I rejoice, not because you were grieved but because you were grieved for repentance, for you were grieved on God's behalf, so that no one of us was forfeited."

His meaning is an enigma wrapped in fractured syntax. But the situation he faced is clear: the Corinthians had not conceded enough for him to declare victory and then move on. He instead seizes on their general willingness to repent ("on God's behalf," whatever that means) as their acknowledgment of his own pain. That amounts to just enough good feeling for him in Corinth, reported back to him by Titus (2 Corinthians 7:5–16), to assuage his pride.

Paul did not refer—in honesty could not refer—to having the Corinthians' offering in hand. He even offered an apology, a unique event in his letters or in Acts. Paul explains his anger by alluding to the riots and his detention in Ephesus just prior to his correspondence with Corinth (2 Corinthians 1:8–9): "We do not want you ignorant, brothers, of our tribulation in Asia, that we were burdened out of measure, beyond our strength, so that we despaired even of living. But we had the sentence of death in ourselves, so that we should not trust in ourselves but in the God who raises the dead."

He excuses his failing to come as he said he would before going to Judea (1:16) by saying he wished to "spare" (1:23–2:4) the Corinthians his wrath. Just shy of his fiftieth birthday, he had learned a little discretion. Paul posed a revealing question, demonstrating how dicey he knew his position was, "For if I grieve you, who rejoices me except the one grieved by me?" (2 Corinthians 2:2) He knows his display of anger was completely impolitic,[4] just as he knows that dividing the community and the movement as he threatened to do only gave an opportunity to "Satan."

That threat became so acute, Paul relented in his obsession with the ministry for Jerusalem's Nazirites. He accepted the hard fact that the Corinthian salons, wealthy though they were, had refused to join in this collection. He still hoped for the support of wealthy individuals, but he had failed in his demand that entire congregations back him up. He reversed his previous stance, ceding his own authority to the Corinthians (2 Corinthians 2:10–11): "Whomever you favor, I do, too: and what I have favored—if I have favored anything—was for your sake in Christ's presence, so that we are not defrauded by Satan, for we are not ignorant of his thoughts."

Climbing down from his towering rage, Paul says that the Corinthians—acting for him personally—can grant anyone the favor of not participating in the collection. After all, he insists, he had only supported that aim for their good. They in effect had disciplined him, as he acknowledged: "Our mouth has opened to you, Corinthians; our heart has widened" (2 Corinthians 6:11).

That was painfully true. The Corinthians had pushed Paul to discover within himself a new generosity and a shared conception of apostolic power. Instead of calling for anyone or any group to be handed over to Satan by the force of his own spirit, Paul accepts that the Corinthians can reverse that spiritual polarity, change his mind, and widen his heart. When Paul made his final preparations in Troas to sail to Jerusalem, he had to rely on other communities and wealthy donors for his collection for the saints. But it was the Corinthians who had done something to his emotions that changed him permanently.

.   .   .

IN TROAS, Paul had gathered considerable resources and a number of people around him. An innovator in developing the tenement church, the guild church, the house church, and the storefront church, he also pioneered a virtual church: a community independent of any one city or constituency, gathering individuals who were moved by Paul's version of the message of Christ to act and contribute[5] on behalf of his collection for the Gentiles.

On the eve of his offering the collection, he spoke frequently and at length to his loyal supporters in Troas. They gathered in improvised settings, back in the tenement rooms above shops. In one passage in Acts, the third-floor space is so cramped that a young man named Eutychus sat on a window ledge.

Any reader of 2 Corinthians can tell you that Paul was in voluble form during this period, and he prolonged his discourse so late one night that Eutychus fell asleep. In fact, he fell not only asleep, but also out the window—and three stories down (Acts 20:1–12). People naturally thought he was dead. But Paul revived the gentle sleeper and went

Stone bench in Miletus (photo courtesy of the author). This inscription is difficult to make out, but reads, "Place of Jews and God-worshipers" (*Topos Eioudeôn tôn kai thesebion*). For a discussion of its meaning and date, see Irina Levinskaya, *The Book of Acts in Its Diaspora Setting:* The Book of Acts in Its First Century Setting 5 (Grand Rapids, MI: Eerdmans, 1996), 63–65.

on to preach and break bread, recalling Jesus' final meal with his disciples.

Bread broken in Jesus' name was a *eukharistia*, a thanksgiving, heralding "the Lord's death, until he comes" (1 Corinthians 11:26). And the Lord did come, in the charismatic experience of Paul and his congregations, with wisdom, prophecy, insight, and a Spirit that healed and revived people like Eutychus, even if they were less attentive than Paul himself might have wished.

Paul's company chartered a boat from Troas, which put out from the port and met up with Paul at Assos, where he had traveled by foot in order to seek out more supporters, further finance for his offering. By ship they made their way from Assos and through a series of short hops to the port city of Miletus (Acts 20:13–16). This was a strategic location, permitting the sympathetic leaders of the Ephesian community of believers to travel and meet with Paul without his running the risk of a physical return to Ephesus.

Acts—with the benefit of hindsight—presents Paul's speech to the Ephesian elders as a highly personal prophecy about his upcoming fate in Jerusalem (20:17–38). The journey did involve risk, but Paul was eager for it, as his letter to the Romans shows. He had collected a substantial sum, and his dozen or so companions represented hundreds of people who were funding his sacrificial pilgrimage. He wanted to get to Jerusalem for Pentecost (Acts 20:16), when Christians there celebrated God's Spirit pouring through the risen Jesus on all humanity. It was the perfect moment for Paul's sacrifice.

· · ·

PAUL DICTATED HIS LETTER to Rome in Miletus in 57 C.E., prior to setting out for Jerusalem. He polished this letter thoroughly: despite his recent troubles, he remained upbeat. The tone differs deliberately from the volatile correspondence with Corinth. In Romans, Paul is writing a letter of introduction for himself, seeking to establish a relationship such as he had enjoyed in Ephesus with a new city—the greatest city in his world.

The letter to the Romans reads as an effortless synthesis of Paul's Stoic intellect and his Christian faith—but if you keep in mind what he had just said to the Corinthians, you realize the enormous, self-mastering effort of will involved. He sounds the familiar motif of Christ as a corporate, all-embracing "body" (Romans 12:4–8), but with a new economy of words, and deploys the classic Stoic trope that earthly rulers are divine ministers "for the good" (13:1–4): "Every being should be submitted to higher authorities, for there is no authority except by God, and they are appointed by God. . . ."

This echoed the position of Seneca, Paul's Stoic contemporary from Asia Minor—and tutor of the emperor Nero. Events would cause Paul to revise his opinion. But it's interesting that a man who had been beaten by lictors three times and was all too aware of the unjust treatment of his fellow believers urged Christians to show obedience to the Roman Empire.

He could take this position because he knew that obedience to any political authority was as temporary as this world. His position was also tactical: by using the language and ideas of Stoicism to describe the cosmic reach of Christ's revelation and by insisting that faith was consistent with imperial law, Paul legitimated Christianity's place in philosophical discourse and helped make the claim for its political legitimacy[6] as well.

Romans closes with the longest list of people of any of Paul's letters (16:1–16, 21–23), including fellow workers and wealthy families with Jewish, pagan, Greek, and Latin names—amounting to at least forty persons altogether. Paul displayed powerful support and implied that Roman congregations of Christians could also enjoy that kind of patronage by allying with him.

Phoebe "the minister" *(diakonos)* heads the list. Paul asks the Romans to receive her warmly and help her materially as she makes her way from Cenchreae (Romans 16:1–2): "And I commend our sister Phoebe to you, who is minister of the church in Cenchrea, so that you receive her in the Lord worthily of the holy ones, and assist her in any concern in which she has need of you, because she has become the protectress of many—and certainly my own!"

On his previous visit to Jerusalem, Paul had stopped in Cenchreae to have his head shaved to fulfill his Nazirite vow (Acts 18:18). Phoebe was part of an advance contingent in Rome, which included Priscilla and Aquila (Romans 16:3–5), for keeping the same vow. She offered the Romans a place in the great sacrifice in the Temple that would unite all the nations in the final victory of Christ.

Through Phoebe, Paul wanted to involve Roman Christians in an offering on an even bigger scale than the one he was about to accomplish. Christ was a "minister of circumcision," a man functioning in historic, territorial Israel, but people like Phoebe and himself were stepping beyond that to include all the Gentiles (Romans 15:7–13) within an Israel now defined by faith alone. For that reason, Paul refers to his own function as a "ritual purveyor of Jesus Christ for the nations, performing priestly service" in the offering of the nations. He refers to the "power of signs and wonders" in this context, because it really is eschatological work that he wants to extend from Jerusalem to the Adriatic Sea through his efforts (15:15–21). Once he has taken his Greek collection to Jerusalem, he plans to make Rome a base of mission to as far west as Spain (15:22–33), which was then the western end of the known world.

His geographical ambition embodies his eschatological hope, and the purpose of Paul's letter to the Romans comes into focus when you keep that in mind. From the outset he writes on a global scale, broadening themes already articulated in earlier letters, framing succinct and penetrating new expressions of his most valued ideas. He wants, he says, to speak of what had been announced already in the prophets, but had not been conveyed to all humanity until the Resurrection of Jesus (1:1–7). His particular desire to come and stay in Rome is quickly asserted (1:10–15), but that does not prevent him from launching into his most sustained tirade against idolatry, linking it explicitly with homosexuality (1:18–32)—including lesbianism this time. Worship an animal, you become an animal; worship a human body, you become a fetishist. There are those who try to wriggle out of this logic while claiming to remain loyal followers of Paul. That can work only if you shoulder the responsibility of specifying where his analysis went wrong.

Alongside the denunciation of idolatry and sexual perversion, Paul sounds another of the letter's characteristic themes from the outset: salvation is for "everyone who believes, both Jew first and then Greek" (1:16). In arguing for the unity of all peoples in Christ's body, he specifically includes circumcised Israel, whose minister Christ himself had become.[7] This Israel alone gave the world Christ in the flesh (Romans 9:4–5), just as Israel's Scriptures uniquely specified what it meant for Jesus and every believer to become a child of God.

Risen from the dead, Christ announces the mutual inheritance and common destiny of all peoples. For that reason Jesus becomes what Paul calls the sacrificial place (the *hilasterion*) where God would take pleasure in the offering of every human being (Romans 3:21–25): "And now apart from Law God's righteousness has been manifested, attested by the Law and the Prophets—God's righteousness through Christ Jesus' faith for all who believe. There is no distinction. For all have sinned and are deficient for the glory of God, yet are made righteous as a gift by his grace through the redemption that is in Jesus Christ, whom God appointed a place of sacrifice through faith in his blood. . . ."

Christ for Paul is the *hilasterion* because he provides the occasion for true worship, an opportunity for the eschatological sacrifice in Jerusalem, the same city in which Jesus shed his blood. That is a guiding principle of Paul's apostolate.[8] Jews and Greeks could indeed offer sacrifice together in Christ (without "distinction"), joined in mutual recognition that the blood he shed was not Jewish blood or Greek blood, but the human suffering that God has decided to transcend. The letter to the Romans maps out the new creation that Paul had described for years, but in a new, precise idiom.

When people started living in their faithful congregations without regard to religion or race or status or gender, Paul saw that as proof of God's new creation. Sin was a reality, but not the last word. Sin came through Adam, and now the undeserved gift of grace came rushing in through Jesus (Romans 5:12–21). This understanding of human solidarity in Adam and in the Messiah was thoroughly Judaic, but then Paul also speaks of believers as dying with Christ and rising with Christ when they were baptized (6:3–11), comparing Christian baptism to the Mysteries of gods like Dionysos.

He spoke to Jews as Jews, to Greeks as Greeks, to all sides at the same time, because he referred to their common goal. The world itself was a broken creature, crying out in travail at a destiny it could not comprehend (Romans 8:22–25). And the inner heart of every person is equally divided, he wrote: "Because I do not know what I am doing; for what I want, this I don't enact, but what I hate, this I enact" (Romans 7:15). You had to be healed; the world had to be healed. Whether at the level of the microcosmic person or the macrocosmic globe, this healing power came from God's Spirit, restoring, refreshing, making new.

. . .

AT THE HEIGHT OF his rhetorical mastery, Paul was nonetheless ill-equipped to cope with the mare's nest of political and religious complications that awaited him in Jerusalem. The city's atmosphere had changed in recent years. James was struggling to maintain his position as a pious Nazirite in the Temple and as Jesus' preeminent disciple.

There were new pressures on James' circle. Jesus' movement had become more prominent because of its success in the Diaspora among uncircumcised Gentiles. This made many of Jerusalem's Jews uneasy. Worse, the high priesthood during these years increasingly sided with factions in the city that wished to purify the Temple of any foreign influences. Being called a "Christian" was demeaning in Antioch; in Jerusalem it had become an outright insult. James was caught in a vice: a growing number of Gentile Christians on one side, and a growing Temple nationalism on the other.

The pinch of this vice was all the more painful because James had sanctioned the baptism of Gentiles without requiring circumcision, and he had also championed enhanced devotion to the Temple. He responded to the pressure by insisting all the more emphatically on the practice of the Nazirite vow, sealing the centrality of the Temple for Jesus' movement and marking the role of Gentiles as secondary. A description of James derives from this period (Eusebius *History of the Church* 2.23.4–7):[9] "He did not drink wine or strong drink, nor did he eat meat; a razor did not mount his head; he did not anoint himself with oil, and he did not make use of a bath. He alone was fitted to enter into the sanctuary, for he did not wear wool but linen. He used to enter alone into the Temple and be found kneeling and praying for forgiveness for the people, so that his knees grew dry in the way of a camel, because he constantly knelt in worship of God and asked forgiveness for the people." Never was Nazirite identity more important to James, because this discipline embraced his identity as an Israelite *and* as the leader (the first bishop) of his brother's community.

When James and Paul met for the last time in Jerusalem during the Pentecost season of 57 C.E., two visions of the risen Jesus, two understandings of Christianity, confronted one another. Ritual purity—the careful observation of what you ate, who you ate it with, what you did with your body—was central to James' Nazirite devotion to Jesus, the heavenly "one like a person." Paul's revelation that the Son of God transcended human differences made some ritual concerns less significant for Jewish believers and of no import whatever for Gentile believers. (Paul still had not explained, and never would explain, why ritual concerns in regard to sexuality were enhanced in Christ, while dietary rules were slackened.) Each man knew that ultimately they could not both be right. Each confronted demanding constituencies: James had to be accepted fully in the Temple in order to put his devotion into practice; Paul needed Jerusalem's authorization to make his way to pagan Rome, the greatest city in the Diaspora.

They never resolved their contradictory visions, yet they did try to coordinate them by means of a single, public act. The vision of James and the vision of Paul found common ground in the Temple, the place from which God would redeem his people. James believed that would happen with the persistent dedication involved in his Nazirite vow; Paul expected redemption when all the nations of the earth made their sacrifice in Jerusalem through him and apostles like him.

In practical terms they could both claim victory if Paul agreed to enter publicly into the Temple in order to participate in the Nazirite vow with some of James' disciples. God would decide finally how to redeem all his people, whether it was through Israel preeminent among the nations or Israel stretching its boundaries to include pagans who believed in Jesus. Either way, James and Paul would start the process by offering in the Temple together. This was James' idea, and Paul readily agreed (Acts 21:18–24) to use his offering to fund the Nazirite vow of believers in Jerusalem, and to enter the Temple with them publicly.

James hoped this visible association with the worship of Israel would launder Paul's reputation in Jerusalem, so people would stop saying he encouraged Jews not to keep the Torah. The rumor that Paul told Jews not to circumcise their children was patently untrue, but it made the rounds in Jerusalem, even among Jews who believed in Jesus (Acts 21:20–21). James needed to distance his brother's movement from all such blasphemy in order for his Nazirite community to continue.

Paul wanted to walk into the Temple as a representative of baptized Gentiles, both God-fearers and pagans, accomplishing his offering for the Gentiles as its apostolic priest. He had actually arrived in Jerusalem with non-Jews in his entourage (Acts 21:29), so it was all too easy for worshipers in the Temple, seeing Paul with a large group of Nazirites and their supporters, to suppose that the leading apostle of the non-Jews had finally consummated his blasphemy by introducing Gentiles into the inner sanctuary that was prohibited to non-Israelites.

Introducing Gentiles into the court Temple reserved for Israel was a sacrilege punishable by death. Josephus refers to inscriptions in stone around the sanctuary, authorized by the Romans, which prescribed the punishment of death for doing that (*Antiquities* 5.417); remains of those plaques have been discovered.[10] So instead of welcoming Paul's display of public piety, a mob in the Temple rioted against him (Acts 21:28): "Israelite men, help! This is the man that teaches everyone everywhere against the people, and the Law, and this place: he has even brought Greeks into the Sanctuary, and profaned this holy place!"

The police of the high priest took Paul from the Temple and beat him. But Paul himself also enjoyed support in the city, and a series of running street battles ensued among his followers, Temple police, and zealots for the purity of the sanctuary (Acts 21:30–36). The Romans could not permit street fights in Jerusalem, and soldiers attempted to restore order by arresting Paul. Acts has the commander permit Paul to make a lengthy public speech at this point (chapter 22). That would have been an unlikely way to restore order; later events show it is more probable that the commander wished to deal with the fracas quietly. The fly in the ointment was that Paul was a Roman citizen (22:24–30): the usual means of interrogating a renegade prophet by means of a good flogging could not be deployed.

This resourceful Roman captain, eventually named as Claudius Lysias (Acts 23:25), nonetheless found a way to resolve the dispute: get the Sanhedrin to see that the charge was moot because Paul had no Gentiles with him when he went into the Temple. Claudius Lysias acted rationally and within the law. The mob wanted Paul executed, and he was a citizen. That went a long way beyond the quasilegal administration of the lictor's rod, as happened in Philippi, Corinth, and Ephesus. Citizens simply could not be dispatched as easily as subject peoples. Much simpler to get the charge removed and get Paul out of Jerusalem.

But in front of the Sanhedrin, Paul undermined Claudius Lysias's stratagem; his mouth got him in trouble again. He insulted the high priest, calling him a whitewashed wall, and claimed that he was being persecuted for believing in the resurrection of the dead. That was untrue, a rhetorical red herring. By focusing on this topic, he stirred up controversy among the Pharisees and Sadducees present, because they had profound differences over the issue of resurrection (Acts 23:1–10). The session even turned violent, and Claudius Lysias had to bring Paul back into custody.

Not even Roman protection could assure his safety. Paul's nephew informed the officer in charge of the Antonia that there was a conspiracy in Jerusalem to kill Paul. Claudius Lysias had no choice but to get Paul out of harm's way with or without the consent of the Sanhedrin; he dispatched him to Felix, the prefect in Caesarea (Acts 23:12–35). Felix reacted by keeping Paul in the elegant praetorian building Herod the Great had built, still hoping to come to an agreement with the high priest. After he heard the accusations against Paul afresh, and Paul's insistence that he was practicing his ancestral religion in good faith, Felix ordered Paul to pay for his own accommodations and remain in Caesarean custody (24:1–27). Felix may have been slightly frustrated by the legal impasse, but any such feeling was more than compensated by the cash cow the goddess Fortuna had brought his way. There the matter languished for a couple of years—even after Porcius Festus replaced Felix, and then well into Festus's tenure.

· · ·

FOR THE FIRST TIME IN HIS LIFE, Paul relied directly on other people for his daily needs. Custody for a citizen did not involve punitive imprisonment, but paying for his housing, food, serving staff, guardians, and occasional bribes to officials quickly depleted Paul's funds. He ate up his remaining "offering of the Gentiles" by rendering Caesar his due and then had to turn to his friends.

His mighty Nazirite sacrifice had proven to be a fiasco—and not a failure of the kind he could write off. This was not just the world's rejection; the Temple had spurned him. James and his colleagues, themselves instigators of Paul's sacrifice, had no standing to intercede with the Romans on his behalf. They had to cut Paul loose, and they did.

Paul needed deep relationships to sustain him. Timothy became his closest friend. He was now much more than just a young assistant willing to do anything—even be circumcised—to help Paul prove a point. He increasingly spoke for Paul and composed letters with him in which he also expressed his own concerns.

Paul's letters become sporadic at this point and he speaks in a new idiom. There are no longer triumphant appeals to the power of the collection to bring on the end of the world, or references to Paul's overwhelming spiritual authority as an apostle. At the close of his triumphant progress to the Temple he had found only ashes, and the result is that in the little he did write, we see Paul's own broken mortality and, at the same time, his growing affective connection to other people.

In 58 C.E., he and Timothy wrote a private letter to a wealthy slaveholder they had met back in Ephesus named Philemon.[11] Paul's whole concern in these twenty-five short verses is with a slave Philemon had loaned him, named Onesimus. Onesimus had stayed on in Caesarea with Paul longer than originally agreed, and Paul wanted to spare the man punishment from an irate Philemon (vv. 8–10): "So having much confidence in Christ to order you what is proper, for love's sake I rather appeal—being Paul the senior, but now also a prisoner for Jesus Christ—I appeal to you concerning my child, whom I begat in my bonds, Onesimus. . . ."

Paul's new tenderness brought no new modesty, false or otherwise, as the opening of this statement shows. But the whole focus is his deep attachment to Onesimus, a feeling he experiences, he says, deep in his body: his viscera or guts *(splangkhna* in Greek). Sadly, modern commentators have tended to weaken the meaning of this term to "heart," but the King James Version bravely uses "bowels." Cut off from his usual, high-voltage activity, the forced repose of custody made him aware of his visceral link (vv. 7, 20) with people as close to him as the children he never had.

IN THE WAY OF BUREAUCRATS, Festus replayed the scenario of his predecessor's interrogation and wanted to take Paul to Jerusalem to stand before the Sanhedrin yet again (Acts 25:1–9). Paul knew that his enemies there had gained in power and influence, and instead he appealed to "Caesar"—that is, for judgment in Rome (v. 10–11). In consultation with King Herod Agrippa II and his sister Bernice (and after another long speech from Paul according to Acts 25:13–26:32), Festus went along with Paul's request.

Festus packed Paul off with a centurion named Julius (Acts 27:1–6). Money became a serious concern because Paul had to meet his own travel expenses as well as the cost of his maintenance. Fortunately, friends took care of him in Sidon, where the ship put in briefly. Julius took Paul and a Thessalonian companion named Aristarchus as far as Myra in Turkey and transferred him to another ship.

Timothy's travel diary in Acts is full and informative, but Paul's letters still ignore his physical surroundings. His mind was now absorbed with his visceral connection to his many children: people like Onesimus whom he had fathered in the service of the gospel. How much time remained to enjoy his sons and daughters in Christ? That question underlies his fullest communication from this period of detention and travel, his letter to the Philippians. Here, too, Timothy is named as a cowriter; when they put into Myra on the way to Rome, they had the opportunity to dispatch it to Philippi.

Despite the hectic anxiety of his custody and appeal, the politics Paul played to stay out of reach of the high priest and get himself to Rome, and the bustle of travel over land and sea, this is his calmest, most limpid piece of writing. He longs for the Philippians, he said, "in the

viscera of Jesus Christ" (Philippians 1:8; see 2:1). Yes, he needed
money, but not much, and he acknowledged (Philippians 4:18) his
European children had already sent him enough money to see him to
Rome.

Timothy—another "child" as Paul calls him (Philippians 2:19–22)—
is the designated emissary for further contact once he has arrived in
Rome, but Epaphroditus—whom Paul calls "your apostle" (2:25)—is
on his way back from Myra to Philippi after an illness (2:25–30). He
had already delivered a gift that seemed lavish to Paul (4:18): "a fragrant
aroma, a sacrifice acceptable, pleasing to God." The connection Paul
once sought to forge with the collection for the saints is now consummated with the concern of the saints for him.

Paul's affection suffuses this letter, as well as his deliberate emphasis
on how to concentrate his thoughts *(phronein)* on people in Philippi
while he is in custody (Philippians 1:3–7). This thinking of himself and
of them, the deliberate orientation of one's own mind and heart in difficulty, is his focus throughout the letter as he refers circumstantially to
the military personnel (1:13) that escorted him.

Paul's mood became so valedictory, he could even refer to his old
competitors with something like affection, although he did not give an
inch when it came to his principles or his pride (1:15–18): "Some herald Christ from jealousy and contention, and some from a good desire.
Those who act from love know that I am destined for a defense of the
gospel; those who act from ambition proclaim Christ, not purely, suppose they raise tribulation by my bonds. So what? As long as in every
way, whether by pretext or truth, Christ is proclaimed—and in this I
rejoice!"

This is no "born again" Paul: he calls people who want to circumcise Gentile believers "dogs," "evil-doers," "the mutilation" (Philippians 3:2). He made his way to Rome with a new maturity, a fresh
reticence, but his adolescent joy in rhetoric never failed him.

What did await him in Rome? Should he hope for life or death? He
doesn't know (Philippians 1:20–22). He lives in a truncated present
where all his expectations have been disappointed, and yet new linea-

ments of affection grow and prosper. To be free of life's concerns entirely and serve Christ in Spirit is his desire, and yet he remembers people like the Philippians themselves (1:23–24): "I am constrained between the two—having the greater and better desire to cast off and be with Christ *and* as more necessary for you to persevere in the flesh."

He entered a netherworld, living on the cusp of life and death, willing for either, accepting both.

The great project of evangelizing the world no longer obsessed him. Now only God's kingdom was on his mind, and his body trembled for the Philippians with "the viscera of Christ." As he concentrates his own attention, he is concerned that the Philippians should do the same (2:1–2; 4:10) and join their souls with his. And here, in exploring this bodily connection of believers in Christ, Paul makes perhaps his greatest contribution to the movement he had joined his life to.

After years of saying that various readers should imitate him, just as he imitates Christ—a touching imperative if you liked Paul, utter arrogance if you did not—with little preamble he tells the Philippians what that whole process is about (2:5–8): "Let this mind be in you, which was also in Christ Jesus; Who, being in the form of God, thought it not robbery to be equal with God: But made himself of no reputation, and took upon him the form of a servant, and was made in the likeness of men: And being found in fashion as a man, he humbled himself, and became obedient unto death, even the death of the cross."

This language is so resonant, it has been described as a hymn—and attributed to a liturgical song that Paul quotes.[12] But even if that is so, Paul is the author who uses this language to speak deliberately of Jesus as God. He has broken through to poetry and enlists the Philippians in working out the deeply affective salvation that was to be their inheritance (2:12–13) by embracing the mind of Christ. The simplicity of the whole achievement is staggering. Paul can now write what is commonly used as a blessing at the close of many, many liturgies, "The peace of God that passes all understanding will keep your hearts and thoughts in Jesus Christ" (4:7). Jesus now becomes the focus of faith because he is divine, and is revealed within the believer so that God's thoughts become human thoughts. "At the name of Jesus every knee shall bow, in heaven, on earth, and in the underworld" (2:10):[13] Christ receives the honor due God, because he makes humanity divine.

Paul is too detached to get into much of a lather anymore. "To write the same things to you is not troublesome to me, but is necessary for you" (3:1). These are not the words of someone burning to write. The force of argument in his prose had been replaced by lyricism. As Paul became more poetic, as the imperative to collect for the ministry for the saints receded into memory, his output decreased markedly. His analysis of the mystical union between Christ and believers was making him into a different kind of writer, a poet in spite of himself.

THE STING OF DEATH

P AUL'S VOYAGE from Myra to Rome compounded disaster with
disaster—complete with a wreck at sea and poisonous snakes
waiting on shore. Timothy passed through this experience with
Paul; Acts includes his vivid reminiscence of what happened to "us"
(Acts 27:6–44), another instance of the "we-sections" of the book.
Timothy had a Greek's knowledge of sailing; he details how the ship's
company escaped, leaving their ship in pieces.

Timothy's detailed diary—incorporated in Acts—came to a close
quickly after the journey's final leg to Rome (Acts 28:1–16). Timothy
observed generally that Paul was to remain in Roman custody for the
next two years (vv. 30–31, the end of the book of Acts), paying his own
rent with the help of patrons until 62 C.E. But the two men obviously
parted soon after their arrival in Rome.

Timothy remained Paul's agent as well as his friend, returning to
Troas and raising funds for Paul there, constantly staying in contact
with loyal supporters in Philippi and other cities. He sent funds along
to Paul, who lived in relative comfort, receiving visitors and teaching
in his hired Roman accommodations.

Rome was the largest, most diverse, and most powerful city in the

Mediterranean world, with a population of 1 million, among them about 50,000 Jews.[1] Paul would once have reveled in such a place. But with Timothy's return to Troas we lose the informant who was most interested in Paul's actions and whereabouts. Paul himself was not. All we know about his final years from Acts (28:30–31) is that the Roman authorities gave him enough slack to teach, provided that he looked after his own expenses.

Why does the Book of Acts end then, in 62 C.E.? Why not with Paul's death a mere two years later? This editorial decision reflects several factors. One major theme of Acts is that the Roman Empire and Christian belief are fully compatible. This was not the emperor Nero's position during the latter years of his reign, so it's a time period that Acts avoids. Moreover, in the year 62, James was killed in Jerusalem; the high priest Ananus ordered him stoned to death. That broke the link with the Temple that was another persistent theme of Acts and signaled the emergence of a new kind of Christianity. That story, everyone involved knew, extended far beyond the lifetimes of James, Peter, and Paul. In aggregate, a book that wanted to depict the Church at relative peace with its secular masters did well to close the story off in 62 C.E.; it would have required literary and logical contortions to write about the rest of that decade and make that argument.

The two years of Paul's life after 62 C.E. were also difficult to relate from the perspective of Acts because they were oddly static. Paul could legally have resumed his travels, and didn't. Acts implies Roman custody was lifted in 62 C.E., and that makes good sense. Ananus's execution of James aroused massive opposition in Jerusalem, so great was James' reputation for piety, so highly regarded his Nazirite practice. Josephus reports that many Jews, horrified by the stoning, petitioned the Roman procurator of Judea to remove Ananus from office (*Antiquities* 20 §§ 200–203). He obliged, and that decision benefited Paul. Imperial authorities didn't want to pursue the case of a recently discredited high priesthood against a citizen, so Paul was free again. Yet he stayed put.

He had once planned to go to Spain, but his last experience in

Jerusalem—capped now by the death of James—quashed any hope of mounting another collection to offer on behalf of Gentiles in the Temple. Paul's prose output, in letters designed largely to make that collection happen, simply dried up with his plans for travel.

Despite the silence of Acts, we do have evidence that Paul pursued an interior journey the last two years of his life. As he visited friendly congregations in Rome, freed of the imperative to raise resources for his massive offering, Paul refined the poetic idiom he had pioneered in his correspondence with Corinth and dedicated himself to in his letter to Philippi. Timothy continued—both at a distance and during sporadic visits to Rome—to connect his withdrawn teacher to the world around him and coax Paul's words onto papyrus. Even after Paul's death, Timothy wrote as Paul's agent on the basis of what he could remember his teacher saying, the written work he could squeeze out of Paul, and his own authority.

Writing in his own name and Paul's years later, Timothy sent a letter to Colossae, a city in Asia Minor. It includes a reference to Paul's time in Rome (Colossians 4:7–18) and represents the outcome of a visit Timothy must have made there a year or so prior to Paul's death. Colossians includes some of Paul's best poetry, without which Timothy would probably have remained purely oral.

The Christ of Colossians projects his cosmic, divine body into the human experience. The theme of solidarity with this body had long been a theme of Paul's, but in Colossians, Christ is the center of the cosmos—natural, social, and supernatural—that created the world and makes the world new each day (Colossians 1:15–20):

> He is the invisible God's image, firstborn of all creation,
>   because within him everything was created,
>   in heaven and on earth, visible and invisible:
>   thrones, dominions, principalities and authorities.
>   Everything through him and for him has been created.
> He is personally before all things, and all things exist in him,
>   and he is personally the head of the body: the Church.

He is the beginning, firstborn from the dead,
  so he becomes in all things precedent.
For in him all the fullness pleased to dwell,
  and through him—and for him—
  to reconcile all things (whether on earth or in heaven),
  as he made peace through the blood of his cross.

The range of Paul's thinking was literally cosmic, and metacosmic, because the viscera of Christ, the mind of Christ, wove all things into the primordial whole that had been their source. To Paul's mind the fulfillment of all things had already been accomplished. Christ had mended the world, and an attuned heart and mind could join in that victory.

Paul—master preacher, oral poet—was welcomed in many Christian communities in and around Rome, albeit not in synagogues (Acts 28:17–29). He still encountered resistance, but he rejoiced in that. He said it was the purpose of the believer to join Christ in suffering (Colossians 1:24), "to fill up what is lacking in the tribulations of Christ." Every drop of a martyr's blood flowed from the veins of Jesus and was shed to reconcile human divisions as decisively as Christ has already reconciled the forces of heaven to the all-consuming love of God. Paul at the end of his life became the first great mystical teacher of union with Christ, the fusion of divine Spirit and human spirit.[2]

Paul had moved completely beyond the collection, now that his offering had been pushed aside. Any sense of dependence upon Jerusalem had left him, and he also let go of one of his cherished Stoic ideas during this period. Even when he had written with Timothy to Philippi when he was in shipboard custody at Myra, he had said, "our citizens' status belongs in heaven" (Philippians 3:20): that loyalty replaced the obedience he had earlier said Christians owed to their rulers (Romans 13:1–7). In Colossians he said even more boldly that God had "rescued us from the authority of darkness, and transferred us into the kingdom of the Son of his love" (Colossians 1:13). If the price of this transfer from human politics into the realm of eternal light happened to be suffering, what did that matter? Christ had stripped away any force from the human and heavenly authorities of this world (Colossians 2:15) by triumphing over death. Every Christian lived out the poetry of Christ (Colossians 2:12): "buried with him in baptism, in which you are also raised with him."

His verbal mastery rendered the rhythm of Christ's victory in words. Timothy got at least some of Paul's poetry into writing, securing his teacher's last literary accomplishment. A few years more might well have seen this new innovation eclipse what Paul had already achieved in the prose letters. Imagine the idiom of Philippians and Colossians extended and deepened to compete in range and depth with 1 Corinthians and Romans. . . .

But while his poetic idiom was still finding its pace, Paul confronted a past master in the cruel art of politics. Nero needed a scapegoat. Without someone to blame, the emperor for all his power had made himself vulnerable.

Fire broke out in Rome in 64 C.E. and decimated the city. Rumor said Nero had ordered the arson, and had forbidden efforts to fight the flames. The cliché of his "fiddling" while Rome burned understates his depravity: he floated down the Tiber on a barge with his prostitutes (Tacitus *Annals* 15.37), pretending to be a great conqueror who ravished his enemies while their city was aflame. The prospect that he could rebuild Rome along any lines he wanted enhanced his pleasure. He even had building plans ready to go. All he needed—to complete his enjoyment and avoid carping criticism—was to find someone else to blame for the fire.

The emperor deflected suspicion from himself by pinning responsibility for the disaster on Christians.[3] Their marginal status must have seemed to him a gift from the gods. They were rounded up, interrogated, often subjected to elaborate torture, and then slaughtered.

Nero's excesses seemed egregious even to those who despised Christianity. Tacitus, the first-century Roman historian, represents an aristocratic perspective on these atrocities (see his *Annals* 15.44): "But neither humanitarian aid, nor imperial largesse, nor propitiations to the

gods, removed the scandalous suspicion that the fire had been an order. To put an end to this rumor, Nero found likely suspects, and inflicted contrived tortures upon people detested for their disgraces,
whom the crowd called Christians. This name came from one
Christus, who was put to death in the reign of Tiberius by the procurator Pontius Pilate; but though checked for the time, the pestilent cult
broke out again, not only in Judea, the origin of the disease, but even
in the capital, where all things heinous and shameful pour in from
every which way and are celebrated."

Tacitus's description of the torture evidently owes nothing to any a
priori sympathy with Jesus' movement: "First those who avowed were
arrested; and upon their information a vast number were condemned,
not so much on the charge of arson as for their hatred of the human
race. Their death was turned into a diversion. They were clothed in
the skins of wild beasts, and torn to pieces by dogs; they were fastened
to crosses, or set up to be burned, so as to serve the purpose of lamps
when daylight failed. Nero gave up his own gardens for this spectacle;
he provided also circus games, during which in the garb of a chario-
teer he mingled with the populace, or took his stand upon a chariot.
But guilty as these men were and worthy of extreme penalty, pity
arose, since they were being destroyed not for public good, but for one
man's savagery."

The debauched emperor created a sympathy for his victims that had
not been there before. He did not extend the rights of a legitimate cult
(a *religio licita*) to Christians, although most of Jesus' followers were
Jews, in Italy and elsewhere, and Judaism was a legal religion. His ruthless cunning isolated Christianity from Judaism and treated Jesus'
movement as a new, autonomous religion. A bad religion (a *superstitio*,
as Tacitus called it), to be sure, but a cult independent of Judaism that
Roman law would never ignore again, whether its attention took the
form of persecution or acceptance. In separating Christianity from
Judaism, Nero's cynical politics anticipated theological changes that
Judaism and Christianity would need another half century to work out.

Nero's evil genius saw thousands of Christians killed in Rome.

Peter, who had come to Rome after James' death to seek help for a now desperate community of believers in Jerusalem, was nailed to a cross and turned upside down to die. Paul's death was more immediate, as befitted a citizen. Rome responded to Christianity's first intellectual and most influential thinker by beheading him.

Gathered up with dozens of Christians camped around him in the ashes of Rome, he no doubt made the kind of sarcastic remark to a Roman officer he once made to Claudius Lysias in Jerusalem (Acts 21:37–39):

> Is this the way you treat a citizen?
> You are a citizen?

To that question the fifty-seven-year-old Tarsan responded with his familiar, proud reply:

> From Tarsus, no mean city.

This time, however, there was no appeal to Caesar. What did that matter? "When this decaying body will clothe itself with incorruption and this mortal body will clothe itself with immortality, then the word that was written shall come to pass, 'Death is swallowed up in victory. Death, where is your victory? Death, where is your sting?'" (1 Corinthians 15:54–55). A nod from an officer instructed a soldier to unsheathe his sword, and Paul's last flash of physical consciousness was as a head separated from its body, even as he entered the body of Christ forever.

· · ·

NERO'S POGROM left Christianity bereft of leaders and without a home. Rome offered them no welcome, with or without the grudging sympathy of aristocrats like Tacitus, while Jerusalem became increasingly inhospitable. Priestly nationalism there grew more extreme until 66 C.E., when the Temple administration announced that priests would no longer accept any offering from Gentiles—including sacrifices the emperor had paid for. Rome understood all too well that this amounted to deliberate insurrection. The Senate dispatched the tenth legion Fretensis, and by 70 C.E., Jerusalem and the Temple would be in ashes. Christians found no natural allies in the midst of this fresh round of disaster. They were squeezed between priests who despised contact with the Gentiles in connection with the Temple and Romans who were prepared to burn anything in their path for the sake of regime change.

Asia Minor and Greece offered better prospects. Among the householders in Philippi, the salons of Corinth, and businesspeople such as Priscilla and Aquila in Ephesus, Rome, and beyond, congregations of Christians endured these changes, local prejudice, and outbreaks of violence that came their way. The networks of travel and communication that Paul had exploited—the Roman Empire's unintended subsidies for this fledgling movement—remained intact and were even extended after Paul's time.

Paul's letters also survived his death. Until the Gospels were produced and circulated, these were the only written sources distinctive to Christianity. That is why they rose to prominence in Christian usage despite the controversy surrounding Paul, and formed the nucleus of what the second-century Church called the New Testament. What we read about Jesus today in Matthew, Mark, Luke, and John was circulating only in oral form during the 60s C.E., and took decades to be consigned to writing. The Bible of Christian worship was the Septuagint, its inheritance from the Diaspora synagogue. Posthumously, Paul filled the vacuum of leadership that plagued Christianity by means of his letters. They were at the right place and at the right time in a way he never managed to be personally.

Many hands copied these letters and got them to congregations sympathetic to Paul and his memory. Amanuenses and assistants had been with Paul when he composed them; these old entourages—in Ephesus, Troas, and Miletus—formed a natural cadre of editors that could correlate their work with copies of correspondence kept by churches in Galatia, Corinth, Rome, and Philippi. Wherever Paul had written from, wherever he had written to, salvaging his words offered guidance to a generation of believers that was battered and disoriented after the catastrophes that unfolded in Rome and Jerusalem.

Timothy played a key role in disseminating the letters in the decades after Paul's death. He had already worked with Paul in the composition of 1 Thessalonians, 2 Corinthians, and Philemon, becoming increasingly influential throughout that progression. Without Timothy's encouragement, support, and editorial initiative, Philippians might not have been written and the poetry of Colossians would have been lost. He was the personal link between the author and the letters that circulated in Paul's name.

With Timothy's growing influence, these letters addressed issues closer to his heart than to Paul's. The beginning of Philippians, for example, includes special greetings to "bishops and deacons," part of the hierarchy that emerged as a result of Timothy's work to consolidate the influence of his teacher. Paul's own characteristic worries did not turn on hierarchical issues, but Timothy had a particular concern for them as the years went on. His influence on the Book of Acts is as obvious as the anachronism involved when Paul and Barnabas ordain men to be clergy (Acts 14:23) just after Paul had been stoned.

Timothy was a young man when Paul circumcised him in 46 C.E.; by 90 C.E., when the collection of Pauline letters was virtually complete, he was well into his sixties. By then most of the letters written up until the time of Paul's imprisonment had been circulating; Timothy consolidated and arranged the fragments that make up 2 Corinthians to enhance the collection. His success in that emboldened him to edit and enlarge the letters to Philemon, to the Philippians, and to the Colossians for general reading: the equivalent of publication.

In Colossians, Paul still speaks of his own concerns, but Timothy also cleans up the apostle's image by having him say (Colossians 2:5): "Because if I am absent in flesh, yet I am with you in spirit, rejoicing and seeing your order and the firmness of your faith in Christ."

This is Timothy's voice rather than Paul's. When the apostle himself spoke of the presence of his own spirit with a congregation, that was more threat than reassurance (1 Corinthians 5:4–5), and he did not trouble about "order" except to warn people about specific problems such as drunkenness, bad teaching, and being stingy.

Neither this new spin on Paul's character nor the organizational concerns of Philippians and Colossians takes away from Timothy's lasting achievement: he made Paul's poetry available together with the earlier prose letters to guide a movement passing through its most difficult period. The capstone of his work is probably the letter to the Ephesians.[4] Here the sweeping image of the cosmic Christ in Colossians is used to address the particular tensions between Gentile and Jewish Christians in Ephesus at a later period (Ephesians 2:11–14): "Therefore remember that you were once Gentiles in flesh, those called foreskin by those called circumcision in flesh—made by hands—because you were in that time apart from Christ, estranged from the citizenship of Israel and foreign to the covenants of the promise, not having hope and godless in the world. But now, in Jesus Christ you who were once far have become near in the blood of Christ. For he personally is our peace: he made the two one and looses the dividing barrier. . . ."

Timothy crafted these words for a community in which Gentiles had become dominant, so they would appreciate that it was only God's gracious inclusion of them within Israel that permitted them to inherit the covenantal promise.[5] Christ's aim was to produce "one new man," joined in "one body for God" (Ephesians 2:15–16). By the time Ephesians was written, the body of Christ had indeed become the body of God for Pauline Christians, so completely had they incorporated Paul's revelation that Jesus was not only God's Son but the cosmic reality of divine nature itself.

. . .

PAUL'S POETRY COULD NOT resolve all the problems of second-generation Christianity. Absent the Temple and the leadership of James, Peter, and Paul, no amount of tinkering with the legacy of sporadic writings to various congregations could explain exactly how churches should face up to challenges that Jesus and his first followers had never confronted. Day to day, how were people supposed to live?

When Timothy edited the core of Paul's letters, adding material of his own, that spurred some Christians to continue writing in Paul's name. They produced these new missives as personal letters of Paul to Timothy and Titus, but scholarship is nearly unanimous in rejecting these attributions.[6] Someone who tried to pass off such works today would be called a forger, but antiquity provides many examples of intellectual enthusiasts who wrote in a great master's name. We know Socrates only from Plato's rosy scenarios, and the *Genesis Apocryphon* from Qumran freely embellishes on what the patriarchs of Israel said and did. The biblical Book of Daniel is pseudepigraphal, written during the second century B.C.E. but attributed to a Jewish sage who lived centuries earlier. Paul had stated openly during his lifetime that he could project his spirit from one place to another (1 Corinthians 5:3–5): he practically invited later disciples to claim his spirit for their own time as well.

The Pastoral Epistles (1 Timothy, 2 Timothy, Titus) took this invitation up, and they deal explicitly with the pastoral imperative to organize, order, and care for congregations. In this, their tone and language is unlike Paul's, and also unlike those letters that have come to us in which Timothy had a hand.

Each claims to address Timothy or Titus personally, but the affectionate language of Philemon and Philippians is missing. Timothy and Titus in the Pastoral Epistles are not presented as coauthors with Paul; instead, they receive categorical, often stern advice. These alleged communiqués are unlike Paul's letters to particular churches (or to a person, in the case of Philemon). Rather, these are epistles, literary productions that try to crystallize Paul's wisdom for the Church at large.

They address the issues of their time, not Paul's. 1 Timothy emphasizes the necessity for prayer on behalf of rulers (1 Timothy 2:1–8), somewhat in the manner of Romans, but against the grain of Paul's proud rejection in Philippians of any citizenship but heaven's, and is particularly concerned to keep women in their place, which this epistle thinks of as bearing children (1 Timothy 2:13–15): "Because Adam was first fashioned, then Eve. And Adam was not deceived, but the misled woman came into transgression. But she will be saved through childbearing, if they remain in faith and love and sanctification with prudence."

This was just the argument from Genesis that Paul had once started to make in a letter to Corinth, then stopping himself (1 Corinthians 11:8–12), because he realized that it contradicted his own principle of equality in Christ. Compunctions of that sort did not distract those who composed the Pastoral Epistles; the agenda of maintaining order overrode the subtleties of Paul's own thinking. At the same time, the concerns of this world (including procreation) intrude much more than they did in Paul's mind.

The proper selection of "bishops" and "deacons" (including women) to govern the Church is supposed to assure good order (1 Timothy 3:1–13). Their central authority devolves through "elders" (both men and women; 1 Timothy 5:1–2, 17–18) and "widows" (1 Timothy 5:3–16), and the epistle gives instructions (vv. 21–22) about their selection and designation by laying on of hands.

Paul himself was interested in seeing to some of the functions these terms refer to, but the Pastoral Epistles consolidated them into hierarchical offices. In all probability Paul had designated some people as bishops. The term *episkopos* means "overseer," like the term *mebaqqer* in Hebrew. Paul needed administrators, especially for his collections, and it made good sense to name them with the same title that James bore in Jerusalem. When a local elder from the synagogue (a *zaken* in Hebrew, a *presbuteros* in Greek) sympathized with him, Paul no doubt embraced this rabbi. And he freely used the word "servant," *diakonos* (in Greek, corresponding to *'eved* in Hebrew), to speak of anyone who helped spread Jesus' message. All the major terms used in the Pastoral Epistles that speak of offices in the Church had their precedents in the life of the synagogue as well as in Paul's life.

For those who wrote these epistles, however, these words didn't just refer to jobs that needed to be done, but to a hierarchy—the template of bishops, priests,[7] and deacons that survives to this day—that alone could preserve the heritage of Paul. In particular, 1 Timothy invoked this hierarchy to warn about teachers who encouraged excessive asceticism (1 Timothy 4:2–3): "Hypocritical pretenders, their own conscience cauterized—forbidding to marry—to abstain from foods, which God created for the faithful who recognize truth to partake with thanksgiving."

An escape into the world of Spirit could become so extreme that it amounted to a denial that God is truly the God of this world as well as of the next. The Pastorals engage this incipient Gnosticism and reflect its origins. So great a threat does this attitude pose, 1 Timothy (1:20) invokes the old stricture of Paul that people who teach this way should be handed over to Satan. But what about Paul himself? Hadn't he said (1 Corinthians 7:1) that it was good for a man not to touch a woman? In shaping Paul's message against Gnostics, the Pastoral Epistles might well be bending Paul against himself.

1 Timothy's enthusiasm for this world and its good order leads to another remark that at first sight looks un-Pauline (1 Timothy 1:8): "We know that the Law is good, if one makes use of it lawfully." This is not at all Paul's way of putting the matter, and is enough by itself to endorse the judgment that Paul did not write 1 Timothy.[8] This is a derivative version of the apostle's message for a new and desperate time.

But derivative as it is, 1 Timothy is also the earliest known attempt to bring some consistency to Paul's teaching about the Law. That was a major achievement, although how to reconcile Paul's various and variable statements about the Torah—as categorical as they are contradictory—is a puzzle to this day.

In Galatians, Paul had boldly given the key to why Abraham had been told in Genesis, "All the Gentiles shall be blessed by you." The prophet Habakkuk said, "The righteous person shall live from faith" (Galatians 3:7–11), and faith for Paul is how people inherit Abraham's blessing. The opposite of this blessing of faith is Torah, which comes with the anathema in the Book of Deuteronomy that anyone who fails to do all the commandments is cursed. No one can really do that, so the Torah curses everyone. This even applies to Jesus, because Deuteronomy also declares that everyone hung on a tree is accursed! So, Paul concludes (Galatians 3:12–14), this curse on Jesus—warranted by Scripture—proves that the promise of the Spirit to all humanity is a blessing of faith, and of faith alone.

Yet this commanding theme of Galatians—becoming righteous by faith alone, apart from "works"—finds no development in 1 Corinthians. Paul does refer to every believer as "made righteous" at the moment of baptism (1 Corinthians 6:11), but there was no danger of his readers in Corinth applying the Torah literally. The salons were mostly made up of non-Jews. So when Paul does cite Scripture in 1 Corinthians, he does so in a *positive* mode, without setting the Bible against itself as he does in the dialectical argument between faith and works in Galatians.

Instead, in writing to the Corinthians, Paul portrays the Scriptures of Israel as being fulfilled as they experienced Christ. God destroys facile wisdom, as Isaiah said (1 Corinthians 1:19), preparing what eye has not seen nor ear heard (1 Corinthians 2:9). Although most of the Scriptures he cites are prophetic, he even invokes the Law of Deuteronomy to insist that any fornicator is to be expunged from the community (1 Corinthians 5:13) and compares the Corinthian communities *directly* to when Israel revolted against Moses in the wilderness (1 Corinthians 10:1–13). Indeed, at that point he tellingly refers to the Israelites as "our fathers" (1 Corinthians 10:1–2) and speaks of their being "baptized into Moses in the cloud and in the sea."

To Paul's mind, writing to the Romans (with the storms in Galatia and Corinth behind him), there was no contradiction between these two stances. The Torah's positive value is purely prophetic, showing the way to righteousness in Christ. Once that righteousness is achieved—even when one is uncircumcised—the Torah has served its purpose (Romans 2:25–29). Paul converted the Torah from an ethical norm into an instrument of prophecy. That move may seem effortless by the time the mature Paul formulated the matter at the age of fifty, but that ease came only with the benefit of his emotional distance from the cruel exchanges with James and Peter. The Scriptures of Israel, on this fully developed estimate, have prophetic value for all believers; they show how each and every believer sees Christ handed over for one's own sin and yet raised for one's own righteousness (Romans 3:19–24). At the moment of baptism, every believer knows that while sin makes one unworthy of salvation, a new possibility of righteousness dawns with the inrushing power of Spirit.

1 Timothy marks an insight that anyone who has tried to organize a group of Christians will find obvious: there is no practical way of explaining the subtleties of baptismal mysticism every time people want to know whether or not to keep the Law. Of course the issue is simplified in the Pastoral Epistles. By speaking of making use of the Law "lawfully," a bishop or priest or deacon could keep order among those preparing for baptism while leaving the opportunity open at a later, more reflective moment to discuss what "lawfully" means.

The Pastoral Epistles also make Paul speak in a way that would make any hagiographer happy. Who could imagine the author of Galatians or 1 Corinthians or Philippians saying that he served God "from ancestral origins with clean conscience" (2 Timothy 1:3)—without mention of his career as a persecutor of Christians?[9] And where is Paul's complex relationship with Moses in this unqualified assertion (2 Timothy 3:16): "All Scripture is God-inspired and useful for teaching, for reproof, for correction, and for training in righteousness"?

Yet that kind of oversimplification pales in comparison to the picture of Paul in the letter to Titus. Here Paul, who seems never to have traveled to Crete, nonetheless leaves Titus there (Titus 1:5) with this warning about the people on the island (Titus 1:12–13): "One of themselves, their own prophet said, 'Cretans are always liars, evil beasts, lazy-bellies.' This testimony is true. . . ."

Paul was never a diplomat, but for him the coin of insult was sarcasm,[10] not calumny. Those who wrote the Pastoral Epistles did not know him and used his letters for their own purposes.

These works trim down Paul's theology more than they continue Paul's thought: they run parallel to his letters, dealing with levels of organization and theological disputes outside of Paul's own experience. It is easy enough to make fun of their bourgeois concern to keep churches ordered, people in line, and the extremes of spiritual enthusiasm under control.[11] But order, convention, and obedience seem to be trivial matters only if you already enjoy their benefits. Persecution without and dissension within plagued churches at the end of the first century, and major renovations of Paul's teaching enabled them to confront those challenges.

The greatest, most elegant[12] post-Pauline epistle is also the last, and deliberately presents Christian faith as independent of Judaism. Hebrews explains that the Temple on earth (which by this time, 95 C.E., had been destroyed) was only a copy[13]—a shadow of the heavenly sanctuary. Moses had seen the very throne of God, which was then approximated on earth in the Temple. That approximation is the "first covenant," and its time has passed. But the heavenly sanctuary offers us a "new covenant" (9:1–15). Christ entered that true sanctuary when he died a sacrificial death (9:24), and its truth—palely reflected in Israel's institutions—is accessible to all who believe in him. Divine vision, the sanctification to stand before God, is in Hebrews the goal of human life, and the only means to such perfection is loyalty to Jesus as the high priest who completes the sacrifice that the practices of Israel could foreshadow but not accomplish.

The epistle to the Hebrews deliberately emphasizes the finality of a perfection from which one must not defect, the heart's only sanctuary (12:22–24): "But you have come up to Zion, mount and city of the living God, heavenly Jerusalem, and to myriads of angels in festal gathering, and to a congregation of firstborn enrolled in heaven, and to a judge—God of all, and to the spirits of righteous people made perfect, and to Jesus the mediator of a pristine covenant, and to sprinkled blood that speaks better than the blood of Abel."

Jesus is the single focus of revelation in Hebrews, and this epistle—unlike Paul—relegates Israel to a thing of the past (8:8–13) because the Son's authority is greater than that of the Scripture. Once, God spoke in many and various ways through the prophets; now, at the end of

days, he speaks to us by a Son (Hebrews 1:1, 2). Scripture is only authoritative to the extent that it attests the salvation mediated by the Son
(1:3–2:4). The argument that animates the whole epistle derives directly from the conviction of the prior authority of the Son of God in
relation to Scripture.

For Hebrews, Christ replaces every major institution within the
Judaism of its time. There is a single center within the theology of
Hebrews. It is not Christ with Moses, Christ with Temple, Christ with
David, Christ with Abraham, Christ with Scripture, Christ with Israel.
Christ is the beginning, middle, and end of theology in Hebrews, just
as he is the same yesterday, today, and forever (Hebrews 13:8).
Everything else is a provisional and expendable type that is consumed
in the fire that is God (12:29).

. . .

MANY OF THESE post-Pauline ideas continue to be attributed to Paul
to this day, making him the apostle many contemporary Christians—
and non-Christians—love to hate. Anyone who wants to complain that
"organized religion" has betrayed Jesus can blame Paul the bureaucrat,
citing the Pastoral Epistles and Acts. Feminist critics can fasten on that
infamous statement in 1 Timothy 2:15 about women overcoming Eve's
curse by bearing children. The Paul of Hebrews is an easy target for
anyone offended by Christianity's claim to supersede Judaism. And
who would want to defend what the Paul of the Letter to Titus says
about people from Crete?

There is good reason to react against these aspects of the Pauline tradition, and some evidence to associate them with Paul himself.
Although he had nothing to do with the gaffe the Letter to Titus attributes to him, he clearly embraced many of the prejudices of his time.
His Letter to Philemon tacitly endorses the institution of slavery, for
example. He was nothing like the organizer that Acts and the Pastoral
Epistles make him into, but he did want to keep his congregations
growing until the apocalypse on Mount Zion ended the world. His
ambivalent attitudes toward women are so confusing that many read-

ers have just written him off as a misogynist, however simplistic that may be. Paul did not think (any more than Jesus did) of Christianity being a separate religion from Judaism, but he relegated the Torah to a position very few of his fellow Jews accepted in his time, and the nearly two millennia since have not changed that.

Paul's ideas remain controversial, disputed to this day. During his life he found no major community of Christians anywhere that would unequivocally back his position against James' or Peter's. His greatest letters—to the Galatians, the Corinthians, the Romans, and even to the Philippians—reflect his defensiveness over that simple fact. After his death, even the writings attributed to him often skewed his perspective. He paid the price for uniqueness on many occasions, in many ways.

Paul could have lived a quieter life. He might have remained a devout Jew in Tarsus, but tried to make himself a Pharisee in Jerusalem. He acquired standing in the priestly wing of that movement, but converted to the heavenly vision and voice that announced itself as Jesus. He could have joined the thousands of observant Jews who acknowledged Jesus as God's Son while obeying the Law, but insisted that the Torah was only a way station to recognizing Jesus as the Christ who would fulfill all the promises to Israel and include the Gentiles in that fulfillment. He might have accepted the pattern of Peter and Barnabas, who extended baptism to God-fearers; but Paul disrupted the fledgling Christian movement by his contact with idolatrous pagans. Maintaining his natural, Stoic regard for the emperor's dignity might have saved his life at the end, and that is just when he rejected his earlier Stoicism and declared that his true citizenship was in heaven, not Rome. All these transitions involved inconvenience and hardship; some brought pain, injury, and mortal danger.

Paul did not invent the message he died for. Jesus remains the genius and founder of Christianity. Jesus' prophetic vision of how God's kingdom will transfigure all things, from Jerusalem outward, became the center of Judaism for his disciples, who joined him on his visionary quest.

But Rabbi Jesus' success was limited to his fellow visionaries: the total number of people immediately after the crucifixion who claimed to have seen him risen from the dead numbered less than a thousand. Yet because they perceived him as alive, Jesus prompted his movement to radical innovations. The Galilean rabbi had never encouraged contact with Gentiles, for example, but Peter insisted on baptizing God-fearers, inspired by his vision in Joppa. Paul's uniquely successful resonance with ordinary non-Jews—living far from Israel and out of touch with synagogues—opened up new territory for the movement. In retrospect it might seem inevitable that the new direction indicated by the risen Jesus in Peter's vision, together with the new ground broken by Paul, would produce a new religion. But that was not the intention of Peter or Paul, who saw their actions as prophetic extensions of Israel, not a break with the people of Abraham.

Paul popularized Jesus' message, providing a new vector of divine apocalypse—the faith of pagans. He also changed the message, shifting the emphasis of Jesus' movement away from realizing the kingdom of God along with Jesus and toward recognizing Jesus himself as the Christ within one's being. Every believer was animated with the Spirit that came from Jesus. Paul claimed to give birth to the divine Son when those who listened to him heard what he said with faith. Jesus is Christianity's founder, but Paul is its maker—he focused the elements of faith on the formation of the Christ within. That paved the way for what emerged after Paul's death, a faith that survived Nero's pogrom and the Roman burning of the Temple.

Baptism turned people into the Israel of God, transformed by the Spirit within them; each of them became "devoted *(euparedros)* to the Lord" (1 Corinthians 7:35). This single word conveys the depth of Paul's conviction that believers lived in a new order of being. In texts outside the New Testament, this term refers to the way that spirits or demons might be helpful for mediums, like a devoted "familiar" serving a sorcerer.[14] Instead of Christ or Spirit coming to the help of the believer, by baptism the believer becomes a *euparedros*,[15] a helpful familiar in the kingdom of Christ that is coming to transform this world.

For Paul, each believer's body was a temple of the Spirit. Contact between the divine and the human level had already been accomplished in baptism. From that moment, divine initiatives were mediated to people by means of the movement of the Holy Spirit within them. They knew God's concerns; they possessed—and were possessed by—the mind of Christ (1 Corinthians 2:16), which gave them a full and intimate revelation of mysteries present and to come. Each person devoted to the Spirit could awaken that Spirit in others, as Christ's *euparedros*.

Deep awareness of one's self, completion by the presence of Spirit, made devotion the deepest pleasure. As far as Paul was concerned, that was all he or anyone like him needed, and he held up that self-sufficiency—or rather Spirit-sufficiency—as a standard. "For I am convinced," he wrote (Romans 8:38–39), "that neither death nor life, neither angels nor principalities, neither present nor coming events, nor powers, neither height nor depth, nor any other created thing shall be able to separate us from the love of God that is in Jesus Christ our Lord."

When in later centuries Christian mystics such as Hildegard of Bingen, Julian of Norwich, and Theresa of Avila explored their relationship to God in Christ, they did so as diarists of their own experience. Their insight joined Paul's in uncovering a pivot of spiritual experience:[16] if you care as God cares, then Christ—the center of the entire cosmos—inhabits the recesses of that inner longing, and nothing can ever separate you from that creative passion.

To arrive at that realization and then articulate it to others represented the height of Paul's intellectual ambition. Beyond that achievement he rejoiced that, for all his faults (2 Corinthians 4:6–7), "the God who said, 'Light shall shine out of darkness,' has shined in our hearts to illumine the knowledge of the glory of God in Christ Jesus' face. But we have this treasure in clay pots, so the eminence of the power is God's, and not ours."

Christ mediated a revelation of God within each human being that was so creative, it was like that first primordial day when God said,

266 · RABBI PAUL

"Let there be light. . . ." The failures of the flesh, the brokenness of Paul's own body, did not disappear in that new reality. His chronic pain and debilitation, his fierce temper and parochial prejudices, were obvious to others—and he could scarcely conceal them from himself. He never found perfection in his own heart and did not expect to find it—there or elsewhere—in this world. Paul knew the ways of the earth of which we are all made, even as he felt within himself the stirrings of a truer self, making peace with God's creation and restoring his own fragmented soul.

A CHRONOLOGY FOR PAUL

334 B.C.E.: Alexander the Great enters Cilicia.

52–50 B.C.E.: Cicero serves from Tarsus as proconsul of Cilicia.

42 B.C.E.: On behalf of the Triumvirate, Mark Antony confirms Tarsus's civic status and grants it exemption from duties.

7 C.E.: Paul is born in Tarsus in Asia Minor into a proudly Jewish family that prospers in the profession of making tents.

28 C.E.: Paul departs Tarsus for Jerusalem, taking the Aramaic name of Saul, to train as a Pharisee.

32 C.E.: Between Passover and Pentecost, the Gospels attest a sequence of Resurrection appearances, and the Book of Acts indicates a series of visions during that summer. After the stoning of Stephen, Paul's vision of the risen Jesus took place (Galatians 1:15–17). He did not return to Jerusalem at that time, but went to Arabia for three years and returned to Damascus. At the end of this period of activity he had to escape Damascus from Aretas IV, king of Nabatea, in a basket lowered over the city wall (2 Corinthians 11:32–33).

35: Three years after his conversion, Paul met with Peter and James, Jesus' brother, in Jerusalem. During a period of fifteen days, he learned what Peter regularly taught those who were baptized in

Jesus' name (Galatians 1:18–20). This was followed by a return to his native land (Galatians 1:21–24), until he joined Barnabas in Antioch.

42: or fourteen years before his correspondence with Corinth (2 Corinthians 12:2–4): Paul says he was taken up into the third heaven. This ecstatic experience corresponds to his prophetic commission in Antioch to take his work among Gentiles into new areas under Barnabas's leadership (Acts 13:1–3). Striking across Cyprus first, Paul and Barnabas accepted the benefaction of Sergius Paulus.

46: or fourteen years after his vision of the risen Jesus: Paul again went to Jerusalem with Barnabas and Titus (Galatians 2:1–10). In addition to determining that circumcision should not be required of Gentile believers, spheres of apostolic influence were a principal concern. Peter's was the territory historically associated with circumcision while Paul's was traditionally Gentile lands (v. 8). At the same time, Paul agreed to meet the needs of the community gathered around James in Jerusalem, which was afflicted by the famine that plagued Judea.

50: Paul met up with Priscilla and Aquila in Corinth (Acts 18:2; 1 Corinthians 16:19) after Claudius's expulsion of many Jews from Rome in 49 C.E. From Corinth, Paul wrote with Silas and Timothy to the Thessalonians.

July 1, 51–July 1, 52: The tenure of Gallio in Corinth (Acts 18:12). In Paul's absence, a meeting in Jerusalem—sealed by a decree from James—stipulates requirements of purity for Gentile believers. Later in 52, the penultimate journey of Paul to Jerusalem (Acts 18:22).

53: The confrontation at Antioch, occasioned by the decree of James (Galatians 2:11–21; and Acts 15:19–24).

53–56: Paul's period in Ephesus (with a retreat to Troas and Macedonia at the end); the composition of Galatians, 1 Corinthians, and 2 Corinthians.

57: Letter to the Romans, written from Miletus, south of Ephesus, and final arrangements for the Sacrifice of the Nations. Paul's arrest in Jerusalem and detention in Caesarea; the composition of Philemon the following year.

59–62: Festus's tenure, overlapping with the tenure of the high priest, Ananus (Acts 25–26). Paul's appeal to the Philippians for help in his letter to that city, written with Timothy and later expanded by Timothy.

62: Paul's release, his final period in Rome, and the composition of poetry later incorporated by Timothy in the letter to the Colossians.

64: Paul's death in Rome under Nero.

70–73: The burning of the Temple by the Roman troops under Titus; the composition of Mark's Gospel in Rome; the end of the revolt against Rome in Palestine.

75: Josephus publishes his *Jewish War.*

80: The composition of Matthew's Gospel, in Damascus.

90: The composition of Luke's Gospel and Acts, in Antioch. Timothy's release of letters written by Paul with his help, together with the Epistle to the Ephesians. The Pastoral Epistles were composed later in the same decade.

93: Josephus publishes his *Antiquities of the Jews.*

95: The Epistle to the Hebrews.

100: The composition of John's Gospel, in Ephesus.

NOTES

Preface

1. At a later period this term was obviously used in a more restricted and technical sense. That is also true of such titles as "apostle," "priest," "bishop," even "church" and "teacher." Historical study always has to allow for such factors as institutionalization that shape and reshape the meanings of words; if you can't do that, you cannot free yourself from the strictures of your own time. See *Rabbi Jesus: An Intimate Biography* (New York: Doubleday, 2000), 109–10, 296.

2. He doesn't even give us his full name. He just signs himself "Paul" in his letters—two names short of the classical Roman style of *praenomen, nomen,* and *cognomen.*

3. For a sober and representative treatment of this question and others, see Raymond E. Brown, *An Introduction to the New Testament,* The Anchor Bible Reference Library (New York: Doubleday, 1997), 225–332.

4. Abraham J. Malherbe has in my opinion struck the right balance in coordinating Acts with Paul's letters; *The Letters to the Thessalonians,* The Anchor Bible 32B (New York: Doubleday, 2000), 55–78. John Knox argued that Paul's letters should be privileged in relation to Acts; *Chapters in a Life of Paul* (New York: Abingdon, 1950). Even William Ramsay's *St. Paul the Traveller and the Roman Citizen* (New York: Putnam's, 1896), still revered as an icon of scholarship among conservative Evangelicals, acknowledges that Acts shapes the story it relates. Where I contradict Acts with Paul in this book (or vice versa), I state my reasons.

5. In detailing that itinerary and its punctuation with visits to Jerusalem, the

place of inference is comparable to the approach I take in *Rabbi Jesus* (see pp. xx–xxii), although the sources involved are as different as Paul is from Jesus. I consciously acknowledge that historians *infer* from evidence and do not really "prove" anything in a scientific or mathematical sense. That is a well-established principle in the study of history, although some students of the New Testament cling to the nineteenth-century myth of historical "objectivity."

1. *Tent-Maker's Son from Tarsus*

1. A woman Paul indicates as being "outstanding among the apostles." That so scandalized later commentators, copyists, and scholars, they turned her into Junias or Julian—a man's name! See C. E. B. Cranfield, *Romans: A Shorter Commentary* (Edinburgh: Clark, 1985), 377, and Joseph A. Fitzmyer, *Romans: A New Translation with Introduction and Commentary*, The Anchor Bible 33 (New York: Doubleday, 1992), 737–38.

2. Because the Cilician plain is alluvial, distances to the Mediterranean have changed over time, but Strabo puts the run to the outlet of the Cydnus at 120 *stadia* (*Geography*, 14.5.11). Rivers aren't straight, and I have pared that estimate down a little. Even the course of the Cydnus has altered since the first century, as a result of a channel project under the emperor Justinian during the sixth century C.E. See *Excavations at Gözlü Kule, Tarsus: The Hellenistic and Roman Periods*, ed. Hetty Goldman (Princeton: Princeton University Press, 1950).

3. Josephus, *Antiquities* 12. 147–53; 13. 145–70 covers the military alliance between Antiochus III and Jonathan Maccabeus and explains the strategic importance of Cilicia to Antiochus.

4. The case of the Maccabees in Jerusalem was aberrant, a unique collision between the arrogance of Antiochus IV in attempting to convert worship in the Temple to Zeus and the uncompromising recalcitrance of Judas Maccabeus and his brothers. Both the Seleucids and the Romans wisely tried to avoid that sort of confrontation with their Jewish subjects. When it came to dealing with the trouble in Tarsus, even Antiochus IV resorted to diplomacy (2 Maccabees 4:30).

5. Plutarch *Antony* 25–28; this is the inspiration behind Shakespeare's lines in *Antony and Cleopatra* that the queen's appearance "beggar'd all description: she did lie / In her pavilion, cloth-of-gold of tissue,— / O'er picturing that Venus where we see / The fancy out-work of nature . . ." (act 2, scene 2, Enobarbus).

6. The classic description, on the basis of numismatic, archaeological, and historical evidence, remains William Ramsay, *The Cities of St. Paul: Their Influence on His Life and Thought* (New York: Hodder & Stoughton, 1907), 137–56.

7. Those commentators who have picked up on the sacrificial imagery have usually thought in terms of *Roman* processions of victory; see Victor Paul Furnish, *II Corinthians: A New Translation with Introduction and Commentary*, The

Anchor Bible 32A (New York: Doubleday, 1984), 187–88. I agree with the majority of them that this particular connection does not work well, and look instead for a sacrificial image that is literally closer to home.

8. The phrase "a Hebrew from Hebrews" in Philippians 3:5 refers to his speaking a Semitic language; in Paul's time and city that language was Aramaic.

9. See the fine discussion in Brian Rapske, *The Book of Acts and Paul in Roman Custody,* The Book of Acts in Its First Century Setting 3 (Grand Rapids: Eerdmans, 1994), 90–108.

10. The order of the Codex Vaticanus divides the works into the categories of history, poetry, and prophecy:

(1) Genesis, Exodus, Leviticus, Numbers, Deuteronomy, Joshua, Judges, Ruth, 1–4 Kings, 1–2 Chronicles, 1–2 Ezra;

(2) Psalms, Proverbs, Ecclesiastes, Song of Songs, Job, Wisdom of Solomon, Wisdom of Sirach, Esther, Judith, Tobit;

(3) Hosea, Amos, Micah, Joel, Obadiah, Jonah, Nahum, Habakkuk, Zephaniah, Haggai, Zechariah, Malachi, Isaiah, Jeremiah, Baruch, Lamentations, Letter of Jeremiah, Ezekiel, Daniel.

Christianity embraced this order, and the Codex Vaticanus was copied for use in the Church, but that does not make the sequence a Christian invention.

11. This was written a century after his death, but its sources are sometimes informative, and in this case there is agreement with Dio Chrysostom, Apollonius's contemporary; see F. C. Conybeare, *Philostatus, The Life of Apollonius of Tyana: The Epistles of Apollonius and the Treatise of Eusebius* (New York: Macmillan, 1912).

12. The treatment of Lillian M. Wilson remains valuable; *The Roman Toga,* The Johns Hopkins University Studies in Archaeology 1 (Baltimore: Johns Hopkins University Press, 1924).

2. *"At the Feet" of Gamaliel, in Service of Caiaphas*

1. Although there is some evidence that the Scriptures in Aramaic and Hebrew influenced Paul, he cited the Septuagint from memory throughout his letters. That in my opinion confirms that he was educated in Tarsus prior to his career as a Pharisee in Jerusalem.

2. For this observation, see Jerome Murphy-O'Connor, *Paul: A Critical Life* (Oxford: Clarendon, 1996), 42–43. He carries it too far, however, in denying that Paul was known as Saul in Jerusalem. The Book of Acts refers to Paul as "Saul" during his time as a Pharisee in Jerusalem, and later—during his sojourns in Damascus, Jerusalem, and Syria, even after his conversion. Then Saul travels to Cyprus and teaches Christianity to Sergius Paulus, a Roman official. From that point (Acts 13:9), Acts calls him "Paul." This pattern suggests where and in what language circles Paul used his Pharisaic name, and where and when he re-

verted to his Greek name. Acts obviously simplifies matters because Paul mixed with Aramaic speakers and Greek speakers—Jews, Christians, and pagans—all his life. His name would have varied with his setting. To avoid confusion, I have decided to call him by his Hellenistic name throughout.

3. *Paul: Apostle to the Gentiles,* trans. O. C. Dean (Louisville: Westminster/ John Knox, 1993), 38–40. Becker fully agrees that Paul was a Pharisee, however, which Philippians 3:5 makes pretty much undeniable. Although I disagree with Becker here, my collation of Acts with Paul's letters often coincides with his treatment, and I appreciate the close company he keeps with the text of Paul's letters. In this regard, however, I side with Murphy-O'Connor, pp. 54–56.

4. To some extent this was the Romans' doing, because in 70 C.E. they destroyed the Temple that had been the power base of the priesthood and exterminated the Essenes during the course of that same war. The Pharisees were guardians of the Judaism left standing after that disaster, along with smaller splinter movements such as the fledgling group called Christians.

5. See *The Judaism of Qumran: A Systemic Reading of the Dead Sea Scrolls,* Judaism in Late Antiquity 5.1 and 5.2/Handbuch der Orientalistik 56 and 57, ed. A. J. Avery-Peck, J. Neusner, B. D. Chilton (Leiden: Brill, 2001). These Essenes later distinguished themselves for their heroism, even under torture, in the war against Rome.

6. This issue arose for Gamaliel's family because they were wealthier than most Pharisees, and that meant they lived near to the lavish dwellings in the priests' neighborhood. For a consideration of the evidence concerning Gamaliel, see Jacob Neusner, *The Rabbinic Traditions about the Pharisees before 70,* South Florida Studies in the History of Judaism (Atlanta: Scholars, 1999).

7. Eveline van Staalduine-Sulman discusses this usage in *The Targum of Samuel,* Studies in the Aramaic Interpretation of Scripture (Leiden: Brill, 2002), 279.

8. This tale is reminiscent of others that speak of the mortal danger of learning esoteric truth. Once, it was said, a Galilean was about to publicly describe the chariot-throne of God (the Merkabah of Ezekiel 1), the transcendent source of the whole creation. Rabbis had long held that the secret of the Merkabah was to be kept among adepts, those who could control their knowledge. But they did not need to worry: A wasp intervened to kill the Galilean before he could divulge his secret knowledge (Shabbath 80b in the Talmud). For similar stories, see the Sources.

9. See *Rabbi Jesus,* 197–289, for a full description of Jesus' motivation from the time of his last pilgrimage to Jerusalem until his death, as well as of the first Resurrection appearances.

10. Acts presents this as occurring in a formal session of the Sanhedrin, but the event makes better sense as mob action, and Acts does have a tendency to make Jewish authorities directly responsible for violence.

11. Jerome Murphy-O'Connor, *Paul: A Critical Life* (Oxford: Clarendon, 1996), 69.

12. The speech of Stephen in Acts also includes a vigorous polemic against the Temple as such, claiming God never sought it from the Israelites. But this aspect of Stephen's discourse reflects later theology more than anything else.

13. Both opponents and proponents of Jesus' Resurrection as a physical event later concocted legends to the effect that the body had been stolen (Matthew 28:11–15) or that, despite the presence of armed guards, the tomb was inspected and found empty (Matthew 27:62–28:6).

3. *On the Road*

1. When Paul writes about his experience (in his letter to the Galatians 1:15–16), he focuses on its significance to the exclusion of explaining what happened. But in this speech as given in Acts to King Herod Agrippa II, some of the circumstances of his vision are attested. But there are two other accounts in Acts as well; the relationship among these differing versions of the story will emerge as I discuss Paul's vision.

2. There is good evidence that 1 Enoch circulated in Greek in the Diaspora as well as in Aramaic in Judea and Galilee (where it influenced both John the Baptist and Jesus). See E. Isaac, "1 (Ethiopic Apocalypse of) Enoch," *The Old Testament Pseudepigrapha* (Doubleday: New York, 1983), 1:5–12.

3. See Mark 1:11 and *Rabbi Jesus*, 41–63.

4. In Acts 26:18, the risen Jesus speaks a pastiche of passages from the book of Isaiah (35:5; 42:7, 16; 61:1) in words that echo a famous prophecy Jesus himself once made about himself in Nazareth (see Luke 4:18–19). Acts of course embellishes what was said to Paul. For example, when the voice says, "It is hard for you to kick against the goads" (Acts 26:14), that is an allusion to the Greek poet Euripides. Alive or risen from the dead, it is hard to imagine that in Rabbi Jesus' thesaurus of quotes, especially when speaking Aramaic! The specificity of Acts sometimes comes at the cost of credibility. But the gist of the commission is confirmed by Paul's own statement in Galatians.

5. Josephus speaks of a different Ananias, a pious merchant whose contacts as far as Adiabene resulted in attracting King Izates to Judaism *(Antiquities* 20.34–48). Ananias convinced him not to circumcise for reasons of state, but to remain a God-fearer.

6. For an overview of a truly vast literature, see Victor Paul Furnish, *II Corinthians: A New Translation with Introduction and Commentary,* The Anchor Bible 32A (New York: Doubleday, 1984), 547–50.

7. See *Rabbi Jesus,* 106–11 for Jesus' development of his healing theory and practice. For the importance of touching within his healing practice, see 84–95, 130–33; in regard to meal practice, see 74–78, 250–56.

8. See Alan F. Segal, *Paul the Convert: The Apostolate and Apostasy of Saul the Pharisee* (New Haven: Yale University Press, 1990), 3–33.

9. Ezra 7:28. So close was this expectation to teachings about Jesus,

Christians composed additions to this book and made it their own. That is how it appears in the Apocrypha (as 2 Esdras). For a good explanation, see B. M. Metzger, "The Fourth Book of Ezra," *The Old Testament Pseudepigrapha,* ed. J. H. Charlesworth (Garden City: Doubleday, 1983), 1:517–24. As he points out, in this section the book develops the themes of the Messiah and the fate of "humanity as a whole, regardless of racial origins" (p. 521), and those themes bear comparison with Paul's thought.

10. See C. K. Barrett, *A Critical and Exegetical Commentary on the Acts of the Apostles,* The International Critical Commentary (Edinburgh: Clark, 1994), 1:467–68; Jacob Jervell, *Die Apostelgeschichte übersetzt und erklärt: Kritisch-exegetischer Kommentar über das Neue Testament* (Göttingen: Vandenhoeck & Ruprecht, 1998), 286–87.

11. In this case Acts seems to me willfully silent, much as Paul managed to avoid naming Ananias. Jerusalem for the Book of Acts is the center of operations, so "Arabia"—that is, the kingdom of the Nabateans—is an inauspicious place for the newly minted apostle to start preaching. Moreover, there is no indication of any successful Christian proselytizing in Nabatea in Acts, although successes in Syria, Egypt and North Africa, Ethiopia, Asia Minor, Greece, and Rome are proudly recorded in Acts. Not mentioning Arabia would be sensible, however, if an apostle dear to Acts had tried to convert people there and gotten nowhere.

12. See Martin Hengel, "Paul in Arabia," *Bulletin for Biblical Research* 12.1 (2002):47–66. He speculates (p. 54) that the Nabatean city of Hagra should be associated with Hagar, following the suggestion of H. Gese. A more secure finding is that a massive project of irrigation was one source of King Aretas's great power and success (p. 49).

13. Here I think there is evidence of delay—not between Paul's conversion and his vocation to reach Gentiles, but between his conversion and his radical criticism of the Torah. This insight seems to me the vital contribution of F. J. Foakes-Jackson, *The Life of Saint Paul: The Man and the Apostle* (New York: Boni & Liveright, 1926), 78–82.

14. For a discussion of this practice, see Segal, *Paul the Convert,* 152–54.

4. *The Petrine Connection*

1. As cover for this move, Aretas complained about Antipas's shameful treatment of Aretas's daughter. Antipas had deserted her—a Nabatean queen!—in order to marry his brother's wife. (I have described this incident in *Rabbi Jesus,* 60–63, because it also brought about the death of John the Baptist.) But that happened years earlier; the emperor Tiberius knew that there was no excuse for Aretas's invasion into Antipas's territory. With typical ruthlessness, Tiberius ordered his Syrian legate to bring Aretas back to him in chains or, failing that, to send along his head *(Antiquities* 18.109–19). Luckily for Aretas, Tiberius died before this order could be carried out, and the king held on to power.

2. For a discussion of Peter's vision, see *Rabbi Jesus,* pp. 281–83.

3. Flame was also associated with rabbis who practiced the vision of the Merkabah; see the Sources for chapter 2.

4. For a full description, see *Rabbi Jesus,* pp. 105–6, 111–15, 225–30.

5. *Paul,* trans. D. M. G. Stalker (London: Hodder and Stoughton, 1971), 28.

6. The term referred to a bird that picks up and scatters seed, and was used of human gossips and babblers; its application to Paul appears in Acts 17:18.

7. *Paul: A Critical Life* (Oxford: Clarendon, 1996), 95–96. Murphy-O'Connor tries to fill in those years with missionary work from a base in Antioch, but that does not explain why Barnabas had to fetch Paul in Tarsus in order to *introduce* him to Antioch (Acts 11:25–26). But Murphy-O'Connor has assembled some fine material on tent-making (pp. 85–89), and this is the period in which I think Paul comes into his own professionally, in the city where his family provided commercial connections.

8. Paul does not mention here the human source of his tradition, but his reference to Peter in Galatians 1:18 seems to settle the matter. For a discussion of the many conceptions of Eucharist in the New Testament, see Chilton, *A Feast of Meanings: Eucharistic Theologies from Jesus through Johannine Circles,* Supplements to *Novum Testamentum* 72 (Leiden: Brill, 1994). Perhaps during this time, his kinfolk Junia and Andronicus (Romans 16:7) encouraged his ideas; see F. J. Foakes-Jackson, *The Life of Saint Paul: The Man and the Apostle* (New York: Boni & Liveright, 1926), 198–99.

9. The Greek language helped him along toward this insight. In the Aramaic that Jesus spoke, the bread was called "flesh" *(bisra).* But Greek makes a distinction between "flesh" *(sarx)* as the generic material from which people and animals are made and "body" *(soma),* a specific example of enfleshed life. John's Gospel renders *bisra* as *sarx;* Paul—along with the first three Gospels—makes the choice of *soma,* "body." Not a great deal hung on that decision at first, but it did encourage Paul to see a link between the "body" offered as sacrifice in the Eucharist and the spiritual "body" of Jesus raised from the dead. By the time John's Gospel was written at the end of the first century, the term "flesh" had prompted non-Jewish believers to think that they were consuming Jesus personally.

10. Jerome Murphy-O'Connor, pp. 62–65, has insisted that Paul *must* have had a wife, since that was the norm in Judaism, and has him marry in Jerusalem (where his wife and children died in an earthquake!). Jerusalem, however, would be an unlikely place for him to have contracted a marriage. That city's Pharisees would not have welcomed an in-law straight in from the Diaspora, and after his conversion the whole notion was moot. The analysis that Paul left the Pharisees at this stage out of "redirected anger" strikes me as ingenious but unconvincing.

11. It is interesting that Gamaliel showed a bit of this attitude. He agreed (Berakhoth 2:5 in the Mishnah) that a bridegroom is exempt from the recitation of the *Shema* on the first night of his marriage. But his disciples nonethe-

less heard him clearly in the wedding chamber on his own wedding night, *"Shema' Yisra'el, Adonai Eloheynu, Adonai Echad. . . ."* When they reminded him of his teaching next morning, he said he didn't want to ignore the kingdom of heaven even for an hour.

5. Antioch

1. See Jacques Leblanc and Grégoire Poccardi, "Étude de la permanence de traces urbains et ruraux antiques à Antioche-sur-l'Oronte," *Syria* 76 (1999): 91–126, and Markus Bockmuehl, "James, Israel and Antioch," *Jewish Law in Gentile Churches* (Edinburgh: Clark, 2000), 49–83, for a discussion of this estimate and the difficulties involved in making one. A Jewish contingent of 25,000 rather than Bockmuehl's 30,000–50,000 seems reasonable to me, and I take it that a few thousand people must have been baptized for the name "Christian" to be coined.

2. See C. K. Barrett, *A Critical and Exegetical Commentary on the Acts of the Apostles,* The International Critical Commentary (Edinburgh: Clark, 1994), 1:556–57, and Anton Dauer, *Paulus und die christliche Gemeinde im syrischen Antiochia,* Bonner Biblische Beiträge 106 (Winhaim: Beltz, 1996).

3. The equivalent word in the Hebrew Bible is *qahal,* an assembly. The English term "church," like *Kirche* in German, derives from the term *kuriakon* in Greek, meaning "belonging to the Lord."

4. See John Ashton, *The Religion of Paul the Apostle* (New Haven: Yale University Press, 2000), 158–62.

5. See, for example, Mark 3:31–35; 13:12–13.

6. This gets lost in the apologetic device of Acts, according to which both Barnabas and Saul/Paul only ever turn "to the Gentiles" (in city after city, never learning from their experience!) after they had been rejected in synagogues. The device is anachronistic in two ways. First, contact with the Gentiles occurred while there was still much positive engagement with the peoples and institutions of Judaism, as ongoing Christian participation in worship in the Temple proves without question. Second, Barnabas and Paul, even though they shared an interest in Gentile belief, did so with differing views of the Torah and different ideas of which Gentiles—God-fearing or pagan—should be contacted.

7. See Stephen Mitchell, *Anatolia: Land, Men, and Gods in Asia Minor* (Oxford: Clarendon, 1993), 2:6–8, and Thomas W. Martin, "Paulus, Sergius," *The Anchor Bible Dictionary,* ed. D. M. Freedman et al. (Garden City: Doubleday, 1992), 5:205–6.

8. Completely out of the league of Antioch on the Orontes in Syria, scholars conventionally call this settlement Pisidian Antioch. See B. W. R. Pearson, "Antioch (Pisidia)." *Dictionary of New Testament Background,* ed. C. A. Evans and S. E. Porter (Downers Grove: InverVarsity, 2000), 31–34, and *Actes du 1er Congrès International sur Antioche de Pisidie,* Collection Archéologique et

Histoire de l'Antiquité, Université Lumière-Lyon 2, ed. Thomas Drew-Bear, Mehmet Tashalan, and Christine M. Thomas (Lyon: Université Lumière-Lyon 2, 2002).

The city had already been developed during the Hellenistic period, but when the Romans made it their own after the first century B.C.E., they restructured the place. The theater was adapted, a grid plan was used for laying out streets, and magnificent aqueducts fed water into a huge fountain. A Roman officer eventually paid for a beautiful bath complex, the best-preserved from the period I have ever visited. A huge temple hewn into the cliff by the Persians to celebrate their dominance was rededicated by the Romans to the divine emperor, Augustus. Imperial opportunism did not stand on pride.

The Romans knew a good investment opportunity, military and economic, when they found one. The colony lay near a range of mountains that protected it from the north, and the coastal escarpment to the south made the area central for a natural line of trade between East and West. Antioch was not the commercial pivot that Tarsus was; it also could not command the status of a free city that Tarsus could, so Roman control was all the more absolute.

9. It is possible that Perga offered the port of landing; see Douglas A. Campbell, "Paul in Pamphylia (Acts 13.13–14a; 14.24b–26): A Critical Note," *NTS* 46 (2000):595–602. But I take my lead from Barnabas's return voyage; Acts 14:25–26.

10. Acts 13:14–49 here follows a favorite apologetic pattern: When Jews reject Paul, then—as in the case of Jesus (Luke 4:14–29)—the result is an opportunity for non-Jews. But even Acts here admits that the apostles then turned not only to God-fearers, but to ordinary Gentiles. This was a change in the very target of preaching, from Israelites and God-fearers in the synagogue to common pagans directly addressed by the apostle Paul.

11. Ward Gasque, "Iconium," *The Anchor Bible Dictionary*, ed. D. M. Freedman et al. (Garden City: Doubleday, 1992), 3:357.

12. For a discussion of stoning among ancient Jews, see *Rabbi Jesus*, 97–102.

6. *On Probation from Jerusalem*

1. Many of the people of this region of Galatia were invading Celts—that is what the word *Galatai* (Galatians) means in Greek.

2. Barnabas's route even shows a symptom of his freedom from his headstrong companion: this time Perga was on the itinerary. On their arrival from Cyprus, Paul had insisted on skipping this beautiful city in his haste to proceed inland, but now Barnabas was free to stop there (Acts 14:25, 26) and then ship back to Antioch on the Orontes from the port of Antalya.

3. I discussed the influence of the Mysteries on Hellenistic understandings of the Eucharist and provided a bibliography in *Rabbi Jesus*, 250–52, 307.

4. Attacks on the eye of herpes zoster often scar the cornea, and Paul had to

deal with much damage and scarring in addition to that as a result of the stoning in Lystra.

5. See Matthew 10:1–16 and *Rabbi Jesus,* 174–79.

6. Both Hebrew *('aral)* and Greek *(akrobustia)* use the direct term "foreskin." English translations persistently water this down to "uncircumcision." But Paul knew what he was talking about, and spoke of it as plainly as the Book of Genesis did.

7. Cephas's supporters could argue the case with the Christian Pharisees in terms of Scripture; while Genesis does speak of circumcising foreign slaves, God-fearers like Cornelius were no slaves.

8. The text reads "the apostles and elders." "Elders" refers to mature teachers, so "senior rabbi" conveys the sense. It is interesting to note that the word for "priest" in English is a contraction of the Greek *presbuteros,* the term for "elder."

9. See Eusebius, *Ecclesiastical History* 2.1.1–6; 2.23.1–19; 7.19. In the first passage he refers to Clement's *Hypotyposeis.*

10. For a treatment of the sources, see *The Brother of Jesus: James the Just and His Mission,* ed. B. D. Chilton and J. N. Neusner (Louisville: Westminster John Knox, 2001). James' history during Jesus' life is woven into the narrative of *Rabbi Jesus.* Like Joses, James was a product of Joseph's first marriage while Jesus, Judas, and Simon were the sons of Joseph and Mary; see *Rabbi Jesus,* 3–30.

11. See *Antiquities* 20.197–203. Hegesippus is cited by Eusebius (see *Ecclesiastical History* 2.23.1–18).

12. See Eliezer Diamond, "An Israelite Self-Offering in the Priestly Code: A New Perspective on the Nazirite," *Jewish Quarterly Review* 88.1–2 (1997):1–18.

13. James' experience of the Resurrection is described in *Rabbi Jesus,* 283–84, on the basis of Jerome's *Liber de Viris Illustribus* 2, quoting from *The Gospel of the Hebrews.* Paul knows that James was among the first people by whom Jesus was seen after his crucifixion (1 Corinthians 15:7), but no text in the New Testament describes his vision. This is typical of the bias of the New Testament and early Christian texts on behalf of Gentiles, which makes the investigation of Christian origins difficult. Fortunately, Jerome had access to the noncanonical *Gospel of the Hebrews,* which does detail James' experience.

14. This strange variation in spelling, the subject of a great deal of scholarly comment, fits the fact that different pronunciations of "Nazirite" were current. A whole tractate in the Mishnah (Nazir) deals with the vow and refers to these pronunciations in 1:1.

15. The Book of Acts includes discussion of another issue here (Acts 15:20–31), but that reflects what happened at another meeting when Paul was not present. As we will see, he was in Greece at the time.

16. James was actually named after this patriarch; the pronunciation of his name in Greek, *Iakobos,* is mangled in English into "James." The fact that this

Scripture from Amos speaks earlier of Jacob (Amos 9:8) and refers to the "tent of David," to whom James and Jesus were related through Joseph, made this one of James' favorite passages.

17. In the literature of the early Church they are called the Ebionites, from the Hebrew term *'evyon,* meaning "poor." Their poverty was often literal, but the word primarily refers to the attitude of humility expressed in the Psalms by those who are "poor." It was a primitive name for Christians: Paul himself talks about his willingness to care for the "poor" in Jerusalem (see below), and over the course of time it was applied to Christian Jews who kept the Torah.

18. This triumvirate alluded back to Jesus' association with Cephas and with James and John (both of them sons of Zebedee) as his three closest disciples. James the son of Zebedee was killed by Herod Agrippa I prior to 44 C.E., and James, Jesus' brother, took up his place in the triad, but in the lead position.

19. Rainer Riesner, *Paul's Early Period: Chronology, Mission Strategy, Theology,* trans. D. Stott (Grand Rapids: Eerdmans, 1998), 187, discusses the difficulty of placing this famine, but I think the reference in Josephus meets the case, and—as Riesner himself points out, pp. 132–36—this accords with Acts.

20. Acts reports the breakup as part of a dispute about whether to bring John Mark along on a return trip to Asia Minor (Acts 15:36–41). Paul did not want him. After all, John Mark had bolted back to Jerusalem as soon as Barnabas and Paul had left Cyprus for Asia Minor; that may well have been one of the provocations that sent the Christian Pharisees to Antioch. But the disagreement between the old partners went deeper.

7. *Excommunicant*

1. The academic jury is still out over whether having a Jewish mother made you a Jew during the first century. At the later period there is no doubt. Shaye J. D. Cohen has denied that the matrilineal principle predates the Mishnah, but admits that "even if Timothy is to be considered a gentile, the reference to the Jewishness of his mother is not irrelevant," amply justifying the language of "hybrid." See *The Beginnings of Jewishness: Boundaries, Varieties, Uncertainties* (Berkeley: University of California Press, 1999), 376 n. 35.

2. Take the example of Jürgen Becker, who says, "The idea that Paul should have him circumcised (Acts 16:3) contradicts so blatantly the Pauline conception (Galatians 2:3; 1 Corinthians 7:18–19) that this note deserves no credence"; *Paul: Apostle to the Gentiles,* trans. O. C. Dean (Louisville: Westminster John Knox, 1993), 127. I can't think of another issue Becker attempts to resolve in so peremptory a way.

3. The text says "Asia," referring to the western Roman province in Asia Minor.

4. The influence of this prophecy on Paul is a major theme of Rainer Riesner's book, *Paul's Early Period: Chronology, Mission Strategy, Theology,* trans.

D. Stott (Grand Rapids: Eerdmans, 1998). He has an excellent discussion of regions mentioned in Isaiah (pp. 245–53).

5. "The walls which guard the wise man are safe from both flame and assault, they provide no means of entrance, are lofty, impregnable, godlike" *(On the Firmness of the Wise* 6.8): for discussion, see Abraham J. Malherbe, *Paul and the Popular Philosophers* (Minneapolis: Fortress, 1989), 91–119.

6. See Peter Oakes, *Philippians: From People to Letter,* Society for New Testament Studies Monograph Series 110 (Cambridge: Cambridge University Press, 2001); Lukas Bormann, *Philippi, Stadt und Christengemeinde zur Zeit des Paulus,* Supplements to *Novum Testamentum* 78 (Leiden: Brill, 1995).

7. Without the evidence of Paul's letters, his power as an exorcist would be difficult to establish. Acts compresses the narrative so much that there is little time for discernment and too much room for doubt. Even the staunchest defender of Acts' accuracy, William M. Ramsay, admitted that its indications of time could not be taken literally as a result of its thematic interests; *St. Paul the Traveller and the Roman Citizen* (New York: G. P. Putnam, 1896), 215–17.

8. The ancient histories that document Claudius's policies are beautifully discussed in Riesner, 105–7, 157–201. The principal sources are Suetonius *(Life of Claudius),* Dio Cassius *(Roman History),* Orosius *(History against the Pagans),* and especially Tacitus *(Annals).*

9. For a detailed description, see Brian Rapske, *The Book of Acts and Paul in Roman Custody,* The Book of Acts in Its First Century Setting 3 (Grand Rapids: Eerdmans, 1994), 261–64.

10. With perhaps fifty thousand inhabitants, this was the largest city in Macedonia; see Christoph vom Brocke, *Thessaloniki: Stadt des Kassander und Gemeinde des Paulus. Eine frühe christliche Gemeinde in ihrer heidnischen Umwelt,* Wissenschaftliche Untersuchungen zum Neuen Testament 125 (Tübingen: Mohr Siebeck, 2001), 72–73. See Abraham J. Malherbe, *The Letters to the Thessalonians,* The Anchor Bible 32B (New York: Doubleday, 2000), 14–15, for a summary of archaeological work.

11. *Iudaios impulsore Chresto adsidue tumultuantes Roma expulsit* (Suetonius *Life of Claudius* 25.4).

12. Acts does not refer to which harbor Paul shipped out from. If the diarist of the "we-sections" was Timothy, that is exactly the kind of information he would not have, since he remained in Berea.

13. In Acts it amounts to a literary trope that Peter, Barnabas, and Paul address Jews first, only to be rebuffed and to head in the direction of the Gentiles as a result. The historical pattern this trope reflects comes from Paul's teaching in moments such as the events in Corinth reveal. His view about the definition of Israel definitely made Jews jealous, not of the Gentiles (as Acts implies), but of their own prerogatives as Israel.

14. See Robert Jewett, *Dating Paul's Life* (London: SCM, 1979), 38–40, on Gallio.

15. In keeping with the practice of the time, he fulfilled his obligation in the land he lived in, Greece, by observing the Nazirite fast and shaving his hair there, and then went to the Temple to join in the offerings of other Nazirites. See Nazir 6:8 in the Mishnah, and Maas Bortien, *Nazir (Nasiräer): Text, Übersetzung und Erklärung nebst einem textkitischen Anhang,* Die Mischna (Berlin: de Gruyter, 1971), 93.

16. In Acts 15, Luke presents James' teaching as if it were articulated during the meeting in 46 C.E. But Acts 15 represents two meetings. One came to a decision about circumcision that Paul agreed with. But the later meeting stipulated rules of purity that Gentile believers had to observe in order to demonstrate their loyalty to the Torah, and the simple fact is that Paul never agreed with the decree James issued and never mentions the rules involved—except to contradict them!

17. See Vincent J. Rosivach, *The System of Public Sacrifice in Fourth-Century Athens*, American Classical Studies 34 (Atlanta: Scholars, 1994).

8. *The Ephesian Catapult*

1. An earthquake in 23 C.E. makes the population estimate of one hundred thousand hazardous, but there is no doubting the importance of the city; L. Michael White, "Urban Development and Social Change in Imperial Ephesos," *EPHESOS, Metropolis of Asia: An Interdisciplinary Approach to Its Archaeology, Religion, and Culture*, Harvard Theological Studies 41, ed. Helmut Koester (Valley Forge: Trinity Press International, 1995), 27–79, 46–47.

2. So Jerome Murphy-O'Connor, *Paul: A Critical Life* (Oxford: Clarendon, 1996), 172–73, 274–76, whose interpretation is an elegant and enduring contribution to scholarship.

3. A principal point of agreement among virtually all teachers in the primitive phase of Christianity was that Jesus represented the fulfillment of the Scriptures of Israel. Of course, the language of fulfilling—frequently used in the New Testament—can carry very different meanings. Does Jesus "fulfill" Scripture because he does everything it says? Perhaps he transcends it, or reinterprets the covenant—how would anyone know? The first Christians went their different ways in understanding fulfillment, but they did arrive at a vital consensus that fulfilling Scripture made Jesus the Messiah. So completely did they accept that, the literature of the fledgling movement (including the New Testament) uses "Christ" interchangeably with Jesus.

4. Acts presents this scene as a set piece of true baptism, down to the detail that there were "about" *twelve* adult males present (Acts 19:7). That is meant to symbolize the clans of Israel.

5. Here I have a little difference with Murphy-O'Connor, p. 275. He thinks Paul laid hands only on the people Apollos baptized. In my view this laying on of hands followed baptism, and Acts remains silent about that immersion for the sake of its picture of primitive Christian unity.

6. Acts raises blandness to an art form. In this case the term "separate" reflects a quasisectarian division. See Paul's one use of the same verb in Galatians 2:12.

7. Miriam Griffin offers a good treatment of the theme of the corporate body in Stoicism; "Seneca and Pliny," *The Cambridge History of Greek and Roman Political Thought*, ed. Christopher Rowe and Malcolm Schofield (Cambridge: Cambridge University Press, 2000), 532–58.

8. See H. G. Haile, *Luther: An Experiment in Biography* (Garden City: Doubleday, 1980), 191.

9. By contrast, see the descriptions of rituals of sometimes baroque proportions in Michael W. Cuneo, *American Exorcism: Expelling Demons in the Land of Plenty* (New York: Doubleday, 2001).

10. For a sensitive treatment of this question, see Richard B. Hays, "Christology and Ethics in Galatians: The Law of Christ," *Catholic Biblical Quarterly* 49.2 (1987):268–90.

11. The technical term is amanuensis, an assistant who took down thoughts by hand, commiting them to a manuscript, and often helping with composition during the entire process of writing a letter. See E. Randolph Richards, *The Secretary in the Letters of Paul*, Wissenschaftliche Untersuchungen zum Neuen Testament 42 (Tübingen: Mohr, 1991).

12. I capitalize here because I think Paul is referring to God. Grammatically, he might be talking about himself, but his point is that there is a single, divine message from a single, divine source.

13. In a time when every written communication was an event, when the arrival of an emissary with a papyrus scroll for one of the little congregations of Christians that dotted cities and towns caused a stir, it just made sense to make them feel good about themselves by referring to their good character and accomplishments.

14. This term refers both to a favor bestowed on a person and the person's response in gratitude. In the cosmic drama Paul had in mind, this favor is not just the warm feeling of acceptance that can come to an individual in prayer; the grace and peace that counted came from God's amazing decision to allow people to have a share in his eternity.

15. See *The Mysticism of Paul the Apostle*, trans. W. Montgomery (New York: Macmillan, 1931).

16. His language of "new creation" is not hyperbole in his own mind but refers to the single eschatological reality that matters; see Chilton, "Galatians 6:15: A Call to Freedom before God," *Expository Times* 89 (1978):311–13.

17. He does not identify the quotes. Sometimes that is because he really can assume that his audience is already familiar with the passages, sometimes because he is talking more to himself than to his audience.

9. Greek Fire

1. The same letter makes it very clear that Apollos continued to be Paul's competitor (1 Corinthians 1:11–12), but it was not in Paul's interests to stress that.

2. Yet the first letter to the Corinthians shows that the habit of sarcasm was still very much with Paul. His listeners in Corinth received the kind of formal flattery aristocrats were accustomed to (1:4–9), only to have it turned around against them later (1 Corinthians 4:10–13): "We are fools for Christ, but you are prudent in Christ; we are weak, but you are strong; you are celebrated, but we are dishonored. Until now, this hour, we hunger and thirst and go ill clad and buffeted and homeless, and labor—working with our own hands! Reviled, we bless, persecuted, we endure, defamed, we encourage. We have become the dirt of the world, the refuse of everything. Until now."

3. For a discussion of the practice in relation to Judaic custom (cf. 2 Maccabees 12:38–45), see Ethelbert Stauffer, *New Testament Theology,* trans. J. Marsh (New York: Macmillan, 1955), 299 n. 544. C. K. Barrett also comes to the conclusion that the vicarious effect of baptism is at issue, *A Commentary on the First Epistle to the Corinthians* (London: Black, 1968), 362–64, although he is somewhat skeptical of Stauffer's analysis. For the use of the term *séance* to describe Christian worship, see Morton Smith, "Pauline Worship as Seen by Pagans," *Harvard Theological Review* (1980):241–49.

4. The only mystery is how this aspect of Paul's religious identity has taken so long to be recognized; see John Ashton, *The Religion of Paul the Apostle* (New Haven: Yale University Press, 2000).

5. See *Rabbi Jesus,* pp. 174–96.

6. Brian S. Rosner, "Temple Prostitution in 1 Corinthians 6:12–20," *Novum Testamentum* 40 (1998):336f.

7. The conventional assumption has been that Sosthenes was in Ephesus at the time, but it is also possible that he simply signed on when the letter arrived in Corinth. Both scenarios presume close links between the two cities as well as between Paul and Sosthenes.

8. He was pressed to use this language, unusual in its time, because in his mind Christ was the only reality that could contain body and self and world, and yet is uncovered within the believer. See C. F. D. Moule, *An Idiom Book of New Testament Greek* (Cambridge: Cambridge University Press, 1988), 75–81.

9. Jesus' teaching is given in Mark 10:1–12; Matthew 19:1–12; Luke 16:18. Paul also states explicitly (1 Corinthians 7:15)—as Jesus implied—that a person divorced by another is no longer bound by the marriage.

10. Fornication and idolatry were metonyms for Paul: not only in his mind, but in his viscera. He reacted so violently against them that what he said amounted to legislating fresh law for the Corinthian communities he wrote to. Just as the man who was overly affectionate with his stepmother was to be ex-

pelled by the power of Paul's transported spirit, so the very strongholds of idolatry and promiscuity were to be laid waste.

10. Sacrifice in the Temple

1. At least, that is my inference. Acts 20:1 does not mention where Paul went, but 20:5–13 assumes that Troas is the staging center of the Macedonian campaign. A letter written in Paul's name after his death alludes to his practical connection with this busy port city (2 Timothy 4:13).

2. One prominent theory finds it necessary to suppose 2 Corinthians includes six different letters. I find that excessive for what is after all a brief epistle. If you look at the present letter, you will find an attempt at reconciliation (chapters 1–7) that includes reference to a letter written "through many tears" (2 Corinthians 2:4) that Paul sent earlier. That tract, an extraordinary, uncontrolled outburst of passion, is reflected in the latter part of 2 Corinthians (chapters 10–13). In between there are two communications about the collection, representing Paul's attempt during this period to build up the offering. So the chronological order of the fragments, as I see it, is 2 Corinthians 8, 2 Corinthians 9, 2 Corinthians 10–13, 2 Corinthians 1–7. For a discussion, see Victor Paul Furnish, *II Corinthians: A New Translation with Introduction and Commentary*, The Anchor Bible 32A (Doubleday: New York, 1984), 35–54.

3. He developed this thought in a simpler way in 1 Corinthians 2:1–5, winding it into a powerful rhetorical effect in 2:6–13; here in 2 Corinthians, he hammers out the theme to justify himself.

4. Titus had managed to cool Paul down (2:12–13; 7:5–7, 13–15). Timothy also joined in the writing of this section of 2 Corinthians (1:1), suggesting that he also—although stung by his bad experience in Corinth—advised his boss to take a temperate line. At last, Paul saw that he could not go on abusing the Corinthians; they were themselves his "letter" (3:2), more eloquent of his achievement in Achaia (for good or ill) than anything he could write.

5. During this period Paul starts to append lists to his letters that praise specific supporters and donors, both men and women. I have used these lists in this book to detail some of the key personnel involved with Paul, but it is notable that they get long and assiduous at this point; see especially Romans 16:1–16, 21–23, but also 1 Corinthians 16:15–20. The list in Romans refers to Phoebe, Priscilla and Aquila, Epainetos, Maria, Andronikos, Junia, Ampliatos, Urban, Stachus, Apelles, Aristobulos, Herodian, Narcissus, Truphaina, Truphosa, Persis, Rufus (with his mother), Asunkritos, Phlegon, Hermes, Patrobas, Hermas (and unnamed brothers), Philologos, Julia, Nereus (and his sister), Olympas, Timothy, Lucius, Jason, Sosipater, Tertius, Gaius, Erastus, and Quartus.

6. The process of making this case took a long time, but Paul was there at the beginning. A century later, Tertullian would say that Seneca frequently agreed with Paul (*De anima* 20.1), and by the third century a spurious corre-

spondence between Seneca and Paul had been "discovered"; Abraham J. Malherbe, *Paul and the Popular Philosophers* (Minneapolis: Fortress, 1989), 67–68.

7. See Romans 15:8. This unity was such that judgment also was to come to "both Jew first and then Greek," whether by the Torah that was Israel's particular inheritance or by the "Law written in the hearts" (Romans 2:10, 12–16) of all people.

8. I have explored this theme in an academic article; see Chilton, "Aramaic and Targumic Antecedents of Pauline 'Justification,' " *The Aramaic Bible: The Targums in Their Historical Context*, Journal for the Study of the Old Testament Supplement Series 166, ed. D. R. G. Beattie and M. J. McNamara (Sheffield: Sheffield Academic Press, 1994), 379–97.

9. Eusebius here quotes Hegesippus, the first Church historian (from the second century). The only element in this description that is implausible is the suggestion that James could enter the sanctuary, which was a high-priestly prerogative.

10. See John J. Rousseau and Rami Arav, *Jesus and His World: An Archaeological and Cultural Dictionary* (Minneapolis: Fortress, 1995), 312–13.

11. Joseph A. Fitzmyer supports the traditional surmise that Philemon came from Colossae, but agrees that he traveled, making Ephesus the likely place of his acquaintance with Paul; *The Letter to Philemon: A New Translation with Introduction and Commentary*, The Anchor Bible 34C (New York: Doubleday, 2000), 12–13.

12. That hymnic quality is beautifully represented in English by the King James Version, which I cite here. For a discussion of the significance of the passage, see James D. G. Dunn, *The Theology of Paul the Apostle* (Grand Rapids, MI: Eerdmans, 1998), 244–52.

13. Paul here paraphrases Isaiah's prediction (45:23) of how *God* will be acknowledged.

11. *The Sting of Death*

1. Colin Wells, *The Roman Empire* (Cambridge: Harvard University Press, 2002), 88, 304–5.

2. Paul assumes that his readers are familiar with the mechanism of this union in his teaching. It is spelled out in 1 Corinthians 2:10–11 (discussed in Chapter 8).

3. One of Paul's recent biographers actually buys Nero's story. A. N. Wilson blames the fire on a Christian's kebab stand! See *Paul: The Mind of the Apostle* (New York and London: Norton, 1977), 4: "Who knows? An accidental fire might well have started in the hutment of some early Christian zealot baking bread or sizzling kebabs."

4. I say "probably" because Timothy is not named at the head of the letter. As a result, other candidates have been proposed for authorship, including Onesimus (the slave for whom Paul had appealed for mercy to Philemon) and

Tychichus (referred to in Ephesians 6:21). During this period, when the Church generally looked to its apostolic past for guidance, it is extremely difficult to specify authorship. But I think the affinity between Colossians and Ephesians points back to Timothy, writing from Troas, as their common author.

5. In tone, what Ephesians says to its community is similar to Paul's own message to the Romans. In the case of Rome c. 57 C.E., Gentile preponderance had been occasioned by the imperial exclusion of Jews from the *pomerium* of the city; by contrast, Gentile Christians had increased in Ephesus by 90 C.E. as a result of shifting demographics within the movement itself.

6. Raymond E. Brown, a cautious scholar, went so far as to italicize his finding that *"about 80 to 90 percent of modern scholars would agree that the Pastorals were written after Paul's lifetime, and of those the majority would accept the period between 80 and 100 as the most plausible context for their composition"*; see *An Introduction to the New Testament,* The Anchor Bible Reference Library (New York: Doubleday, 1997), 668.

7. In English, this term is a shortened form of *presbuteros* in Greek, which means "elder." It refers to the same function of teaching and guidance exercised by a rabbi in a synagogue.

8. See the uncharacteristically severe remark of C. F. D. Moule, that Paul's own perspective was that Law is "liable to abuse precisely when it is used 'lawfully'!"; "The Problem of the Pastoral Epistles: A Reappraisal," *Essays in New Testament Interpretation* (Cambridge: Cambridge University Press, 1982), 113–32, 115.

9. The RSV finesses this by saying "as did my fathers," but that is a paraphrase.

10. And he would never call Epimenides (the author of these words in *de Oraculis*) a "prophet."

11. Another such work, 2 Thessalonians, has Paul exclaim: "If anyone doesn't want to work, neither will he eat!" (2 Thessalonians 3:10) That is another example of dealing with attitudes that may well have derived from Paul. After all, if the form of this world is passing away (1 Corinthians 7:31), what incentive is there to make a living?

12. This work doesn't even mention Paul's name, but winds up with a reference to Timothy and to Italy (Hebrews 13:22–25) that implies Pauline authorship.

13. The term Hebrews use is "type" *(tupos),* which refers to the imprint an object might make in a malleable material such as sand or clay.

14. See the discussion in Morton Smith, "Pauline Worship as Seen by Pagans," *Harvard Theological Review* 73 (1980):243–44.

15. Even sexuality is to be redirected, in Paul's mind. That is the reason for his unusual advice (1 Corinthians 7:32–34): "The unmarried man worries over the Lord's concerns, how he pleases the Lord. The married man worries over the world's concerns, how he pleases the wife: and he is divided. The unmarried woman also—the virgin, too—worries over the Lord's concerns, so she is

holy in both body and spirit, but the married woman worries over the world's concerns, how she pleases the husband." Paul could not have put matters more clearly, embarrassed his liberal commentators more thoroughly, or discomfited the Corinthians more comprehensively. He is clearly talking about a union with God through Christ as the only relationship fully consistent with the Spirit.

16. See Matthew Fox, *Original Blessing: A Primer in Creation Spirituality* (New York: Putnam, 2000).

SOURCES

Preface

Two approaches to Paul's letters have prevailed in scholarship. One is the way of commentary, dissecting every phrase; the other is the way of systematic theology, fitting the arguments of each letter into a doctrinal whole. Both of those ways are valid; the adage about not seeing the wood for the trees applies here. But there is a loss in limiting our understanding to these alternatives. Whether looking at the trees of commentary or at the forest of theology, scholarship has made Paul appear more wooden than he was. Paul did not write his letters as a system of doctrine or as belles lettres. Some of them are so crude, he would have been embarrassed by the thought that they could be compiled into an addendum to the Scriptures of Israel. Who would willingly go down in history as telling his opponents (Galatians 5:12) to cut off their penises? In Paul's case you cannot know the literature apart from the person, apart from appreciating the dynamics of his interaction with others. Then you can savor both his magnificent insights and his brutal rages.

For a lucid description of the impact of discussion in regard to the relationship of Acts and Paul's letters, see Donald Harman Akenson, *Saint Saul: A Skeleton Key to the Historical Jesus* (Oxford: Oxford University Press, 2000), 134–43. From these considerations, Akenson evolves a chronology comparable to that followed here (pp. 144–45), based in its turn on the work of Gerd Lüdemann, *Paul, Apostle to the Gentiles: Studies in Chronology,* trans. F. S. Jones (London: SCM, 1984). Lüdemann (p. 99) follows the suggestion of J. B. Lightfoot, originally published in 1865, that Galatians was written later than most scholars place it; see *St. Paul's Epistle to the Galatians* (Peabody, MA:

Hendrickson, 1999), 36–56. I follow the view of the majority. All recent discussions of chronology are greatly indebted to Robert Jewett, *Dating Paul's Life*
(London: SCM, 1979).

1. Tent-Maker's Son from Tarsus

Key among the ancient sources are Strabo—see *The Geography*, The Loeb
Classical Library, trans. H. L. Jones (New York: Putnam, 1917–32)—and Dio
Chrysostom—see his two speeches to the Tarsans in *Dio Chrysostom III*, The
Loeb Classical Library, trans. J. W. Cohoon and H. Lamar Crosby (Cambridge:
Harvard University Press, 1940). For a discussion, see the study of William
Ramsay, *The Cities of St. Paul: Their Influence on His Life and Thought* (New
York: Hodder & Stoughton, 1907). Ramsay's approach has been continued by
works such as Henri Metzger, *St. Paul's Journeys in the Greek Orient*, trans. S. H.
Hook (New York: Philosophical Library, 1955); W. Ward Gasque, "Tarsus,"
The Anchor Bible Dictionary, ed. D. M. Freedman et al. (Garden City:
Doubleday, 1992), 6:333–34; Stephen Mitchell, *Anatolia: Land, Men, and Gods
in Asia Minor* (Oxford: Clarendon, 1993); and Rainer Riesner, *Paul's Early
Period: Chronology, Mission Strategy, Theology*, trans. D. Stott (Grand Rapids, MI:
Eerdmans, 1998).

Jerome Murphy-O'Connor argues that Paul's family had acquired citizenship only during the first century B.C.E., having been enslaved by the Romans
in Galilee and exiled to Rome, where his father became a citizen prior to
moving to Tarsus; see *Paul: A Critical Life* (Oxford: Clarendon, 1996), 37–39.
While all that is not impossible, the entire reconstruction rests on a fourth-
century legend. Not only is it late: It is handed on by St. Jerome *(De viris illustribus* 5), whose speculations about the family relations of major figures in
the New Testament are notoriously weak. After all, it is he who turned Jesus'
brothers and sisters into his "cousins" to protect the emerging doctrine of the
Virgin Birth. (Lightfoot devastated this argument, although attempts have been
made to revive it from time to time; *St. Paul's Epistle to the Galatians* [Peabody,
MA: Hendrickson, 1999], 252–91). In the case of Paul, Jerome uses the legend
to tie the apostle as closely as possible to Galilee, the native territory of Jesus.
Yet for all his bragging about his Jewish pedigree, Paul himself never mentioned family ties to Galilee or Judea. Such modesty in his case would be
unique. I cannot see him passing up reference to his own Galilean roots in the
midst of controversy with the positions of Peter and James, and so remain
skeptical about Jerome's legend. Ramsay may be going too far in calling
Jerome's story "impossible"—*The Cities of St. Paul: Their Influence on His Life
and Thought* (New York: Hodder & Stoughton, 1907), 185—but only a step
too far.

I agree with Murphy-O'Connor (p. 52) in regard to Paul's age when he
went to Jerusalem for the first time, but he places Paul's journey in 15 C.E.
That then gives Paul more than fifteen years as a Pharisee in Jerusalem prior

to his conversion. During that time, in Murphy-O'Connor's original reconstruction, Paul married, had children, and lost his whole family in an earthquake (pp. 52–70). In addition to the problems of inventing such a rich
private life without evidence—and against Paul's own assertion in regard to
his marital state (1 Corinthians 7:1–7, 9:5)—Murphy-O'Connor's chronology
has Paul executed at the age of seventy-three (pp. 1–31). Vigorous people in
their seventies are common, but I know none as active as Paul was at that
stage. And although Paul complains about his physical condition in some detail, he never mentions advanced age as a burden. My dating comports with
the reference to Paul as a young man at the time of Stephen's death (Acts
7:58) in 32 C.E.

Henry Barclay Swete was able to show at the last turn of the century that
the ordering of the Septuagint into history, poetry, and prophecy goes back
to the Jewish community in Alexandria, where the Greek Bible originated.
See *An Introduction to the Old Testament in Greek* (Cambridge: Cambridge
University Press, 1902), 197–230, especially pp. 201, 217–19. The widely di-
verging orders of the Hebrew and Greek Bibles resulted in the divergences
among the Vulgate, Luther's Bible, and the English Bible. A great deal of
scholarship has been focused in recent years on the Septuagint. See, for example, Eugene Ulrich, "Origen's Old Testament Text: The Transmission History
of the Septuagint to the Third Century C.E.," *The Dead Sea Scrolls and the
Origins of the Bible* (Grand Rapids, MI, and Leiden, Netherlands: Eerdmans
and Brill, 1999), 202–23; and (more generally) Julio Trebolle Barrera, *The
Jewish Bible and the Christian Bible* (Leiden and Grand Rapids: Brill and
Eerdmans, 1998), 301–23. Albert I. Baugarten describes the enthusiasm for
Aristeas in the Diaspora in "Bilingual Jews and the Greek Bible," *Shem in the
Tents of Japhet: Essays on the Encounter of Judaism and Hellenism*, Supplements to
the *Journal for the Study of Judaism* 74, ed. J. L. Kugel (Leiden: Brill, 2002),
14–29. For a translation, see R. J. H. Shutt, "Letter of Aristeas (Third Century
B.C.–First Century A.D.): A New Translation and Introduction," *The Old
Testament Pseudepigrapha*, ed. J. H. Charlesworth (Garden City: Doubleday,
1985), 2:7–34.

2. *"At the Feet" of Gamaliel, in Service of Caiaphas*

For a grounding in Rabbinic sources, see Jacob Neusner, *Introduction to Rabbinic
Literature*, The Anchor Bible Reference Library (New York: Doubleday, 1994).
The Judaism of the New Testament period is treated in Oskar Skarsaune, *In the
Shadow of the Temple: Jewish Influences on Early Christianity* (Downers Grove, IL:
InterVarsity, 2002).

Both major Talmuds of Judaism (Yerushalmi Chagigah 2.77a–b; 14b in the
Babylonian Talmud, here paraphrased) tell the story of Paul's younger contemporary, Yochanan ben Zakkai. As he was traveling along one day mounted on
a donkey, a disciple named Eleazar ben Arach was walking beside and slightly

behind him, urging the animal along while the two sages talked. Describe God's chariot-throne—the Merkabah—for me, Eleazar asked his rabbi. You know that is forbidden, Yochanan replied, unless the student is in control of his learning.

Yochanan was citing a well-known axiom: Contemplating the chariot-throne by means of entering into the text and the vision of Ezekiel 1 was fraught with danger. Moses had learned that no man could see God's *face* and live (Exodus 33:20). He and his companions did see God's throne (Exodus 24:10), but that revelation on Sinai was ringed with a fire that few could penetrate. The Scriptures of Israel enshrined the primordial principle of Near Eastern religion: Contact with the divine world could easily prove fatal.

In a well-known legend, when four mystics entered the paradise adjacent to the divine Merkabah, one died, one went mad, and one taught heresy; only the fourth returned safely, in control of his own learning. He was safe after entering paradise because his learning was secure beforehand: Vision was only for those who were prepared. Rabbinic tradition over the centuries showed itself to be keenly aware of the dangers of undisciplined vision.

Yet Eleazar ben Arach persisted that day on the road. He proposed: If you will not describe the Merkabah to me, Rabbi, then let me explain it to you. Yochanan agreed, dismounted his ass, and sat under an olive tree, arranging his cloak and hood to cover his head entirely. Eleazar asked: Why has my teacher dismounted? Yochanan grunted back an answer from beneath his cloak: You are about to detail the presence of God and his holy angels, and you think I'm going to schlep along on a donkey?

And Eleazar did recount the Merkabah-vision of Ezekiel 1. The angels descended like fire in the fields around Yochanan and Eleazar, much as tongues of fire appeared over Jesus' disciples at Pentecost. These angels danced, sang the praises of God, and commended Eleazar for his exceptional advance in the *ma'aseh* Merkabah, "the work of the Chariot."

Eleazar and Yochanan were not alone in this kind of angelic vision. The Talmuds speak in the same passage of two other rabbis in connection with a similar experience. In their case the angels who surrounded them invited them into the third heaven, where a celestial banquet awaited.

The idea that Paul practiced the Merkabah is now a conventional opinion. See the brilliant article by John W. Bowker, " 'Merkabah' Visions and the Visions of Paul," *Journal of Semitic Studies* 16 (1971): 157–75, richly updated in Alan F. Segal, *Paul the Convert: The Apostolate and Apostasy of Saul the Pharisee* (New Haven: Yale University Press, 1990), 34–71, in a chapter entitled "Paul's Ecstasy." This work is summarized, and collated with some additional evidence from the Dead Sea Scrolls by James M. Scott, "Throne-Chariot Mysticism in Qumran and in Paul," *Eschatology, Messianism, and the Dead Sea Scrolls*, Studies in the Dead Sea Scrolls and Related Literature, ed. C. A. Evans and P. W. Flint (Grand Rapids, MI: Eerdmans, 1997), 101–19.

In *Rabbi Jesus*, I demonstrated that Jesus' practice of prayer involved connections with the Merkabah in Rabbinic Judaism on the basis of clearly vision-ary passages in the Gospels—such as his baptism and Transfiguration, his vision of Satan falling like lightning, and his Temptations. Both Jesus' baptism and Paul's conversion on his way to Damascus with his companions involved en-counters with the divine world that had visionary and auditory elements. But religious experiences are as complex and varied as any range of human percep-tion. While Jesus' contact with the mysticism of Ezekiel's chariot can be docu-mented, that doesn't mean that *Paul's* practice had to involve the Merkabah any more than St. Francis's long after Jesus, or Abraham's long before Jesus. Mystical experiences and practices vary according to times, cultures, and people.

Some similarities between Paul's experience and the practice of the Merkabah are indeed striking, but there has been a tendency to exaggerate them. (See Peter Schäfer, "New Testament and Hekhalot Literature: The Journey into Heaven in Paul and in Merkavah Mysticism," *Journal of Jewish Studies* 35.1 [1985]: 19–35. As he remarks in closing, any such comparison is a matter "of taking account of the fact that we have to do with differing *litera-tures*," so "no direct historical conclusions" are to be drawn. I take it that this is generally the case when we deal with ancient Christian and Rabbinic docu-ments: They concern issues that are not shaped by our understanding of history, so that any historical findings we might offer are by way of inference: What we believe happened to produce the texts as we can read them.) Why should any scholar make Paul a Merkabah mystic on dramatically less evidence than he would want for the case of Jesus? As sometimes happens, this is a case of theo-logical fashion masquerading as academic judgment. Paul can be the irrational mystic that Jesus is not allowed to be, because vision is as dangerous as it is sub-jective.

3. On the Road

An example of the visionary spirituality of the Diaspora is offered by *The Life of Adam and Eve*, a text from the first or second century C.E. Adam tells his son Seth (25:1–3):

> After your mother and I had been driven out of paradise, while we were praying, Michael the archangel and messenger of God came to me. And I saw a chariot like the wind and its wheels were fiery. I was carried off into the Paradise of righteousness, and I saw the LORD sitting and his ap-pearance was unbearable flaming fire.

The name "Adam" in Hebrew simply means "man": Such traditions suggest that humans as a species—not only experts in the Merkabah, not only Israelites—have access to divine presence. Interest in the chariot vision was in no sense a Pharisaic (or later, Rabbinic) peculiarity.

Cicero occupies a special place within Stoicism, well described by Marcia L.

Colish in *The Stoic Tradition from Antiquity to the Early Middle Ages*, vol. 1, *Stoicism in Classical Latin Literature* (Leiden: Brill, 1990).

For Saul's experience as a conversion, see Alan F. Segal, *Paul the Convert: The Apostolate and Apostasy of Saul the Pharisee* (New Haven: Yale University Press, 1990)—as complete, judicious, and convincing a treatment as one could wish. He consciously replies to the seminal challenge of Krister Stendahl that this was "Call Rather than Conversion," *Paul among Jews and Gentiles and Other Essays* (Philadelphia: Fortress, 1987), 7–23. Segal makes it clear, for example, that Saul's initial attraction to Pharisaism (hardly an obvious option in the Diaspora) constitutes significant evidence for Paul's predisposition toward conversion "since it implies either that Paul was a religious quester or that his parents instilled an unusually strict training in him" (pp. 25–26). In this sense, the appearance of the risen Jesus to Saul was his second conversion. Fundamental to this understanding is the recognition that conversion was an important feature of the Judaism of the period (see "Conversion in Paul's Society," pp. 72–114).

Segal is masterful in his presentation of "Paul's Ecstasy" (pp. 34–71) in terms of its biblical and Judaic precedents, and his argument that the Merkabah and apocalyptic thought were intimately connected is judicious. Still, a distinction should be made in my opinion between first-century oral practice of the Merkabah in territorial Israel and literary apocalypses available in the Diaspora, and that distinction helps account for differences of visionary experience among Jesus, Peter, James, and Paul. In regard to the Merkabah at Qumran, see Carol Newsome, "Mysticism," *Encyclopedia of the Dead Sea Scrolls*, ed. Lawrence H. Schiffman and James C. VanderKam (Oxford: Oxford University Press, 2000), 1:591–94.

Segal holds that Paul came to see his vocation as to the Gentiles only gradually, after his conversion. To make his case he quotes Galatians 1:15–16, observing, "Paul does not say explicitly that his gentile mission came immediately after his conversion" (p. 13). That is true, but something of a cavil, since Paul does not refer to any interval of time here: His apostolate was nothing other than the announcement of God's Son among the Gentiles, and Segal agrees that the content of the apostolate was given in Paul's conversion (p. 19). I think an interval was required, however, for Paul to work out the consequences of his conversion in terms of the Torah; see H. G. Wood, "The Conversion of St. Paul: Its Nature, Antecedents and Consequences," *Jesus in the Twentieth Century* (London: Lutterworth, 1960), 159–68.

4. The Petrine Connection

F. F. Bruce argued that Paul's activity in Nabatea annoyed Aretas, and also that Paul's retreat to Tarsus brought him isolation; see *The Acts of the Apostles: The Greek Text with Introduction and Commentary* (Grand Rapids, MI: Eerdmans, 1986), 205, 207–8. My principal guide to the city of Damascus has been

Dorothée Sack, *Damaskus: Einwicklung und Struktur einer orientalisch-islamischen Stadt,* Damaszener Forschungen 1 (Mainz am Rhein: Philipp von Zabern, 1989). See also Martin Hengel and Anna Maria Schwemer, *Paul between Damascus and Antioch: The Unknown Years,* trans. J. Bowden (London: SCM, 1997).

Robert Jewett makes a good case for dating Saul's escape from Damascus later than I do, under Gaius just prior to Aretas's death in 39 C.E.; *Dating Paul's Life* (London: SCM, 1979), 30–33. The escape obviously had to have happened before that, but I think it also occurred before Aretas's war with Antipas in 36 C.E. That is when, at the peak of his power, Aretas could influence events in Damascus. Jewett's reference to Acts at this point takes no account of the fact that Acts says nothing of Paul's sojourn in Arabia (which must have won him Aretas's antipathy); evidently, Acts takes up the story after that point. Jewett's fine introduction (pp. 1–6) indicates the range of methodological options that have been explored. As I look over my disagreements with Jewett, I see that I am inclined to find the testimony of Acts in more agreement with Paul's letters than he suggests is the case (pp. 7–24). Even here, however, I would wish to emphasize that Jewett wrote during a period of profound skepticism in regard to the value of Acts, which he wisely resisted. Indeed, in arguing for the identity of the author of Acts ("Luke") with the travel diarist (cf. 16:11–13; 17:1–9, 10, 14, 15; 20:4–21:26; 27:1–28:16; cf. pp. 13, 17), Jewett goes further than I would.

Jewett acknowledges that he is operating on the basis of received opinion in positing that the crucifixion occurred either in the year 30 or the year 33 (pp. 26–29). Both dates are calculated on the basis of Passover falling on a Friday. But once that factoid from John's Gospel is accepted to be theological—as Jewett admits it is—the better route is to infer the date on the basis of a consideration of Roman politics alone, which would yield a date of 32 C.E.; see Rainer Riesner, *Paul's Early Period: Chronology, Mission Strategy, Theology,* trans. D. Stott (Grand Rapids, MI: Eerdmans, 1998), 63. I find against Jewett (pp. 29–30) that the list of Resurrection appearances Paul gives in 1 Corinthians 15 does not support the surmise of an eighteen-month delay between his experience and the first appearance of Jesus risen from the dead.

The decision not to marry could not have come easily, but even the circle of Gamaliel remembered some odd attitudes toward marriage on the part of their teacher. When his wife died, Gamaliel washed on the first night after the death of his wife (Berakhoth 2:6). His *talmidim* remonstrated: Did not our master teach us that it is forbidden for a mourner to wash? He said to them, "I am not like other men, I am frail."

Paul and Gamaliel both developed attitudes toward marriage that are comparable, and you could scarcely call them romantic. Gamaliel's school was willing to take a single slave's testimony on the death of a husband, in order to find that the woman was free to marry (Yebamoth 16:7 in the Mishnah). The Apostle Paul used the image of a woman free from the constraints of marriage

298 · Sources

because of the death of her husband as an example of how wonderful it was to
be liberated by faith (Romans 7:1–3). What she could not do before without
being an adulteress, she could now engage in freely! Paul expected that people
would latch on to that moment as a time of rejoicing.

Paul goes his own way in comparison to Gamaliel, when he opines in another letter that, although marriage is acceptable as a remedy for sexual passion,
on the whole it is better to avoid the trouble involved (1 Corinthians 7).
Scholars have debated whether Paul was ever married. He specifically points out
in 1 Corinthians (9:5) that, unlike other apostles, he is single; to his mind the
absence of a wife makes him freer to serve the Lord (1 Corinthians 7:32–40) and
less of a burden on the communities that he serves (1 Corinthians 9:4–18).
Although those claims are not direct assertions that he had *never* been married,
it seems to me that there would be little to brag about if it were well known in
Corinth that Paul had once been married.

The obligations of God-fearers to the Torah are discussed in Alan F. Segal,
Paul the Convert: The Apostolate and Apostasy of Saul the Pharisee (New Haven:
Yale University Press, 1990), 194–201. Riesner discusses the disproportionately
large number of women among God-fearers, which he posits on the basis of
grave inscriptions; *Paul's Early Period*, 351.

5. Antioch

Pharisees and Rabbis saw Antioch as a Jewish home: Some of them claimed that
those living there had to pay tithes as if they dwelled in the land of Israel (see
Hallah 4:7 in the Mishnah). See Markus Bockmuehl, "James, Israel and
Antioch," *Jewish Law in Gentile Churches* (Edinburgh: Clark, 2000), 49–83, and
Glanville Downey, *A History of Antioch in Syria from Seleucus to the Arab Conquest*
(Princeton: Princeton University Press, 1961). For some of the archaeological
evidence, see *Antioch on the Orontes*, vol. 1, *The Excavations of 1932*, ed. George
W. Elderkin (Princeton: Princeton University Press, 1934); Jean Lassus, *Antioch
on the Orontes*, vol. 5, *Les portiques d'Antioche* (Princeton: Princeton University
Press, 1972).

For the visionary idioms of Diaspora Judaism in relation to Paul's religious
experience, see James D. Tabor, *Things Unutterable: Paul's Ascent to Paradise in Its
Greco-Roman, Judaic, and Early Christian Contexts*, Studies in Judaism (Lanham,
MD: University Press of America, 1986); David E. Aune, *Prophecy in Early
Christianity and the Ancient Mediterranean World* (Grand Rapids, MI: Eerdmans,
1983); *Visionaries and Their Apocalypses*, Issues in Religion and Theology 4, ed.
Paul D. Hanson (Philadelphia: Fortress, 1983). Philo of Alexandria believed that
the highest attainment was prophetic. Taking the example of Moses as a truly
good man, Philo observes that "what the mind misses, this prophecy attains"
(*Moses* 2.6). The Antiochene prophets agreed entirely and sent Barnabas and
Paul out as apostles of their community. For a treatment of Philo as representing prophetic practice in the Diaspora, see John Ashton, *The Religion of Paul the*

Apostle (New Haven: Yale University Press, 2000), 183–84, 205–6. For reasons already mentioned, I would not conflate the Merkabah and prophecy as easily as Ashton does (nor do I think that "shamanism" can be used without differentiation as a category of religious experience). But I have no doubt that, for a man of his background, nothing could have been more moving to Paul than his spiritual transport in Antioch. Pharisees told a similar story about the great rabbi named Hillel (Tosefta Sotah 13:3; see Jacob Neusner, *The Peripatetic Saying: The Problem of the Thrice-Told Tale in Talmudic Literature*, Brown Judaic Studies 89 [Chico: Scholars Press, 1985], 114–15, and Chilton, *Profiles of a Rabbi: Synoptic Opportunities in Reading about Jesus*, Brown Judaic Studies 177 [Atlanta: Scholars Press, 1989], 77–89):

> When the latter prophets died—Haggai, Zechariah, and Malachi—then the Holy Spirit came to an end in Israel. But a heavenly echo was heard. Sages gathered together in the upper room of the house of Guria in Jericho, and a heavenly echo came forth and said to them, There is a man among you who is worthy to receive the Holy Spirit, but his generation is unworthy of such an honor. They all set their eyes upon Hillel the elder.

Paul had joined himself to a movement that rejoiced in receiving the same Spirit that not even Hillel could attain to, and now that Spirit—in the presence of other apostles—spoke his own name, dispatched him as Antioch's apostle together with Barnabas. See Nicholas Taylor, *Paul, Antioch and Jerusalem: A Study in Relationships and Authority in Earliest Christianity*, Journal for the Study of the New Testament Supplement Series 66 (Sheffield: Sheffield Academic Press, 1992).

For an earlier treatment that emphasizes the mystical element of Paul's identity, see Samuel Sandmel, *The Genius of Paul: A Study of History* (New York: Schocken, 1970). On the magical side of such practices, see Rebecca Macy Lesses, *Ritual Practices to Gain Power: Angels, Incantations, and Revelation in Early Jewish Mysticism*, Harvard Theological Studies 44 (Harrisburg: Trinity, 1998).

6. On Probation from Jerusalem

I owe the suggestion of herpes zoster to a friend. After she explained the symptoms to me, I was struck by how swelling, disfigurement, pain, and blindness could be produced at intervals as well as by the relationship of attacks to stress. Recent studies document the severity of cases, even in the young; see Lee-Ellen C. Copstead and Jacquelyn L. Banasik, *Pathophysiology: Biological and Behavior Perspectives* (Philadelphia: Saunders, 2000), 1186–88.

Acts does not like to break up witnesses to the gospel from one another, and for that reason has a badly wounded Paul returning by land with Barnabas (Acts 14:19–26). In the case of Jesus, Luke's Gospel has the young man return home docilely to Nazareth from the Temple in Jerusalem, although his family had set out home without him and despite the fact that Jesus next appears in Judea, not Galilee, with John the Baptist (Luke 2:39–52; see *Rabbi Jesus*, pp. 23–40). In the case of Paul, Luke postulates an impossibly short recovery time and has him meandering back through cities that had already proved deadly, so as not to break up the partnership with Barnabas, his fellow apostle. Yet even Luke will admit that after this trip, this partnership was over. C. K. Barrett, commenting on this passage, remarked in a nice turn of phrase, "Luke has not fully thought through the tradition he found, but this does not rob it of all historical value"; see *A Critical and Exegetical Commentary on the Acts of the Apostles*, The International Critical Commentary (Edinburgh: Clark, 1994), 1:665.

On the religions of mystery, see *The Ancient Mysteries, a Sourcebook: Sacred Texts of the Mystery Religions of the Ancient Mediterranean World*, ed. Marvin W. Meyer (San Francisco: HarperSanFrancisco, 1987); Walter Burkert, *Ancient Mystery Cults* (Cambridge: Harvard University Press, 1987); and David Ulansey, *The Origins of the Mithraic Mysteries: Cosmology and Salvation in the Ancient World* (New York: Oxford University Press, 1989).

For a more technical study of James, see *James the Just and Christian Origins*, Supplements to *Novum Testamentum* 98, ed. B. D. Chilton and C. A. Evans (Leiden: Brill, 1999). For the role of the *mebaqqer* in relation to the tradition of James, see George J. Brooke, "James, Letter of," *Encyclopedia of the Dead Sea Scrolls*, ed. Lawrence H. Schiffman and James C. VanderKam (Oxford: Oxford University Press, 2000), 1:396–97.

The recent publication of an ossuary bearing the inscription "James, son of Joseph, brother of Jesus" has sparked a controversy that is not likely to be settled soon. If you do not know where an artifact has come from, it is not really an archaeological discovery at all—only an item on the collectors' market. Context alone can explain what precisely an artifact was used for, the conditions it has been submitted to, its meaning for the people who deposited it, and the chain of possession that reaches from its deposit to its possession by the current owner. All those considerations are involved in the issue of authenticity, and many of them are more interesting than whether or not a given object is a forgery. But the owner's arrest on suspicion of forgery in 2003 after an investigation by the Israel Antiquities Authority makes it silly and irresponsible to assume the ossuary is authentic.

Whoever took this piece from its cave (if that is where it *was* found) not only looted the ossuary itself but looted our knowledge of what the ossuary really means. We cannot remove the possibility that we are dealing with a forgery until we can say where it came from. There is a change in epigraphic style in the inscription, but that does not by itself prove fraud. Grave markers are subject to emendation over time, as you can see from visiting many family tombs from antiquity until today. "James, son of Joseph" might have been inscribed when James' bones were put in the box, and "the brother of Jesus" could have been added later. It is worth remembering that the first historian of Christianity, Hegesippus, refers to a monument being set up for James in Jerusalem. Jerome Murphy-O'Connor explores this possibility in "Where Was James Buried?" *Bible Review* 19.3 (2003):34–42. Was this bone box part of the memorial, built-in above or below ground? That is the kind of question that should be asked alongside the obvious ones: Is the ossuary genuine? Is it a fake?

If it is not fake, it is either the original ossuary of James or part of a monument to him. It could also be both. That would make this artifact evidence of the earliest identifiable Christian grave site—and until we find out where the piece came from, we will be unable to say where that is. Anomalies remain, on any reading. Why is the reference simply to "Jesus" when the titles "Messiah," "Son of Man," and "Lord" were applied to him in Aramaic from a very early period? There, too, we are up against a wall of uncertainty, until someone lets us into the place where the ossuary was found.

7. *Excommunicant*

Paul's circumcision of Timothy contradicts the conventional opinion that he rejected the ritual commandments of Moses. A great deal of traditional theology hangs on this opinion, because the difference between "moral" and "ritual" commandments has been Christian doctrine for a millennium. The idea that Christ's coming absolved people from the "ritual" Law and confirmed the validity of the "moral" Law became dogma by the time of the Middle Ages, and is still repeated today. It is a way for Christians to say that they do the things that count in the Law (the "moral" part) while Jews and other "primitive," "legalistic," or otherwise "backward" people adhere to the "ritual" (or "ceremonial") part of the Law. Once this distinction is made, one denomination of Christians can apply it against another denomination, charging that they stand on ceremony. Protestants frequently make the charge, for example, that Catholics ignore Paul by upholding ritual or ceremonial concerns.

The simple fact is that much Christian custom and law is grounded in "ritual" constraints. If you marry a close relation or eat the carcass of an animal you have found by accident, you are literally breaking the law in most Western communities. But those regulations derive from commandments about purity, which is exactly how the Torah refers to marrying close relatives (Leviticus 18:6–18) and consuming carrion (Leviticus 17:15–16). Western science can rationalize these rules—in terms of genetics and hygiene, for example—but their origins are not scientific, but ritual. Anyone who believes Christians do not care about rites should try—in any church, any Sunday—to change the order of worship.

By the same token, Christians have very cheerfully ignored key provisions of the moral side of the Torah over the centuries. By looking at current economic practice, who would have thought, for example, that Moses' Law requires farmers to leave some of their fields unharvested for the benefit of the poor, and to pay hired hands on the same day that they work (Leviticus 19:9–10, 13)? And in what country in the world can it be said that courts judge the poor and the wealthy *equally*, as Leviticus 19:15 explicitly requires? Traditional Judaism actively discusses those commandments and their morality; traditional Christianity has conveniently managed to forget them by labeling anything troubling as "ritual."

The image of Paul in the West has helped along the deception that "we" are "moral" while "they" are "ritual." He—it is widely maintained—had nothing to do with "ceremonial" legalism. His agreement in Jerusalem to support the community that sacrificed in the Temple there obviously embarrasses this picture, so some theologians explain away his collection for the Nazirites as simple charity. But they can't get around the vivid picture of Paul slicing off Timothy's foreskin. In this case, something has to give: either the medieval dichotomy between "moral" and "ritual," or the Book of Acts. Purity turns out to be a foundational element in religious praxis, embedded in ethical sensibility; cf. Robert Parker, *MIASMA: Pollution and Purification in Early Greek Religion* (Oxford: Clarendon, 1996), and Chilton, *The Temple of Jesus: His Sacrificial Program within a Cultural History of Sacrifice* (University Park: Pennsylvania State University Press, 1992). An attempt has recently been made to revive the old dichotomy in the study of Judaism, in my view unsuccessfully; cf. Jonathan Klawans, *Impurity and Sin in Ancient Judaism* (Oxford: Oxford University Press, 2000), and my review in *Review of Rabbinic Judaism* 4.2 (2001):350–55.

One of the shadowiest figures in the New Testament, Silas nonetheless exerts a palpable influence in several of its writings (usually under the Latin form of his name, Silvanus). He reshaped the profile of Paul's activities. That is manifest in Acts, and also in 1 Thessalonians, which Silas wrote with Paul and Timothy (1 Thessalonians 1:1). Later, his association with Paul behind him, Silas appears with Peter (1 Peter 5:12), writing a letter to a circle of churches in Asia Minor. I follow the majority of scholars in seeing this work as written after the death of Peter, but his influence and Silas's seem clear from the point of view of its content. Similarly, 2 Thessalonians is an example of Silas's later eschatology (as in my opinion is Mark 13, a chapter assembled after the destruction of the Temple in 70 C.E.). So Silas engaged in two vital programs (Pauline and Petrine) for promulgating faith in Jesus among Gentiles in a way that upholds the Torah. Whether Silas appears in association with Paul or Peter, a strong element of apocalypticism always makes its appearance when he is involved in writing a letter. Silas motivated his theology with the strong appeal of his calendar of the end of time.

Rainer Riesner, *Paul's Early Period: Chronology, Mission Strategy, Theology*, trans. D. Stott (Grand Rapids, MI: Eerdmans, 1998), 235–56, especially stresses the importance of Isaiah's prophecies within Paul's itinerary. I think he succeeds in showing Paul's interest in getting to Rome and in explaining his westward orientation as derived from Isaiah 66:19. But at times Riesner's application of the passage to Paul's itinerary, point by point, seems mechanical to me, as does his assumption that this itinerary was a part of the revelation on the road to Damascus.

The Stoic teaching of *ekpurosis*, comparable in some ways to Paul's eschatology, is discussed contextually in David Sedley, "Stoicism," *Routledge Encyclopedia of Philosophy*, ed. Edward Craig (London: Routledge, 1998), 9:141–61.

Could Paul have avoided the lictor's rod in Philippi? After all, Roman citizens were not supposed to be subjected to the humiliation of punishment without due process. Technically that is true, but Roman history provides actual examples of citizens being beaten on the spot at a magistrate's order, whatever the law might say; see Brian Rapske, *The Book of Acts and Paul in Roman Custody*, The Book of Acts in Its First Century Setting 3 (Grand Rapids, MI: Eerdmans, 1994), 123–27. Power governed the empire; law was its handmaid and its ornament, never its true ruler. From the lictor rods to the cross that any military bureaucrat could hang noncitizen criminals on, the Roman Empire exerted its authority by means of terror. Organized across its wide domains, terror reconquered any bit of the empire that seemed recalcitrant, took new taxes, new prisoners, new slaves, and renewed the imperial hegemony. Even *if* Paul could have pleaded his way out of this rough justice, that would have left Silas alone with the certainty of punishment. Paul had no real choice but to take his beating. Given the presence of the mob, the decision of magistrates to inflict official punishment might in any case have spared the apostles' lives, and detaining them in prison could have been as protective as it was humiliating and punitive.

On conditions in Athens and Corinth, see Judith Perlzweig, *Lamps of the Roman Period*, The Athenian Agora VII (Princeton: American School of Classical Studies at Athens, 1961); Robert Scranton, Joseph W. Shaw, Leila Ibrahim, *KENCHREAI, Eastern Port of Corinth: Results of Investigations by the University of Chicago and Indiana University for The American School of Classical Studies at Athens*, vol. 1, *Topography and Architecture* (Leiden: Brill, 1978); Hector Williams, *KENCHREAI, Eastern Port of Corinth: Results of Investigations by the University of Chicago and Indiana University for The American School of Classical Studies at Athens*, vol. 5, *The Lamps* (Leiden: Brill, 1981).

There is an interesting pattern in Acts' presentation of Paul in Jerusalem. He goes with Barnabas in Acts 11, but virtually nothing is reported of the visit. Then chapter 15 conflates the discussion of that visit with the meeting that decided to send an encyclical to the Gentiles about their purity. Acts 18:22 is a bigger blank than 11:29–30. But then 21:23–25 speaks both of James' report to Paul that he had sent the encyclical and of the Nazirite arrangements that resulted in Paul's arrest. Why does Acts empty two meetings (chapters 11 and 18) of an agenda and overfill two meeting (chapters 15 and 21)? William B. Ramsay answered this question in principle (but not in practice). Although a defender of Acts' author, whom he takes to be Luke and a great historian of the stature of Thucydides, he admits that the chronology of the work is loose; see *St. Paul the*

Traveller and the Roman Citizen (New York: Putnam's, 1896), 3–28. Rather, Acts has a habit of associating events thematically rather than when they happened over time. Ramsay wrote (p. 7):

> True historical genius lies in selecting the great crises, the great agents, and the great movements, in making these clear to the reader in their real nature, in passing over with the lightest and slightest touch numerous events and many persons, but always keeping clear before the reader the plan of composition. The historian may dismiss years with a word, and devote considerable space to a single incident.

Whether or not this is genius, it sounds like Acts, and the characterization also accounts for the extreme compression of what Acts says in narrative about Paul's staying in a given place, even when it specifies that a considerable period of time was involved. Ramsay's estimation of Acts seems to me far-fetched, but he does provide the key in my opinion to the puzzle of its chronology.

For an intelligent retooling of Ramsay's approach, see Anna Maria Schwemer, "Paulus in Antiochien," *Biblische Zeitschrift* 42 (1998):161–80, p. 175: "Wenn wir diesen Zusammenstoß in Antiochien nicht direkt nach dem Apostelkonzil ansetzen, sondern mit der Apg 18, 21–32 gesschilderten Reise des Paulus von Ephesus auf dem Seeweg nach Caesarea, dann nach Jerusalem und schließlich nach Antiochien verbinden, werden die Zusammenhänge verständlicher."

Why was the question of who ate with whom so fraught in Antioch? Daniel Boyarin succinctly distills a great deal of scholarly discussion in *A Radical Jew: Paul and the Politics of Identity* (Berkeley: University of California Press, 1994), 291:

> If Peter had been eating with those gentile Christians, then certainly it means that he was eating the same food as they, and if they were exempted from the Jewish food laws, then he also was eating nonkosher food, which constitutes in itself a renunciation of the Law.

For a similar albeit less categorical analysis, see Segal, 230–33.

8. The Ephesian Catapult

Brief though the mention of Apollos in Acts is, it opens a window on a Christianity different from Paul's and Peter's and James' during the fifties of the first century. Alexandria by this time had already seen the work of Philo—a brilliant synthesis of Judaism and Platonism—emerge and prosper. Philo taught that the practices of the Torah were to be maintained and at the same time he saw in each of them a deep, philosophical meaning. When circumcision became an issue, for example, he acknowledged that the ritual was a symbol of obedience, but he also insisted that you needed to engage in the practice to achieve the obedience (see *The Migration of Abraham*, 89–93). In this he aligned himself with the teaching of the *Letter of Aristeas*, where legends about the high priest and his contacts with the Egyptian court express the hope of a synthesis of philosophical and practical Judaism. Philo set up his Judaism against those who saw the Torah as purely symbolic and wished to relax its actual practice for that reason. He refers to some Jews in Alexandria, who saw the Torah as a matter of allegory rather than practical behavior and so stopped practicing circumcision, but he opposed them. Apollos practiced Philo's kind of Judaism, complete with regular, ritual immersion, which he saw as authorized by the example of Jesus.

Apollos obviously did not learn of Jesus by means of Peter. His alternative view of baptism makes that clear beyond a doubt. Acts keeps silent about which apostle first contacted Alexandria, but it does relate how the apostle Philip baptized Samaritans (see Acts 8:5–13) and even an Ethiopian official (8:26–40). Like Apollos, Philip immersed people in water, but did not teach the association between baptism and receiving Spirit. As a result, Acts describes Peter as following Philip into Samaria and laying hands on people Philip had baptized so that Spirit would come upon them (8:14–25). Just as the Galilean apostle Philip could have contacts with Samaritans and Ethiopians, we can easily imagine other apostles contacting Egyptians, so that the teaching in regard to Jesus found its way to Alexandria. (People from Egypt, Libya, and Cyrene appear as witnesses of the dramatic Pentecost in 32 C.E. [Acts 2:10], but of course that is the kind of tradition—emphatically focusing on the Spirit that comes through Jesus' Resurrection and motivates baptism—that did *not* influence Apollos.) I find it interesting that Luke's Gospel—written within the same community as Acts—omits one of the names of the twelve apostles that appear in other Gospels, Thaddeus. (See both Luke 6:14–16 and Acts 1:13 in comparison to Mark 3:16–19; Matthew 10:2–4. To make up the number, Luke adds "Judas the son of James," which may originally have been an alternative way of referring to Judas Iscariot.) That may be a case of convenient amnesia, a forgetfulness of a genuinely Galilean stream of tradition, deeply committed to Jesus but divergent from the practice of Peter, which had made its way to Alexandria and influenced teachers such as Apollos.

However the message of Jesus came to Alexandria, and however Apollos came to Ephesus, Ephesus clearly offered hospitality to this Alexandrian brand of Christianity. A generation later, the Gospel according to John would be composed in Ephesus, opening with an overture on the "Word" of God, which is directly comparable to Philo's earlier teaching on the creativity of the divine *logos* that was also the very image of humanity itself. Philo saw the creation as the icon of the human-shaped "Word" that was the template of the cosmos; Johannine Christianity went on to identify that *logos* when it walked the earth as Jesus. Apollos initiated these deep connections between Alexandria and Ephesus, although his difference from Peter caused Acts to reduce his importance to nearly zero. Influential though Apollos proved to be, you could argue that his greatest impact may have been in cementing the alliance Paul had forged in Corinth with Priscilla and Aquila.

Paul's technique of exorcism and Jesus'—or rather, the relative absence of a technique—stands in contrast to stories about Apollonius of Tyana, a popular philosopher of the late first century. It is said that Apollonius was immune to imprisonment and took charge of demons. The stress in the stories about Apollonius resides in his command of natural forces, whether in his soul or in the world. He elaborately removes his leg from a shackle and puts it back in again (Philostratus *Life of Apollonius* 7.38), demonstrating his total self-control. When he commands a demon to prove its departure from a possessed young man, the thing enters a statue and throws it to the ground *(Life of Apollonius* 4.20). For the demon there is no disputing the exorcist's power, as in the cases of the spirits that yelled back at Jesus or in the assaults of Satan that Paul describes.

The realization of the promise of faith to Abraham by belief in Jesus within baptism leaves an open question: the exact place of the Law. Paul addresses that question in Galatians 3:15–18. The promise is compared to a will, which can't be changed once the provisions have been made. The promise to Abraham was made to his "seed": the singular rather than the plural is used in the Book of Genesis, and Paul has no interest in seeing the usage as collective (see Genesis 13:15; 17:8; 24:7). That seed, Paul asserts, is Christ, the point of the promise that cannot be annulled by the intervention of the Law some 430 years after Abraham.

Up until this point then, Paul's assessment of the Law has been negative. It is the principle of Scripture that can seem to overrule the promise, but which in fact does not. "What, then, is the law?" (Galatians 3:19–25) is precisely the question Paul proceeds to answer in more positive terms. His answer to the issue of Law's function is literally pedagogical. As the function of a pedagogue in antiquity was to lead children to school, so the Law was intended to keep humanity under its constraint until the promise of belief could be fulfilled by faith. The climax is inevitable, but also resonant (Galatians 3:26–29): "For you are all God's Sons through faith in Jesus Christ. Because as you were immersed in Christ, you clothed yourselves with Christ. There is not a single Jew or Greek, not a single slave or freedman, not a single male or female, because you are all one in Jesus Christ. And if you are of Christ, then you are Abraham's seed, inheritors by promise." The constraint of the Law, because it is provisional, comes to an end in the fulfillment of the promise by means of faith.

This method of argumentation paradoxically betrays Paul's Judaic background, as remarked by Dan Cohn-Sherbok, "Paul and Rabbinic Exegesis," *Scottish Journal of Theology* 35 (1982):117–32 (p. 132):

Of course certain aspects of rabbinic exegesis, such as the expansion of Scriptural law, are absent from the epistles. Yet like the rabbis, Paul attempted to show that Scripture is sacred, that it is susceptible of interpretation, and that properly understood, it guides the life of the worthy. In proclaiming his Christian message, he employed standard techniques of Scriptural exegesis, occasionally even using some of the rules of rabbinic hermeneutics. In this sense Paul's teaching and preaching are rooted in Pharisaic Judaism.

Even Paul's understanding of salvation in terms of being made righteous is precedented within the Judaism of his time; see Markus Bockmuehl, "1QS and Salvation at Qumran," *Justification and Variegated Nomism*, vol. 1, *The Complexities of Second Temple Judaism,* ed. D. A. Carson, Peter T. O'Brien, and Mark A. Seifrid (Tübingen and Grand Rapids, MI: Mohr and Baker, 2001), 381–414, 398–99. Bockmuehl goes on to observe (p. 401) that "The community's worship here becomes the 'pleasant aroma of righteousness'; its perfection of behavior will be as a freewill offering; and some scholars have gone so far as to see two disputed passages (1QS 9:3–6; cf. 8:5–6) as evidence of the *yachad* itself taking on the role of the temple's inner sanctuary or 'Holy of Holies.' "

9. Greek Fire

Morton Smith stresses the magical environment of Corinth in "Pauline Worship as Seen by Pagans," *Harvard Theological Review* 73 (1980):241–49, 243–44. As Smith describes the matter:

Christianity was allied with another type of magic, that by which recalled spirits *(not* resurrected bodies) of executed criminals and of persons who had died unmarried or childless were invoked to aid the magician. Jesus belonged to all three of these categories. The spirits of such persons were the most powerful of the *nekydaimones,* "spirits of the dead," who might be acquired as *paredroi*—spirits in attendance on the magician and ready to obey his orders, so that no considerable rite was needed to activate them. Such a "familiar"—to use the old English term—might play a role in the magician's life not dissimilar to that of "the spirit" in Paul's life. That Paul recognized the similarity is shown by his recommendation of celibacy on the ground that it would free the Christian from distractions and make him *euparedron* for the Lord—well suited to be joined with Jesus as a *paredros*. In modern terms, the lack of normal sexual satisfaction is likely to lead to compensatory connections with spirits, hence the requirement of celibacy by many shamanistic and priestly groups has probably some functional justification. The medicine man is more likely to get the spirit if he forgoes the flesh. It is worth noting that the ordinary magician got a spirit as *his paredros,* but Paul wants the Christian to be the *paredros of* the spirit (i.e., of Jesus).

I am indebted to Smith's insight and admire his description of the religious environment in which Paul thrived. In his later book *Jesus the Magician* (San Francisco: Harper & Row, 1978), he placed Jesus in the same environment, however, and in my view that is an anachronism.

Smith's explanation of Paul's behavior in terms of magical practice needs to be complemented with Stoic views of the power of intellectual masters. Stoic theory held that a human being could come to embody the underlying logic that undergirds the universe. When a teacher accomplished that, he could become a window into that logic for others by means of his personal presence and example, his verbal instruction (oral or written), and even his projection of himself through time and space. As Seneca said, "Happy is the man who can make others better, not merely when he is in their company, but even when he is in their thoughts!" *(Epistle* 11.9); Abraham J. Malherbe, "Paul: Hellenistic Philosopher or Christian Pastor?" *Anglican Theological Review* 68:1 (1986):3–13, 5. Examples of a deliberate projection of oneself in a corporeal way, the obvious precedent for what Paul is speaking of in Corinthians, include Seneca's "Dream of Scipio" and Apollonius of Tyana *(Life of Apollonius* 8.31). Those precedents take us right into Paul's period, and Apollonius was also a native of Asia Minor. Apollonius, like Paul, represents the fusion of magic and philosophy that the first century occasioned. Paul's new twist in this thinking was not the fusion of these two forms of being and acting, but his explanation that this occurs by means of divine Spirit.

What may seem an outburst from a completely different context in 1 Corinthians 9 in fact makes sense in the setting of Stoic argument; see Abraham J. Malherbe, "Determination and Free Will in Paul: The Argument of 1 Corinthians 8 and 9," *Paul in His Hellenistic Context*, ed. Troels Engberg-Pedersen (Minneapolis: Fortress, 1994), 231–55, and Leon Hermann, *Sénèque et les premiers chrétiens*, Collection Latomus 167 (Bruxelles: Latomus, 1976). To be "free"—as Paul insists he is in chapter 9—was the capacity not to be deceived by external impressions. The opposite of this cognitive power is the condition of being weak, exactly what Paul calls people who do not realize that idols do not truly exist (so 1 Corinthians 8:10–11). As an apostle, Paul claims the mantle of a true philosopher, taking up here in chapter 9 a theme he has already sounded earlier when he sarcastically praised the Corinthians for their wisdom.

E. Earle Ellis, "Traditions in 1 Corinthians," *New Testament Studies* 32 (1986):481–502, offers a survey of materials commonly held to have been incorporated by Paul in his letter. The parade examples are Paul's reference to Jesus' final meal with his disciples (11:23–26) and to his Resurrection (15:1–8). The language there used, of handing over a tradition (*paradidomi* in Greek, *masar* in Hebrew/Aramaic) and holding it fast (*paralambano* in Greek, *qabal* in Hebrew/Aramaic), reinforces the impression of a commonsense reading of the passages. Ellis (p. 483) is appropriately skeptical of the claim that, every time the phrase "The Lord says" is used, a saying of Christian prophets is in play. After all, that is a suitable way to introduce a passage of Scripture, a saying of Jesus, a revelation, or an interpretation. On the other hand, Ellis stretches credulity with his analysis that, when Paul uses such expressions as "Do you not know?" or "I want you to know" or "it is not (the case that)" they refer to a specific, early tradition. Any speaker, in antiquity or today, might use such rhetoric. Here is an example of scholarship pressing the case for the usage of traditional materials too far.

Paul's evaluation of prophecy in 1 Corinthians is well presented by C. K. Barrett, *A Commentary on the First Epistle to the Corinthians* (New York: Harper & Row, 1968), 316, who has pointed out that we need to correct traditional translations of 14:5. The text does not say that he who prophesies is greater than he who speaks in tongues, unless *someone* interprets, but unless *he* interprets his own ecstatic speech. In other words, speaking in a tongue is an ecstatic utterance, not a use of conventional language. This view of glossolalia is supported by the work of Felicitas D. Goodman, *Speaking in Tongues: A Cross-Cultural Study in Glossolalia* (Chicago, 1972), 152. The basic point has been elaborated on by A. C. Thiselton, "The 'Interpretation' of Tongues: A New Suggestion in the Light of Greek Usage in Philo and Josephus," *Journal of Theological Studies* 30 (1979):15–36, where (following consultation with the present writer) Thiselton suggested that *diermeneuo* in Greek might mean "articulate" as well as "interpret." Especially striking is Philo's comparison of word and music (*On the Posterity of Cain* 108). For Paul, as for Philo, accurate speech gives voice and concept to what is otherwise ineffable.

Daniel Boyarin, *A Radical Jew: Paul and the Politics of Identity* (Berkeley: University of California Press, 1994), 57–85, deals with Resurrection in making out the "major thesis" of his book (85):

> Paul's genius was not as a philosopher, which he was not, but in his realization that the common dualist theology—ontology, anthropology, and hermeneutics—which together for him formed a christology, provided the answer to the theological problem that troubled him the most: How do the rest of the people in God's world fit into the plan of salvation revealed to the Jews through their Torah?

10. *Sacrifice in the Temple*

Wolfgang Wiefel has discussed the situation in Rome that Paul addressed, "The Jewish Community in Ancient Rome and the Origins of Roman Christianity," *The Romans Debate,* ed. Karl P. Donfried (Minneapolis: Augsburg, 1977, and Peabody, MA: Hendrickson, 2001 [revised and expanded edition]), 100–119, and see H. Dixon Slingerland, *Claudian Policymaking and the Early Imperial Repression of Judaism at Rome*, South Florida Studies in the History of Judaism (Atlanta: Scholars, 1997).

In the middle of this letter, Paul launches into an ornate discussion of how the Israel of Christ and Israel after the flesh (Jews) are related to one another. Once the Scriptural ornament of this section (Romans 9–11) is accounted for, the basic argument is simple:

> There is now no distinction between Jew and Greek in the matter of salvation: if you confess the Lord Jesus and believe God raised him from the dead, you will be saved [10:1–21, v. 9]. Those who are believers must not, however, imagine that God has rejected his people. After all, there are Jews who do believe in Jesus [11:1–10], and even those who do not believe have, in their lack of faith, provided an opportunity for Gentiles [11:11–24]. Once the fullness of the Gentiles is accomplished, all Israel, including both Jews and Gentiles, will be seen to be saved [11:25–36].

There are, of course, crucial facets within each of the statements that can be explored, but they are subsidiary to the main lines of the argument. What becomes unmistakably clear when we boil Paul's ornate speech down to its essentials is that he is making a case for a particular view of how God's saving activity in Christ Jesus is consistent with his election of Israel; Chilton, "Romans 9–11 as Scriptural Interpretation and Dialogue with Judaism," *Ex Auditu* 4 (1988):27–37. Once it is clear that Israel is elected, not sovereign, that divine choice is operative rather than divine right, Paul's observations follow logically.

This argument reflects Paul's struggle to maintain the "advantage" of Judaism while insisting upon its integration within a spiritually defined Israel. He hopes in Romans to coordinate his own passion with the needs of the community. Claudius's edict in 49 C.E. had put Jewish believers in the minority: here Paul could reverse his usual rhetorical weakness in the face of a majority Jewish community, and come to the rescue of a minority all the while helping Roman Christians to strengthen their community. The integration of this concern with Paul's eschatological perspective is beautifully brought out in Jacques Schlosser, "L'espérance de la creation (Rm 8, 18–22)," *Ce Dieu qui vient: Mélanges offerts à Bernard Renaud*, Lectio Divina 159, ed. Raymond Kuntzmann (Paris: Cerf, 1995), and it is also treated in N. T. Wright, *The Climax of the Covenant: Christ and the Law in Pauline Theology* (Minneapolis: Fortress, 1991).

Other works related to Romans or Paul's concerns in Romans that I have found particularly useful include C. E. B. Cranfield, *Romans: A Shorter Commentary* (Grand Rapids, MI: Eerdmans, 1985); Glenn N. Davies, *Faith and Obedience in Romans: A Study in Romans 1–4, Journal for the Study of the New Testament Supplement Series 39* (Sheffield: Sheffield Academic Press, 1990); Neil Elliott, *The Rhetoric of Romans: Argumentative Constraint and Strategy and Paul's Dialogue with Judaism, Journal for the Study of the New Testament*

Supplement Series 45 (Sheffield: Sheffield Academic Press, 1990); L. Ann Jervis, *The Purpose of Romans: A Comparative Letter Structure Investigation*, *Journal for the Study of the New Testament* Supplement Series 55 (Sheffield: Sheffield Academic Press, 1991); John G. Lodge, *Romans 9–11: A Reader-Response Analysis*, International Studies in Formative Christianity and Judaism (Atlanta: Scholars Press, 1996); David A. Renwick, *Paul, the Temple, and the Presence of God*, Brown Judaic Studies 224 (Atlanta: Scholars Press, 1991); and John A. T. Robinson, *Wrestling with Romans* (Philadelphia: Westminster, 1979).

The setting and purpose of Philippians is developed in L. Gregory Bloomquist, *The Function of Suffering in Philippians*, *Journal for the Study of the New Testament* Supplement Series 78 (Sheffield: Sheffield Academic Press, 1993). The supposition that the letter was originally written from Myra suits the variables to be accounted for better, in my opinion, than the other options that have been posited (Caesarea, Corinth, Ephesus, and Rome); see G. F. Hawthorne, *Dictionary of Paul and His Letters*, ed. Gerald F. Hawthorne and Ralph P. Martin (Downers Grove, IL: InterVarsity, 1993), 707–13. Roman custody was consistent with Paul's writing letters during this period; Brian Rapske, *The Book of Acts and Paul in Roman Custody*, The Book of Acts in Its First Century Setting 3 (Grand Rapids, MI: Eerdmans, 1994), 358. So the issue of provenience remains open.

11. *The Sting of Death*

Paul spelled out the theory of Spirit that animates his later thinking in 1 Corinthians. The fire he wanted to kindle burned within each believer and was not a matter of one's own status or accomplishment. Paul explains his position by quoting a passage from Isaiah, which speaks of things beyond human understanding that God has readied for those who love him (in 1 Corinthians 2:9). He then goes on to say (2:10–11): "But to us God has uncovered through the Spirit, because the Spirit searches all things, even the depths of God. For among people who knows a person's concerns except the spirit of the person that is in one? So also no one has known God's concerns except the Spirit of God." As Paul sees human relations, one person can know what another thinks and feels only on the basis of their shared "spirit." "Spirit" is the name for what links one person with another, and by means of that link we can also know what God thinks and feels. The Spirit at issue in knowing God is not "the spirit of the world," but "the Spirit that is from God" (1 Corinthians 2:12). The human spirit that is the medium of ordinary, human exchange becomes the vehicle of divine revelation, the Greek fire Paul catapulted into Corinth. That is why Paul's perspective demanded that "Those who have wives should be as those who have not, those weeping as those not weeping, those rejoicing as not rejoicing, those acquiring as not possessing, those involved in the world as not obsessed" (1 Corinthians 7:29–31).

Useful breakdowns of what Paul did and did not write include *The Writings of St. Paul,* A Norton Critical Edition, ed. Wayne A. Meeks (New York: Norton, 1972); Donald Harman Akenson, *Saint Saul: A Skeleton Key to the Historical Jesus* (Oxford: Oxford University Press, 2000), 125–34; Richard J. Cassidy, *Paul in Chains: Roman Imprisonment and the Letters of St. Paul* (New York: Crossroad, 2001).

Daniel Boyarin has in my opinion identified the source of Paul's struggle over the issue of the Torah; *A Radical Jew: Paul and the Politics of Identity* (Berkeley: University of California Press, 1994), 52:

Paul was, therefore, troubled by, critical of, the "ethnocentrism" of biblical and post-biblical religion, and particularly the way it implicitly and explicitly created hierarchies between nations, genders, social classes. Despite this powerful, nearly irresistible concern for universal "Man" and critique of "Judaism," Paul nevertheless remained convinced that the Hebrew Scriptures contained God's revelation and that the Jews had been at least the vehicle for the communication of that revelation.

As Richard B. Hays remarks in a more theological vein, Paul replaced Moses with Christ, and the Torah with the Law of Christ, but "law" in a refined sense; "Christology and Ethics in Galatians: The Law of Christ," *Catholic Biblical Quarterly* 49.2 (1987): 268–90, 275:

Contrary to the opinion of Dodd, this expression should not be taken as evidence that Paul regarded the sayings of Jesus as the basis for a new torah; it simply means that Paul acknowledges (or, in this case, affirms) that he is under obligation of obedience to Christ, that he is not "lawless" (=autonomous). The expression *ennomos Christou* appears to be framed by Paul as a witty (though serious) response to a negative judgment on his apostolic ministry.

Hays's reference is to C. H. Dodd's essay, "ENNOMOS CHRISTOU," *More New Testament Studies* (Manchester: Manchester University, 1968), 134–38.

Timothy's concern was not limited to Church hierarchy in giving Paul his new look. In Colossians he also has Paul refer lovingly to John Mark, Barnabas's nephew, with whom he had not had contact in years (Colossians 4:10). Here, too, Timothy has Paul name "Luke, the beloved physician" (Colossians 4:14), the putative author of the Book of Acts. Mark may well have been in Rome at the time Paul was and could have met his former colleague, but Timothy has Paul go beyond reference to a simple meeting so as to champion the letters of Paul as offering direction to the Church at large, not only those few congregations that agreed with him. At the same time, the letters produced by Timothy, and more especially the Pastoral Epistles, treat Gnosticism as a threat to Paul's inheritance. On this issue, and for a fine discussion of Ephesians and Colossians, see Markus Barth and Helmut Blanke, *Colossians: A New Translation with Introduction and Commentary*, The Anchor Bible 34B, trans. Astrid B. Beck (New York: Doubleday, 1994). But there is a paradox here, because Paul himself inspired Gnostic forms of Christianity; see Elaine Pagels, *The Gnostic Paul* (Philadelphia: Trinity Press International, 1992). For a more conservative treatment that nonetheless allows for considerable editorial revision in the production of the Pauline corpus, see Michael J. Gorman, *Apostle of the Crucified Lord: A Theological Introduction to Paul and His Letters* (Grand Rapids, MI: Eerdmans, 2004).

ACKNOWLEDGMENTS

Ever since my teachers at the General Theological Seminary in New York introduced me to Greek, Paul's letters have enthralled me. Before then, I read them as a duty; in their native Koine, they still give me deep pleasure. Two professors in particular, Frederick Houk Borsch and Orlando Sydney Barr, helped me acquire a lifelong taste for Paul.

Andrew Corbin at Doubleday, in a series of discussions, provided the incentive, encouragement, and prodding necessary to turn my enjoyment of reading Paul into a book about his life. I am grateful for him as a reader. He shares an awareness of the dark shadows in Paul's makeup that are too often covered up by hagiographers, or exaggerated by Christianity's detractors. Colleagues within New Testament scholarship—especially Karl Donfried, Robert Jewett, Amy-Jill Levine, and Alan Segal—have helped me strike a balance of light and shade in a complex, vigorous thinker. Jacob Neusner continues to provide profound incentive to my thought, as our new article in *The Bulletin for Biblical Research* 14.1 (2004) shows.

Paul's spirituality is easily overlooked in the midst of the doctrinal controversies that have swirled around him. Members of the Institute of Advanced Theology, by their careful hearing of my lectures on Paul and their prodding questions, helped me focus on the spiritual identity that is the enduring legacy of his life. Marguerite Hayes gave a manuscript of this book a very thorough and helpful consideration from this angle, and the Research Council of Bard College provided material support.

As in the case of *Rabbi Jesus,* I have particularly to thank Kenneth Wapner. It is amazing how many different ways you can say something you know, only to have it completely befuddle the reader. Ken continues to stay on my case; I remain a willing and lumbering patient under the hands of his physiotherapy in prose.

INDEX

1 Kings (cont.)
18:42, 37
19:13, 37

Letters to Friends (Cicero), 23
Leviticus 18:6–18, 15, 169
Life of Apollonius (Philostratus), 24
Lucius of Cyrene, 112, 114
Luke, Gospel of
4:1–13, 184
10:18, 183
10:38–42, 35
Luther, Martin, 127, 184, 186
Lydia, 151, 215
Lysias, Claudius, 239–40, 252
Lystra, 120–23, 124–25

Mark, Gospel of
angelic vision by women at the tomb, 46
Temple as house for all nations, 81, 83, 136
vision of Jesus with Moses and Elijah, 80, 115
1:12–13, 184
3:21, 95, 115
6:56, 36
9:2–9, 80, 96, 114
11:17, 81, 83, 135
16:1–8, 46
marriage, 15, 211–12
Matthew, Gospel of
4:1–11, 96, 184
12:28, 183
13:55, 18
23:8–9, 108
23:15, 18
Mazar, Eilat and Benjamin, 38
Menachem, 112, 114

Mishnah, 35
Aboth, 34
Bekhorot 6:9, 40
Erubin 6:2, 33
Ketubot 13:10, 93
Makkot 3:10–13, 84
Makkot 3:14, 85
Sanhedrin 6:4, 123
Sanhedrin 7:5, 43
Sheqalim 3:3, 40
Sheqalim 6:2, 39
Moral Epistles (Seneca), 23
Moses, 34, 52, 69–70, 75, 206
Murphy-O'Connor, Jerome, 44, 88
Myra, Turkey, 242, 249

Nabatea, 60, 65–69, 76, 77, 78
Aretas IV, 76–77, 78, 79
Nazirite practice, 136–37
Nero, 250–52
Nicolas of Antioch, 102
Nike, 182, 219
Noah, 14, 15, 132

Onesimus, 241–42
On the Life of Moses (Philo), 206
On Tranquility of Mind (Seneca), 23
Osiris, 11, 129

paganism
Antioch and, 100–113
apotheosis in, 10
centers of, first century, 26
death and resurrection in, 10–11, 129
Greco-Roman, 109–10
Mysteries, 129, 236
sexual indulgence, 206, 235

330 · Index

Bruce Chilton is the Bernard Iddings Bell Professor of Religion at Bard College in Annandale-on-Hudson and priest at the Free Church of Saint John in Barrytown, New York. He is the author of many scholarly articles and books, including the widely acclaimed *Rabbi Jesus*.